LOOK IN,
LOOK UP,
LOOK OUT!

LOOK IN, LOOK UP, LOOK OUT!

Be the Person You Were Meant to Be

Joyce L. Vedral, Ph.D.

WARNER BOOKS

A Time Warner Company

Warner Books, Inc., 1271 Avenue of the Americas, New York, NY 10020

A Time Warner Company

Printed in the United States of America

ISBN 0-446-51863-8

Book design by Giorgetta Bell McRee

To those who have a dream, be it big or small
I dedicate this book to you—
and I trust that with God's help you will use it
to propel yourself on to the next step . . .
and then the next, and then the next.
It's up to you!

Acknowledgments

To Joann Davis, for your enthusiastic belief in this project—and for your priceless perspicacity.

To Mel Berger, my agent, for your sage advice.

To Edna Farly, for your willingness to go the extra, extra mile in publicity.

To Grace Sullivan for your affable and willing assistance.

To Diane Luger and Jacki Merri Meyer for your dedication to the cover art.

To Larry Kirshbaum, Nanscy Neiman, and Emi Battaglia for backing me up "to the hilt."

To family and friends for your continual love and support.

To you, the women and men who have written to me requesting such a book. This one's for you.

Contents

LOOK IN, LOOK UP, LOOK OUT!

1

LOOK IN, LOOK UP—
LOOK OUT!

Help. I'm stuck. I'm not happy with my life, but I can't seem to find the motivation to make something happen." I've heard these words from thousands of readers, asking me to help them to move on to a better life—involving everything from getting in shape or finding the right relationship to building self-esteem and finding peace of mind and a worthy goal.

How can you get unstuck and begin to move on to the life you really want, the life of your dreams? First, you have to *look in*—look to yourself, for there you will learn to develop the first seven of the eight golden keys that will give you the power to take action and enable you to achieve your goals and dreams. You'll find out how to listen to and trust your inner voice. You'll learn how to build your self-esteem. You'll find out how to let go of the past and begin to take responsibility for your actions, past, present, and future. You'll discover how to use your will to overcome virtually any obstacle you meet. You'll learn how to do things alone, without the help of others. You'll discover how to motivate yourself by developing your own "personal bag of tricks."

But then you'll learn use the eighth and most important key of all—the key that asks you to *look up!* You'll find out how to tap into your spirituality and, by a simple prayer of faith, to take advantage of the most powerful force in the universe. And after that, *look out!* Nothing will be impossible for you.

Yes. It is the eighth and final golden key that holds the secret, the missing link that, up until now, perhaps has been preventing you from moving ahead. You'll be able to tap into the all-knowing, all-caring source of power, a force that can gently lead you into the most fulfilling life you can possibly have and assure you of accomplishing the purposes for which you were born—if only you ask. You'll understand how, when, and why to pray, and here you may be in for some very important surprises.

And then, I tell you, you had better look out. Because after you have looked in and gained your personal power, and looked up and accessed divine wisdom, finally, you'll be able to "look out" clearly, to look ahead and see without obstruction the road in front of you so that you can accomplish what you believe you should achieve in this life. In the long run, you will not have wasted your talent or your potential, but in fact will have become the person you were meant to be! And when that happens, then the world will have to look out, and I do mean look out—look out for you! You will be in full force, armed with the feeling that nothing can stop you. Physically, psychologically, spiritually—finally it will all come together for you. But you have to get "in tune" first. This book will show you how.

WHY SHOULD YOU LISTEN TO ME?

Okay. Let's all put the cards on the table. Who am I, Joyce Vedral? And why should you listen to me? I'm not a psychologist. My Ph.D. is in English Literature—albeit with a specialization in psychology. But a psychoanalyst I'm not. True, after writing best-selling fitness and relationship books, answering the many letters I've received asking for my advice, and teaching high school and college for over twenty years, I've functioned many times, in a sense, as a lay therapist. But I'm not a psychologist. So why should you listen to me?

The answer is simple. I did it myself. By the grace of God, and by acts of will, I was able to transform myself from a person whom, by all accounts, the odds were against, to a person who was able to achieve self-fulfillment and success. I was able to make my inner dreams happen, and be the person I was meant to be—instead of being the fearful, insecure, unsuccessful person I had been, and I did it in spite of the odds against me. I believe that if I did it, you can do it too. What you are about to read about me may surprise you.

I'm not going to offer you in-depth psychological studies or rules for mental health. Such things you may get from an abundance of books, many of them written by people who may have the education but not the experience. What you're going to read instead are specific guidelines for changing your life—in spite of the odds. Those guidelines will be based largely upon my personal experience, how I, who, perhaps like you, was once a hurting soul, came through the flames and ended up where I am today.

I DID IT AND YOU CAN DO IT TOO

Unlike so many who get their degrees in the privileged Ivy League, I got my education from the oldest and most prestigious school in the world, a school that accepts no applications, a school that plucks its students from the great pool of humanity—whether we like it or not. It's the "School of Hard Knocks." I'm a graduate of that school, but up until now I never thought of telling anyone about it. I just took my life and my history for granted, made the best of them, and continued to struggle toward self-fulfillment or self-actualization (trying to become who I sensed I really was deep down inside). Yet I never thought of discussing my personal past in my books.

But I kept getting letters from the readers of my fitness and relationship books. "Where do you get your motivation? Did you always have such high self-esteem?" they would ask. "You seem so happy. What is the secret of your joy?" they would inquire. "You've accomplished so much. How did you do it?" they would implore.

So I began to think about it. I began to realize that what I have taken for granted for so long—my background and how I became the person I am—could be of value to others. And when I thought about it, I certainly wasn't always happy. I certainly didn't always have high self-esteem, and I wasn't always successful. In fact, there was a time in my life when my prospects for success were very dim. If anything, I was well on my way to a life of anger, failure, depression, and worse.

This person, who is now a two-time New York Times best-selling author, a Ph.D. in English Literature, a former teacher, a well-known talk-show guest and motivator and sought-after lecturer and even "role model," was not born with a silver spoon in her mouth. I'll tell you a little bit about myself here—and a lot more as you read the book.

I REMEMBER WONDERING . . .

I was born in the poorest of poor areas of the Bronx in New York City, in a furnished room that I shared with my mother and infant sister—and some unwelcome roaches and an occasional rat. My mother worked hard doing piecework at home (making belts) to support us. My father was not there until my later years. I went to ghetto schools with cracked ceilings and water leaking from the radiators, where the teacher spent most of her time screaming at the class.

I remember wondering if the schools described in my first-grade reader really existed—where everything seemed so clean, and the teachers really taught, and the students sat at their desks and listened rather than throwing things at the teacher when her back was turned—and what it would be like to go to such a school. Yet I remember being a somewhat cheerful soul; I always had a ready smile. Part of me was content, grateful for what I did have.

Higher education? Who had time for such lofty ambitions? We were too poor even to think of such things. "College? Are you crazy?" I was told. I recall looking out the window of my fifth-grade classroom as I viewed the garbage-strewn vacant lots, thinking, "Maybe, just maybe, I'll find a way to be somebody someday."

I never felt safe. Small in stature and afraid to fight, I learned early in life, with heart pounding, to talk my way out of getting beaten up. When that didn't work, I learned to run faster than anyone you could ever meet. In fact, looking back, I did an awful lot of running in the first thirteen years of my life.

I was running from "the enemy"—the drunken bums sleeping behind the stairs and on the roof landing—running from the law (I managed to get into some trouble in this area), and, most of all, running from myself, a self I didn't know or trust—or respect. The best I could do, I thought, would be to cover my back and keep going.

I recall thinking, "What does it feel like to be normal? I wonder if everyone feels like I do about themselves?" I suspected that some people felt good about themselves, and I dreamed of a day when perhaps I too could feel that way—but it felt so very far away from me. Yet there was a part of me that was happy. I remember beaming with joy whenever anyone in school would befriend me, say a kind word, or laugh at one of my jokes. Those were the times when my hope for a joyful and fulfilling life would surge.

In my teen years, many of my closest friends died of drug overdoses. Often I would look at the sky and wonder what the future could possibly hold for me. And with that as my foundation, I eventually grew up.

I then got married, got fat, got in a rut, and got depressed. I'll tell you more about that later, but for now, suffice it to say that everything became too much for me. Discouraged and disillusioned, I recall thinking, "Is that all there is?" I even toyed with the idea of suicide.

THE SOURCE OF YOUR POWER

How did I go from the ghetto to a Ph.D. in English Literature and grow from a fearful person with low self-esteem into a woman of courage with a solid sense of self? How did I break through the barriers of anger at parents and things past and free myself to make my dreams happen?

How was I able to motivate myself to make the changes that needed to be made without the help of others and how did I find the glue that holds it all together—a simple faith in a loving, wise God who is ever willing, ready, and able to help? How did I do it? I have been asked all these questions, but the most important question is, How can you do it?

In a nutshell, here is the secret. I realized that in spite of the odds against me, I had the power *within myself* to make something happen, and that it was up to me to use that power. I learned that even though at times my power was very limited and the changes I was trying to make came very slowly, some changes eventually came if I didn't give up. I learned that as long as I was still breathing—as long as I had the precious gift of life—anything could happen.

My secrets are found in the following chapters. They are secrets that you can use to reach down deep inside yourself and tap your inner strength so that you too can get, do, and be what you want in life—in spite of the odds. In short, you can make your inner dreams happen and become the person you were meant to be.

THE EIGHT GOLDEN POWER KEYS

Looking back at my life, and reviewing the many self-help and psychology books that were influential in the making of who I am today, I see that there were eight golden keys that I had to develop and put on my "inner-strength key ring" to give me the power to make my life go in the direction I had in mind.

I believe that separately, but especially in combination, these keys will open up the doors to your dreams—no matter how small or how grand. They are:

Key #1 The power of your inner voice. Know and trust yourself.

Key #2 The power of self-esteem. Respect, value, and love yourself.

Key #3 The power of letting go of the past and moving on. Liberate and free yourself.

Key #4 The power of admitting it—owning up and taking responsibility. Mature yourself.

Key #5 The power of your will. Strengthen yourself.

Key #6 The power of doing, being alone. Autonomize yourself.

Key #7 The power of getting yourself to do what you want. Motivate yourself.

Key #8 The power of spirituality and prayer. Inspire yourself.

WHAT CAN YOU ACCOMPLISH BY USING THE GOLDEN POWER KEYS?

By developing and using the eight golden power keys—putting them on your "inner-strength key ring"—you'll be able to accomplish what is important to you, whether modest or grand. For example, you'll be able to get yourself in great physical shape and stay that way. You'll be able, once and for all, to find the power to advance in your career, or even to change careers if deep down inside you know you are on the wrong path. You'll be able to drop "friends" or acquaintances who are bad for you and meet the people who are in tune with your true self. You'll be able to let go of a negative romantic relationship and move on, and to find the right one later. You'll discover how to use your time alone to reach inward and renew and energize yourself.

You'll be able to find a more fulfilling, meaningful life, a more peaceful, joyful day-to-day existence. And in the end, you'll be able to say without a doubt that you accomplished the purposes for which you were born. Indeed, when the time comes to let go of this life, as it will for every one of us, you will not face death with "empty hands," but rather "go gently into that good night" with an armload of kind deeds and solid accomplishments, and with the knowledge that you have used your potential to the fullest.

FORGING THE SELF
YOU WERE MEANT TO BE

The word *forge* is very appropriate when we think of the growth of the self. It means "to form or shape with blows or pressure from a hammer or press—usually after beating." After reading this book and applying the eight golden power keys to your own life, you will have learned that just as there are "odds," there are also opportunities. You'll be able to use the problems and difficulties of your past and present literally to "forge" the self that is inside you, the self that has been gently whispering to you over the years, "This is what I really want to be. This is how I really want to feel. This is what I really want to do." In short, finally, you'll feel very comfortable and have inner joy and peace of mind because you will be yourself. Yes—you'll be the person you were meant to be.

HOW TO READ THIS BOOK

The best way to read this book is in the order it is written—but that is not an absolute necessity. If a particular chapter title appeals to you, by all means read it first. If you feel compelled to read another chapter, you can do it. Then go back to the beginning of the book and read the chapters in order, skipping the chapters that you have already read or, better, rereading those chapters.

After reading this book, it is my hope and in fact belief that you will find the power to move on to the next step in your life. I want you to write to me and tell me exactly what happened to you after reading this book. My address is listed on page 272. You are not alone. I'm sticking with you for the journey, and even though I've never met you, you are already in my prayers.

2

THE POWER OF YOUR INNER VOICE

We all have an "inner voice," a still, small sensation that speaks to us from deep within when we are about to do the wrong thing or to not do something we should do. At times, this gentle voice also quietly tries to prepare us for some future event, or to warn us to be cautious so as to avoid some potential trouble. We can't hear the voice with our ears, but rather with our minds. In fact, it's almost a feeling, and not a voice at all, but we call it a voice because it gives us a quick, clear message—so quick that it's almost a flicker, sometimes causing us to brush it aside. Yet, it is so clear that when we ignore it, we can always remember that we heard it, and that we ignored it, and we *always* regret it.

YOUR INNER VOICE IS ABOUT TRUSTING YOURSELF

Your inner voice is "you," the part of you that knows you so well that it can tenderly alert you in various situations that come up in your life—and in essence help you to make wise choices. By learning to listen to your inner voice, you come to know and trust yourself: "know" because you begin to learn what is and isn't right for your life, and "trust" because you realize that you have the answers to the problems that face you already at hand—right within yourself.

Scientists can't prove the existence of the inner voice, but it is as real as the nose on your face. Ask the next ten people you meet if they've ever had the experience of hearing an inner voice that told them to do or not to do something—and ask them how they responded. I predict that nine out of ten of them will know exactly what you are talking about and have a story to tell—a story with the moral. "I listened and I'm glad," or "I didn't listen and I wish I had."

The renowned psychologist Carl Rogers admits to listening to what sounds to me like an inner voice, although he doesn't use those words. He says, "I have never regretted moving in directions which 'felt' right, even though I have often felt lonely or foolish at the time. I have found that when I have trusted some inner non-intellectual sensing, I have discovered the wisdom of that move."[1]

WHY WE HESITATE TO LISTEN TO OUR INNER VOICES

Carl Rogers, an extremely educated man, seems to put his finger on the very reason we sometimes ignore our inner voice. We feel "foolish" listening to it, because we can't prove that it really exists. But why do we feel foolish—and anyway, who would know if we listened to our inner voice? After all, we don't have to make a public announcement each day, "Today I listened to my inner voice." The truth is, we don't want to make fools of ourselves even to ourselves. Just in case it is our imagination, we don't want to follow something that can't be proven scientifically.

But there is another reason why many of us don't listen to our inner voice—and that is because we may be running from what is called "consciousness," or, to put it another way, awareness. In fact, we may not trust ourselves, and we may not want to believe that our inner voice is "wise." Perhaps our inner voice is trying to alert us to something we do not want to face. At such times, it is tempting to ignore our inner voice, to brush it aside, or drown it out in various ways: with an excess of "business," with alcohol or other mind-altering substances, or even with food.

Thankfully, however, sooner or later many of us do learn to trust ourselves enough to listen to our inner voice, and in time, like Carl Rogers and many other highly intelligent people, we find out, always in retrospect, "the wisdom of that move." In short, we learn that you can't go wrong when you at least listen to your inner voice, for if nothing else, at least listening helps you to see that you do have choices. You don't have to go headlong into potential problems and disasters that lie ahead; you can possibly sidestep the problem.

WHEN YOUR INNER VOICE WHISPERS

Sometimes your inner voice whispers. At other times it shouts. When you are about to make a small mistake, something that is not life-and-death, something that will not affect your entire future, your inner voice speaks quietly. Following are some reasons your inner voice may speak to you, and some examples of such times.

TO SAVE YOU AGGRAVATION

You may be about to drive to work and you get a strong feeling that the weather is going to be bad later on, even though it is sunny now and the weather report says it is going to be fair all day. You know from experience that if it does rain later on, you will wish you had taken public transportation (since traffic always backs up two hours in the rain). You are about to get into your car and drive toward the highway, but again you get that "feeling" that you should instead head toward the train station. But you hate to take the train, and you feel foolish changing your mind on the basis of a "feeling," so you ignore the voice, using logic to silence it and saying to yourself, "But the weather report says it will be fine."

Later on, when caught in traffic on the way home, you think, "I knew I should have taken the train today. Why didn't I listen to myself?" But what exactly was that "self" you didn't listen to? It was your inner voice, gently whispering to you, trying to save you from aggravation. But why did it whisper rather than shout? Why did a thought pop into your mind only two or three times rather than obsess you until you were forced to take notice? Your inner voice shouts only in dire situations. We'll talk about that later in this chapter.

Let me give you a recent example from my own life in which I ignored my gentle inner voice and later regretted it. Not too long ago, during tax season, I had been reading the paper and noticed an interesting income-tax table. "I should clip this table," I thought. "But why?" I second-guessed myself. "My tax man is coming in three days, and he has the table. It's stupid." "But the table is so clear, and you can use it for yourself now—to look up your income and see where you fall," I answered myself. "I don't care. I'm not doing it," I argued back. And I threw out the paper.

Three days later, my tax man came, and the first thing I asked him was, "Do you have the table that shows the income brackets?" After fumbling about in his briefcase, he said, apologetically, "I forgot it, but we can still do the basic work." Very upset, I said, "No. What good is it to me to do the work now if after we finish, I still won't know if I owe money or if I'm getting a refund? Let's postpone the meeting until next week." He then spent thirty minutes fumbling with his computer to pull up a table (which he never did) while I rummaged through the recycling bin trying to find the tax table (which I never found). Needless to say, in time I found out where I stood, but I could have saved myself a lot of frustration had I listened to my inner voice.

Just the other day I had the opposite type of experience, where I did listen to my inner voice—and I was happy as a result. I tell this story at the risk of sounding silly, but I believe that you will know exactly what I'm talking about. In fact, I have a feeling similar things have happened to you.

I had come home from an evening out and was transferring money from a rather small purse back to my wallet. Suddenly, I got a strong urge to leave one twenty-dollar bill in the bag's zipper compartment. "I'm being foolish," I first thought. But then I stopped and quietly "felt" what I was sensing. Again, I got a strong feeling to leave one twenty-dollar bill in the zipper compartment. I thought about it and said to myself, "What is the harm of leaving the bill there? If this is your inner voice, you'll clearly know at some future date why you did it, and you'll be glad you listened." So I left the bill there.

As it turned out, a girlfriend invited me several weeks later to meet her at a dance, and that purse was the perfect match to my outfit. Knowing that I usually leave my purse unattended on a table while dancing, I didn't want to bring too much money, so I threw in only two twenties. While waiting for my friend at the bar, I ordered a glass of champagne that cost $15 with the tip. I had already spent ten dollars on a taxi, so that left me only $15. It cost $10 to get into the dance. That would leave me with only five dollars—I wouldn't even be able to buy myself another drink! My friend was also short on money and couldn't help me—and neither of us had brought along a credit card.

I began to berate myself for not bringing more money. "What a pain," I thought. Going back home for credit cards or money was out of the question, so in desperation, I recounted my change. Happily, I discovered that I had $20 more than I thought I had. Then, with joy, I remembered the "inner voice" that had prompted me to leave that money in the purse.

Let's look at an example where the inner voice functions like radar, or a "sixth sense," to pick up negative energy. Did you ever feel uncomfortable sitting in a waiting room or on a bus or train—and then realize that it was the person next to you who was making you feel unsettled? How did you realize it? I'm not talking about a person who smelled or dressed strangely. I'm talking about someone who in every way seemed perfectly normal—yet you could "sense" something, and you had the urge to move away from that person. If you're anything like me, you did move. What happened as soon as you moved? You immediately felt more comfortable. Your inner voice was right, but you could never prove why.

But what can you do in a situation where you can't get up and move, because you are comfortably seated, and there are no more seats, and you are very tired? You try to read your book or think your own thoughts, but that "feeling" won't go away and you are very ill at ease sitting next to the person. Somehow, you feel that this person has transmitted negative or even perhaps potentially harmful energy to you.

Try this experiment. Think these words and direct them mentally toward the person next to you: "Go away. Leave now." Say the words again and again, completely concentrating your thought on this person, and mentally directing the words at him or her. Picture a force of energy pushing the person out of the seat and to the other side of the room. Picture him or her getting up and moving. Nine out of ten times the person will first start fidgeting, and finally get up and move.

I know this sounds crazy—and in fact, there's no way I can prove that it works. Quite frankly, it doesn't always work. But when it does work, I notice that it is when I am completely centered and determined—and focused—and I'm totally concentrating, picturing the energy pushing him or her away. When it does work, I think it works because the person senses something—and begins to feel uncomfortable. What that "something" is cannot yet be proven scientifically.

Another idea is to envision an impenetrable glass wall rising up between you and the unpleasant person. Imagine that this person's energy cannot touch you. In other words, mentally "protect" yourself from this person. Keep imagining the glass wall every time you feel the uneasy feeling— and soon you will not feel the discomfort of this person's energy. This is an excellent method to get you through times when you cannot get away from a person (packed bus, long line you cannot leave, etc.).

TO SAVE YOUR CREATIVE ENERGY BY PROTECTING YOU FROM CERTAIN PEOPLE

Your inner voice can also tip you off to someone in your life who has negative energy, someone who by their presence is bringing you down. This person has the effect of a rain shower on a campfire. Every time you leave his or her presence, your "fire is out," and you don't know why. I believe that the let-down feeling is a quiet warning from your inner voice that this person is not good for you.

Think. Who in your life is gifted at bringing out the negative side of everything? Who in your life always has "an answer" as to why "it won't work," why "it isn't worth trying"? Is there someone in your life who you now realize does not share your values—someone you think will hinder you from reaching your full potential? You don't need friends or acquaintances who drain your energy and hinder your creativity. Having such people around you is like trying to run with a thirty-pound sack on your back. You can do it, but it really slows you down.

The renowned psychologist and philosopher Carl Jung put his finger right on the problem when he said of his own life: "I was able to become intensely interested in many people; but as soon as I had seen through them, the magic was gone. In this way I made many enemies. A creative person has little power over his own life. He is not free. He is driven by his daimon."[2]

You have to be honest with yourself. There may be a person in your life who is perhaps a wonderful, fun-loving individual, but he or she may be a hindrance to you. Will allowing this person to remain in your life cost you the precious time that you need to achieve your goals? Ask yourself, Does this person's presence in my life drain precious creative energy? If so, if like Carl Jung you "see through them," you may need to let go of that person. You may realize that it is important for you to think of the big picture, and in so doing, take steps to protect your creative gift, what Carl Jung calls your "daimon." You can save your own life by weeding out this person.

But what if that negative influence is someone from whom you can't escape, such as someone you must live with—for whatever reason—perhaps a parent? Well, you can "turn them off," at least their negative parts. You can select what you "let in," and in fact this sifting process can be fun. At times when that negative influence is being projected, you can mentally put a soundproof, impenetrable, Plexiglas wall around yourself. When you begin to feel the negative influence being projected toward you, picture the words and energy coming from them as not being able to penetrate your thick, soundproof, impermeable wall.

TO RESTORE CREATIVE ENERGY BY URGING YOU TO GET PHYSICALLY FIT

Your inner voice also watches out for your physical body. You see, the mind-body connection cannot be severed. When your body is overweight, weak, ailing, and generally "out of shape," your mind does not function at its optimum level. This connection can even be seen in the foods we eat. Overload the body with too much sugar and fat, and the brain will not be as alert as it would be if you fed it a balanced diet. Starve the brain of complex carbohydrates, and the brain is less able to focus—to concentrate. In fact, if you let your complex-carbohydrate intake get too low, you literally can't think straight.

But it goes farther than that. If you are out of shape and are feeling sluggish and unhealthy, you waste a lot of creative energy feeling upset about the condition of your body—energy that could be better channeled into achieving your goals. For this reason, your inner voice will not let up on gently urging you to get in shape.

I know this from the thousands of letters I've gotten from readers of my fitness books, both male and female. Time and again they write, "I've tried to be happy, fat, and out of shape, but it just isn't me. Something keeps telling me that I'll never be content until I get this out of the way." And I've also gotten letters from people who did get in shape, and who tell me they have gotten promotions in their jobs, moved out of negative relationships, and even gone back to school. In fact, one man told me that after getting in shape, he gained such energy and renewed confidence that he went back to school to finish his law degree.

And why wouldn't your inner voice urge you to do something that would make your daily life flow with more ease and help you to be more productive, energetic, confident, and at peace with yourself? Isn't it true that when your body is out of shape, you feel that it no longer represents "you" and is a contradiction of your "self"? When you look in the mirror, your appearance says, "I'm lazy. I'm sloppy. I don't care." But your "self" is not lazy or sloppy or indifferent; rather it is creative, intelligent, and capable.

How do you know that your inner voice is urging you to do something about it? You will know that your inner voice is speaking to you when (1) you find yourself apologizing for your appearance all the time; (2) you find yourself dreading comments from friends and relatives on your weight gain; (3) you head off conversation by saying, "I really have to go on a diet"; (4) you catch yourself, in intimate situations, saying, "Wait. That light is bothering me. Let me turn it out," and you hide beneath the covers claiming to be "cold," when all the time you love the light and are really too warm as it is. Clearly, your inner voice has set up a continual undertone: "This is not you. You belong 'in shape.' Do something about it."

When your ears perk up every time you hear about a new diet, when you get excited every time you spot a new workout book or video or read an article in the paper about obesity, it is not just you being neurotic. It's not just "society" expecting you to look a certain way. It's not just "vanity," or your supposed obsession with your body. It's unfinished business, something that you have to do. And until you do it, your inner voice will not stop gently urging you to get fit, because your inner voice knows you. It is the voice of your "self," and it perceives that you are wasting precious creative time and energy on an extraneous issue that has taken over and become a major issue.

WHEN YOUR INNER VOICE SHOUTS

Sometimes your inner voice does not gently whisper or nag you, but rather shouts at you, seeming to set off an alarm system with sirens loudly screaming and red lights flashing.

It does this when you may be about to make a major mistake that will affect the rest of your life, or when your physical body is in danger.

WHEN YOU'RE ABOUT TO MAKE A BIG MISTAKE

I can give you an example from my own life. In 1965 I had become engaged, and as the wedding grew closer and closer, a heaviness set upon me that I couldn't shake. Every time I thought of the wedding, instead of being happy, a dreadful foreboding overtook me, a deep sadness, as if I were walking into a dark tunnel where I couldn't breathe. When I walked through the marriage in my mind I would feel as if, in some strange way, I was selling myself out—and a loud, clear voice in my mind seemed to say, "Call if off. Don't do it."

"What in the world can this be?" I wondered, ignoring the fact that I was clearly not in love with my fiancé and I was marrying him because we shared religious values. I had just gotten "saved"—had become a "born-again Christian"—and in my fervor to do what I thought at the time was God's will (without, of course, ever consulting God), I determined to marry a preacher. My future husband had just graduated from Bible school and seemed an excellent partner. I wanted to devote my life to winning converts to the church.

I wished I could talk to someone, but to whom? I dared not reveal my secret to anyone for fear that they would think I was either flaky or going berserk. So I kept it to myself all the time, the gloomy feeling getting worse and worse, and the voice shouting louder and louder. I drowned it out by keeping myself busy with planning the details of the wedding.

But the voice kept shouting. As the wedding approached, my heart grew heavier and heavier. Thoughts came to me loud and clear: "Don't do it. You're about to make a dreadful mistake," and I felt as if I were about to walk off a cliff. It scared me. I wondered if I were losing my mind. But instead of trying to listen to the voice, I couldn't wait until the wedding day was over so that I could have peace of mind again.

Up until two days before my wedding, the voice kept shouting. It was Thursday, and I was to be married on Saturday. I was in Macy's buying some last-minute items for my honeymoon. I remember exactly where I was in the store when it happened. I was standing by the makeup counter, having awful thoughts about the wedding, when suddenly the room blurred and seemed to start to spin. I became light-headed and couldn't catch my breath. My heart started beating faster and faster. When it slowed down, my mouth was dry. I felt suspended in time. A feeling of seminausea overtook me. I gripped the counter and said to the makeup clerk, who was looking at me with curiosity, "I think I'm going crazy. I'm supposed to get married in two days and something tells me not to do it." The clerk laughed and said, "Oh, it's just the jitters."

We talked for a while and she comforted me. I managed to regain my composure and my sanity. But as I walked home, I felt as if I were doing a slow walk toward a firing squad that would kill my soul. I managed to get home, where I was able to distract myself by showing my mother what I had bought and being hastened to the dinner table.

After that, the feeling slowly subsided, and did not return. On my wedding day I felt nothing but excitement and anticipation. Why had my inner voice shouted so loudly on Thursday, giving me what I now know was an anxiety attack, and then seemed to disappear? Why didn't the "voice" continue to badger me right up until the moment when I walked down the aisle?

I believe that our inner voice knows us so well that it "realizes" what is and what is not possible and realistic for us to do, given our individual psyche and our total situation. I believe that my inner voice knew that for me, there was no way I would call off the wedding unless I at least had time to call everyone first, that I would not just refuse to show up at the church on my wedding day. I believe that with the wedding imminent, my inner voice knew that for me there was no turning back.

Three weeks after the wedding, my inner voice again began to shout. I guess it knew that I could have had the marriage annulled, that I had it in me to do that. But once again, I refused to listen. We had come back from our honeymoon and had been in our apartment for two weeks—and were already fighting every day. One evening, and I remember it as a "moment in time," I walked out of our apartment and into the city streets, in a semidaze and looking up at the sky. I knew I had made a mistake. "What have I done? I've ruined my life," I thought. And then came the thought, "No. Get it annulled. Do it before it's too late." But I was afraid even to think about an annulment. How could I embarrass my husband this way? What would my parents think? How humiliating to face all of my friends. So once again I squashed the voice, going home and making up with my husband. And for the next ten years, I busied myself with a life that I hated, a life that was not meant for me from the first day of our marriage until the day of our divorce.

In defense of my ex-husband, I must tell you that he is a wonderful man, and in fact such an amenable person that we got along in many ways. Now that I think of it, this is probably why it took me ten years to gain the courage and will to leave him. But he was the wrong man for me, and I was the wrong woman for him. Yes, marrying him did produce a wonderful daughter. "Perhaps you are the reason I married Daddy," I often tell her. "I think God knew that only the combination of the two of us could have produced you."

But that marriage cost me ten years of my life, ten years off perhaps another path—a time when I could have been fulfilling the purpose for which I was born. But fortunately I was able to retrieve myself and regain my destiny. I'll talk more about this later and also tell you how to refind your path if you have strayed from it.

We all have an inner voice. We can drown it out with rationalizations. We can try to drink it under the table. We can busy it out of our consciousness. But the inner voice will not be permanently silenced. It may play possum for a while, knowing that it is temporarily wasting its breath, but it won't give up on you. It will always be there for you—if you want to avail yourself of it. It is our "sixth sense," or what some people call intuition, and I believe it is what keeps many of us from danger, and even from death.

WHEN YOUR LIFE OR PERSON IS IN DANGER

Your inner voice can protect you from dangers that come up in daily life. I am reminded of what happened to my daughter not long ago. It was broad daylight. She was merrily walking to her car in the parking lot of the mall, rejoicing in the purchases that she had just made, when she "felt something" behind her. She got a very strong urge to turn around, but when she did, all she saw was a man walking quickly behind her. She gave him a long, hard look, but could find nothing visibly wrong. He seemed simply to be in a hurry, and it appeared that he might be racing to pass her by on the way to his car. So she kept walking. Again, she got a very strong feeling that something was wrong. She tried to ignore it, but couldn't, and was forced to turn and once again check out the immediate field behind her— so she looked over her shoulder. Again she could "see" nothing wrong, but was impelled to put the strap of her shoulder bag across her chest—and instead of arguing this time, she did it. Immediately, the man did an about-face and began running in the opposite direction.

Clearly there was something warning my daughter of danger, but what was it? It was a sensation, a feeling, a "vibe." Call it what you will, but it was very real. I've had the experience many times myself, where I'll be walking down a street and I'll "feel" someone behind me. When this happens, I'll usually stop and look in a store window, and sure enough, the person will hesitate and linger, waiting for me to walk on. That's when I cross the street or go into a store—to get away from what I am sure is a potential mugger. I believe that my inner voice has saved me more than once from being mugged.

Your inner voice can also warn you to be alert a few hours ahead of time so that you can ward off potential danger—but you have to be careful not to misinterpret the message. For example, did you ever get a "premonition" that something bad was going to happen, then later in the day it happened? Probably later, when the negative event occurred, you said to yourself, "I knew that was going to happen. I was forewarned." But perhaps you misinterpreted what you felt, and took what was meant to be a warning of caution by your inner voice to be an inevitable prophecy. The message was given to you, not to prepare you for a "fact," but to give you the opportunity to prevent the negative event from happening by being cautious. Let me give you an example.

I was daydreaming in my kitchen one morning when suddenly a thought flashed through my mind that I would get into a car accident that day. I acknowledged the thought, but barely, and in fact forgot that I had even had the thought, until later, when I was in my mother's house telling her about the car accident I had gotten into (my car was badly damaged but, thankfully, I wasn't hurt).

A few weeks later I got another premonition: that I was going to get mugged on my way home from my night teaching job at the university. But by now I had spoken to a friend who told me that whenever you get a thought of something bad happening, you can prevent it from actually occurring by rejecting it on the spot. She told me to picture the event mentally, and then, in my mind, to draw a big X over the event, and at the same time, to say "No!" out loud. I did something extra. I shot up a simple prayer to God—just a thought, actually. "Please protect me, God," I implored.

So when I had this thought of being mugged, and I caught myself thinking, "Oh my God, how awful," and in a sense, accepting or "claiming" the dreadful event, I instead drew an **X** over it and said "No!" Later that night, on the train, I was about to get into a subway car—but as I was stepping in, I noticed that the car was empty except for a lone man who was already eyeing me furtively. Instead, I turned on my heels, making believe I had forgotten something (not that I owed him an explanation, but I didn't want him to think he was "suspect," just in case he was not planning to do anything). I waited for the next train, and this time I made sure I got into a car with a bunch of other people. I arrived home safe and sound that evening.

I have had many other "premonitions." But instead of accepting them, instead of "claiming" them, in a manner of speaking, and in essence turning them into self-fulfilling prophecies, I rejected them. For example, I know that there are times when you're going to get sick and there's just nothing you can do about it. For one reason or another, a germ or virus has invaded your body and it just has to run its course. But I must say, I believe I've been able to ward off many an illness by being aware of my mental process as soon as I began to feel ill, and doing everything in my power to send it in another direction.

For example, more than once I've begun to feel under the weather, as if a cold or fever were coming on, and that I was about to get sick and miss an upcoming planned vacation, an important meeting, or some such event, but instead of mentally accepting the idea, I would immediately put an **X** over the image of myself being sick, and say "No." In addition, I would take the time to get a little extra sleep and, in a sense, pamper myself, so as to give my body every chance to reverse the direction of the illness. I'm not saying that this always works, but it certainly can't hurt to try it.

YOUR INNER VOICE GUIDES YOU

Your inner voice does more than whisper or shout to help you to avoid aggravation, wasted energy, or danger. Throughout your life, your inner voice struggles to be heard—over the noisy din of your own thoughts; the pressures put upon you by personal responsibilities, family, and friends; and the confusion of the many choices that surround you. It tries to give you guidance or direction in finding the path that you should walk, so you can best utilize your talent and fulfill the purpose for which you were born.

It is your inner voice that quietly nags or even badgers you if you have stepped off your path and are not living up to your potential. No matter what the reason—whether out of laziness, or fear, or weakness, or circumstance—if you are off "the path," or are not being true to your purposes in life, your inner voice will not leave you in peace. In speaking about the inner voice as it urges us toward self-actualization, psychologist Abraham Maslow says:

> It insists that we be true to our inner nature, and that we do not deny it out of weakness or advantage, or for any other reason. He who belies his talent, the born painter who sells stockings instead, the intelligent man who lives a stupid life, the man who sees the truth and keeps his mouth shut, the coward who gives up his manliness, all these people perceive in a deep way that they have done wrong to themselves and *despise themselves for it.* Out of this self-punishment may come only neurosis, but there may equally well come renewed courage, righteous indignation, increased self-respect because of thereafter doing the right thing.[3] (Italics mine)

The point made by Maslow is clear. The inner voice is the guardian of the "self." When we have strayed from that which we know in our hearts we must do, it is our inner voice that will continually shine the light on our darkness. As a faithful friend, it can cause us to feel so uncomfortable that we have no choice but either to "despise ourselves" or to give in to the truth that is being spoken to us, and do "the right thing" with our lives.

Ironically, I had an unusual experience just as I was contemplating this chapter. I went for a manicure, something I rarely do because I have no patience to sit in the salon. But this day I went, and sitting next to me was a young lady who told me that she had just quit her job in the garment center. "Why did you do that?" I asked, only mildly curious, but willing to pass the time in polite conversation and thinking, "Who knows? Maybe I can offer her a word of encouragement."

She then told me that she really wanted to be doing something else. Sociology had been her major in college, she said, "but my parents felt I should go into practical work—where you can make some money."

"Well, what are you going to do now?" I asked.

"I don't know," she said. "It's too late for me."

Surprised to hear that, I said, "What do you mean? Are you saying that you missed your path?"

With this question she became energized and turned to face me, her eyes lighting up as if to say, *How did you know?* and she answered, "Yes. That's it, and now it's too late for me. I missed my path."

She proceeded to tell me that she was twenty-two-years old and had worked in the garment center for a year. At this I smiled and said, "And why does a twenty-two-year-old feel that it's too late to get back on her path?" Now she was smiling, too, but she said, "I don't know. I feel as if it's too late."

We talked for a while, tossing ideas around, and it turned out that she really wanted to work with children. I suggested that she apply for a job in the local nursery school— at least for a start (we had both noticed the "Help Wanted" sign). But she had a list of other possibilities too: the hospital where abandoned children were left, an ad she had seen in the paper for a graduate course that gave "in the field" training, and so on. By the time our nails had dried, she was very excited about her prospects.

What had caused this young woman to quit her job in the garment center, to strike up a conversation with me, to notice an ad in the paper about in-the-field training in social work? I am certain it was her inner voice, gently urging her to find her path in life.

But why did the young woman feel as if it was too late after only about a year in the wrong direction? The answer to this is very clear to me. Our lives are so precious, and every day is so valuable, that when we are off our paths for a few months, for a year, for two years, we "know" we are wasting the precious time we were given on this earth—and we feel a heavy burden of guilt that distorts our perception. Also, on some level, we know that days and months off our paths can slip into years—and then a wasted life. So we feel guilty and we allow that guilt to cause us to believe wrongly that "it is too late." But the truth is, it's never too late. The only thing it is too late to do is to regain the time we have already spent on the wrong path.

It isn't too late if you're twenty, or thirty, or forty, or fifty, or even if you're in your eighties—for even at that age, there is still something that is "right on the money" that you can do with your time and energy that would insure that you do not go out of this world with what I shall later explain as "empty hands." But it takes a courageous person to admit that he or she has made a mistake, and to take the pains necessary to correct the situation.

IS IT REALLY MY INNER VOICE— OR IS IT MY IMAGINATION?

But how can one tell the difference between a thought that is erroneous or merely superstitious, and one that is truly coming from the inner voice, the voice that knows the self, the voice that one can trust? Someone I met in a local fitness center recently made me think of this. While I was working out, a young man exercising next to me told me he worked for a local newspaper. "Do you like it?" I asked, wanting to be polite.

"I hate it," he said.

"Then why don't you try something else?" I asked.

"Well, I'd like to become a cop. I've wanted to for a long time."

I stopped working out and gave him a long look. "You look like you'd make a great cop," I said.

He became very excited about that remark and said, "Really? Do you think so? Everyone says that. I just took the test and I'm waiting for the results. I can't wait to see what happens."

With that I said, "Don't worry. If it is what you really want, don't give up until you get it."

"I won't," he said—and sprinted across the gym to his next machine.

Clearly this young man's inner voice was urging him to go in a different direction, to move from being a newspaperman to becoming a police officer. He was definitely not a victim of his imagination or hearing a false message. Here's why: (1) He was getting the message from a variety of sources (notice that when I said "You look like you'd make a great cop," he replied, "Everyone says that"); (2) He tried to ignore it, and admittedly, he was miserable; (3) When he tried to move in the direction that his inner voice was urging him to go, he felt not only more comfortable, but energized (he had taken the police exam, and enthusiastically said, "I can't wait to see what happens").

The bottom line is, when your inner voice is speaking to you, you can find out if it is a true inner voice by testing it out—by trial and error. As human beings, we are complex and have many talents, and can be good at more than one thing in life, but we may feel happier and more fulfilled doing certain things. I believe that experimenting is in fact the only real way to end up where we truly belong. You are a multifaceted person, and if it is time to move on, start making forays in other directions. There will probably be more than one confirmation to let you know if you are on the right track.

BE TRUE TO YOURSELF AND YOU WILL BE TRUE TO THE WORLD

Sometimes it is not being in the wrong job that is the problem, but refusing to listen to your inner voice because you are afraid to displease certain people. If your inner voice has been prodding you to change your career or your job, don't fall into the trap of convincing yourself that "it is best for all concerned" that you just keep doing what you're doing. Don't believe the lines you throw yourself, like "Oh, it's not that bad." It *is* that bad. It's worse. Betraying yourself is the worst thing you can do to yourself.

When you betray yourself in this way—by not finding your path and doing what you were born to do, or restrict yourself by saying, "How dare I try this?"—you also rob the world. How so? You steal from the world the gift that you have to give it. The world misses out on your talent. So, ironically, we start out thinking, "Isn't it selfish for me to do X, Y, or Z in order finally to become what I know I should become?" Chances are your decision will affect the lives of people in your immediate surroundings. But you have to think of the big picture. In the long run you can't be true to others unless you are first true to yourself. The fact is, if we are true to ourselves, we will be happier, more content, and more excited about whatever we do—and that in itself will make us more effective—and indeed, more happy.

I am reminded here of how my dog behaves when I want to take his old, raggedy bone away—a bone he has been working on for days, which is really no longer of use to him. If I approach it he will growl and snap and defend his bone. But if I approach him with a new juicy bone with lots of meat on it, he will focus on the new bone and let go of the old bone. But unless I hand him that new bone first, he won't let go of the old.

The trouble is, in life we are not handed the new bone first. Very often we must first, by faith, let go of the old bone. It is only then that we are handed the new, more juicy bone. If we refuse to let go of the old bone, we may never know what new bone we were missing!

But what do you do in a situation where listening to your inner voice may prove very costly to the people around you? For example, suppose the young man I met at the gym were married and had two young children. Suppose he was earning a substantial salary at the newspaper and would have to take a significant salary cut to become a police officer. Suppose that his wife did not want him to become a police officer because she felt that she would be worried about his safety all the time. What should he do then?

It would depend a great deal upon how strongly he felt about the unpleasantness of his job and/or how deep was his desire to become a police officer. If his feelings were very intense, he would eventually have to find a way to move in the direction that would allow him to feel fulfilled—self-actualized—even if it would mean some temporary sacrifices for his family. He could compromise by working a part-time job to supplement the lost income—at least until his policeman's salary came up to what he was making on the paper. He could also study diligently for the promotions that are offered in the police department and increase his salary that way.

The point is, I don't believe that we should just say, "Let the devil take the hindmost," throw all caution to the wind, and dart ahead in the direction that we feel is best for our fulfillment. I think we should consider carefully and perhaps make some necessary compromises. But under no circumstances do I believe that we should permanently give up our dreams just because they will inconvenience others.

WHY DO WE RUN FROM OUR GIFT?

Very early in life, we each begin to realize that we have certain talents or "gifts," yet instead of following the early clues and developing our aptitudes into a career, so many of us run from them. Many of us would rather do anything but what we were born to do, taking as many side roads as possible to avoid our gift. It is as if we sense that developing our gift will involve a lot of work. It's almost as if we fear that our gift will consume us. Still others run from their gift because they suffer from low self-esteem and the fear of challenge, conflict, or change that goes along with it. "Who am I," they think, "to deign even to dream of such ambitions?" and they go every which way except in the direction of their gift. (Chapter 3 will help you to build self-esteem.)

At a very early age it was apparent that I had a talent for writing and speaking. I can remember that, way back in the Bronx, in the fifth grade at PS 42, my poetry and compositions would end up in the school magazine—and on the bulletin board of the local library. In junior high school I won the "English Medal" for writing. And my mother reminds me that at the age of eleven, I taught an entire Bible class for adults in our church. "You were a good speaker even then," she says.

Yet as I approached my final years in high school, I decided to become a secretary. After a year of hating my job and my life, I decided to go back to school, but instead of daring to major in what I loved best, writing and English literature, I took a commercial course and majored in retailing. After getting a straight-A average and being asked to serve as president of the Retailing Club, I decided to apply for City College. But still I dared not go for my true love. I took up elementary-school teaching and went for a bachelor of science in Education. What was my problem? Why did I keep sidestepping my real goal? I can clearly remember thinking, "It's one thing to get straight As in business or education courses. Everyone knows they're easy. I could never do that in English courses. I probably couldn't even keep up with the work. I'm just not smart enough. I could never be an English teacher."

But let's take a closer look at what happened to me. Was I really completely sidestepping my goal or was I really in fact circling around it, getting closer and closer to my path? Looking back at my life, I now see that I always knew deep in my heart that I wanted to teach, write, and do public speaking; I just didn't believe that I was capable or even worthy of such high ambitions. Instead of daring to go straight for what I wanted, I circled around it for a long time.

But then I started to gain confidence, because I did well in my courses and because I was a good teacher, and the students loved me and I loved them. It was at this point that I began to dare to think directly in terms of what I wanted to do, and eventually I switched to teaching high school and then college—and writing books and lecturing, and doing television appearances. But what took me so long?

If I knew then what I know now about the inner voice, I believe I would have gotten on my path sooner. But I didn't listen to my inner voice because I didn't believe that there was such a thing. No one had ever talked to me

about it—and at that point I had never read about it anywhere.

But the main reason it took me so long to get on my true
path is very clear to me now: lack of self-esteem. As mentioned above, whenever the idea of becoming a teacher or
a writer would go through my mind, I said to myself, "Who
are you kidding? You're not intelligent or talented enough."

So I took what at the time felt like more "realistic" roads,
roads that I believed I could walk. But my inner voice
never let me forget that these side roads were just that, and
that I had a higher calling. And my inner voice continued
to urge me on until eventually I ended up where I am now,
dead-center on my path, feeling as if I wouldn't rather be
anywhere else in the world, doing anything else in the
world, or being anyone else in the world.

But notice that for me, self-esteem was a big problem. It
caused me to take more side roads than I would have perhaps taken had I had a stronger sense of self. For this reason, I devote a whole chapter to self-esteem in the hope
that if you suffer from a lack in this area, you will be able
to identify and remedy the problem, and not waste any
more of your precious life. In fact, that's why I am writing
this book: to help you to get there sooner than I did.

Another thing that stopped me from listening to my inner
voice—and it may be stopping you now—is misplaced
guilt. I felt guilty not contributing to the household fi-
nances, going to school when my parents were struggling
financially. So I went to work as a secretary. Later I realized
that I could do both, and when I went back to school, I
worked part time and went to school full time. Where there
is a will there is a way, but I had to suffer going off the
path. I had to feel that I was off my path, to think, "It's too
late," and then realize, "No. It's never too late. I can always
get back on my path." I finally learned to listen to the gentle but continual urging of my inner voice—the voice that
was always there—guiding me in the direction of my gift.

You have a gift too—and if you follow your inner voice, you will eventually develop your gift and become what you are supposed to become in this life. In fact, the Bible talks about this idea. It says, "A man's gift maketh room for him and bringeth him before great men" (Proverbs 18:16). This means that if we acknowledge and develop our gift, it will take us exactly where we are supposed to go in life.

ALL THINGS WORK TOGETHER FOR GOOD

But what about all of the "side roads" that so many of us take before we finally get on the best path for our lives? Was it all a complete waste of time? Of course not. You'll discover that once you are finally doing what you were born to do, all of the side roads will appear to have been "meant to be" in one way or another. You will see how they helped you to become the person you are now, and in some ways helped you to do what you were born to do better than you would have been able to do it had you not taken those detours. We need to prepare for our ultimate destiny, to build on knowledge and experience, and some of that preparation is not what we would have chosen—yet it's exactly what we needed.

I feel that had I not had such difficulty in finding my path—teacher, writer, and speaker—had I been "lucky" and become those things without struggle, I would not be able to offer conviction and hope to others. For example, if I was dead-center on my path from day one, how could I know to tell you that it is never too late get on track? I couldn't do it. But I can do it because I know what it is like to feel lost and confused—and unhappy with my life—and to feel a nagging voice in the center of my being say, "No. This is not what you were meant to be or do." And I know now, having finally arrived where I am, that the "nagging voice" was not my imagination, but in fact my inner voice, trying to nudge me gently along—and sometimes even shoving me—to get me to the life I was meant to live.

When I come to think of it, I didn't feel that I was really "on track" until I was in my late thirties or early forties. Since then, it's been a continual refining of that track, until now, as mentioned before, I feel I'm "dead-center" and moving in the direction of fulfilling the rest of what I was born to do. I tell you this not to encourage you to use my life-pattern as your example, because every one of us has a different road, but rather for your information.

So all of the things that happened to me worked together for the good of the big picture, and although for you, and for each of us, the details will be different, the result will be the same—but there is a big "if." The result will come if, and only if, you start listening to your inner voice.

HOW TO GET BACK ON TRACK

A good way to begin finding your path or destiny is to ask yourself what you value and to start pursuing or doing more of it. For example, if you are very artistic but are working in a chocolate factory, begin practicing your artwork in your spare time, and on the weekends attend art exhibits—and show your creations. If you have strong feeling for the homeless, volunteer to work in a shelter, even for an hour a week. If your heart goes out to abandoned children, you might think of being a foster parent. If you are concerned with the educational system, there are hundreds of volunteer positions you can apply for in your local school.

If you take small steps in the direction of your gifts, I believe one thing will lead to another, and you'll eventually find yourself doing what you were meant to do with your life. In fact, all of the above examples are not just examples. They are actual cases of people I know who started out just experimenting—and ended up being paid to do something they loved but thought they could not afford to do full time.

Another way to find your path or destiny is to ask yourself what you really wanted to do when you were younger, and then to determine where and why you went off your path. I have a friend who did this. She was working as a secretary for a music company in Los Angeles, and in many ways enjoyed the glamorous life: free tickets to concerts, continually meeting stars, wonderful parties. But deep down inside she was not happy. Something was missing. After much soul-searching, she admitted to herself that she had always wanted to be an elementary-school teacher. In fact, she had gotten her degree in this field, but when she moved to Los Angeles, she got caught up in the glamour scene and had strayed from her course.

After wrestling with her inner voice and trying to outshout it with protests such as "I can't afford the pay cut" and "I'll miss the many perks of my job" and "How do I know I could even pass the teacher's exam after all this time?" she decided to take the teacher's exam "just for the fun of it." And to her surprise, not only did she pass it, but she got one of the highest marks of the group taking the test that day.

Next, she thought, "Why not see if there are any teaching positions open in elementary school in my district?" Partially relieved, and partially disappointed, she found that there were none. One administrator informed her that there was an overabundance of teachers in that area, and that she should forget about it for any time in the near future. But at this point she couldn't stop herself from checking into surrounding communities. One day she got a call from a principal who told her that an unexpected position had opened up. Would she be interested?

To make a long story short, she accepted the job, taking a chance that she would like teaching, be a good teacher, and cope with the salary cut. Now, two years later, she is making more than she did when she worked for the recording company—and what's more, she met and married a man she describes as her soul mate. Their combined salaries make her feel as if she is "living in the lap of luxury."

But how did all of this happen for my friend? She took a chance. The chance is the risk of security—and, almost always, money. We are so deluded by trinkets at times that they can blind us to the future. We may ask, "Won't I be in poverty if I dare to go for the path that I know, deep down inside, I should follow?" but making a major life change, when you come down to it, always involves a chance. In the end, you have to bet on yourself and let the chips fall where they may.

And thankfully, the likelihood is that if you do take a chance, your ultimate situation will probably be quite the opposite of poverty. You may be better off financially than you were before because when you follow what you really believe in, you do it with all your heart. And when you do anything with passion and energy, the result is always bounty—perhaps financial, and definitely spiritual. On the other hand, if you spend your life doing something you don't really love, something for which you have no passion, you will hold back. You'll give it the least amount of effort, and you will reap meager rewards—and you may also reap anger, regret, and self-contempt. There is a biblical proverb that demonstrates this principle: "He becometh poor who dealeth with a slack hand: but the hand of the diligent maketh rich" (Proverbs 10:4).

But it's not a simple formula. There's no guarantee that if you follow your path you will automatically be financially prosperous. There may be a test period, a time when you may have to take a cut in income temporarily, or you may never be affluent. But even if that financial cut is permanent, can you really put a price on the daily joy that fills your soul when you know you are doing exactly what you were born to do, when, as a general rule, every morning you wake up and think, "I can't wait to get to work today" instead of, day after day, awakening to the thought of, "I wish it were five o'clock already—and my workday was over," and, in a sense, wishing your life away?

EMPTY HANDS

Picture yourself at the end of your life. You are on your deathbed. You have continued to follow the path that you're on now until the day you are about to die. You are looking at the ceiling, reviewing your life. How do you feel? Is it okay to die? Did you fulfill the many purposes for which you were born? If you can say yes to that question, you are in a good position. Chances are, you have been listening to your inner voice—and are where you should be.

But if your answer is no, it would not be okay to die, you would not have fulfilled your purposes, you need to ask yourself, "What would I change?" and change it. In fact, let's take the above analogy a step farther. Let's make believe that the above is only a bad dream. Now you wake up and you see that you have your life back. You are given a second chance. Now what will you do to make sure that you would feel comfortable at the end of your life? To me, it is very important to resolve this issue, because, like Carl Jung, I feel that

> When I die, my deeds will follow along with me—that is how I imagine it. I will bring with me what I have done. In the meantime it is important to me that I do not stand at the end with empty hands.[4]

There you have it—your opportunity to take your life back and do what you were born to do, to get excited about life and live it to the fullest, so that when you die you will not face death with empty hands.

ϙ **Key #1.** The power of your inner voice. Know and trust yourself.

NOTES

1. Carl R. Rogers, *On Becoming a Person* (Boston: Houghton Mifflin, 1961), p. 22.

2. Carl G. Jung, *Memories, Dreams, Reflections*, ed. Anelia Jaffe (New York: Vintage Books, 1965), p. 357.

3. Abraham Maslow, *Toward a Psychology of Being*, 2d ed. (New York: Van Nostrand, 1968), p. 7.

4. Carl G. Jung, *Memories, Dreams, Reflections*, ed. Anelia Jaffe (New York: Vintage Books, 1965), p. 318.

3

THE POWER OF
SELF-ESTEEM

It is with great emotion that I write this chapter because it forces me to remember how hard I struggled for my self-esteem as a child growing up and through my early adult life. It was a long, hard journey, yet, having done it myself, and having come out of the other side of the tunnel (for surely there is a light at the end of that tunnel), I feel that I can help you.

I can encourage you to "struggle for your sanity," as it were, if self-esteem, for a moment, can be equated with sanity and mental health. I can encourage you to engage in this battle because if you do, you will eventually win. You will raise your self-esteem. The day will come when you finally say, "Whew. I am actually okay. There's nothing really wrong with me. In fact, I am quite a gal (or guy)." You will be able to live and enjoy life in peace, and to pursue your goals without guilt or shame. In short, all the clouds that have hovered over you all your life will finally lift— and the sun will permanently shine from the center of your being. You'll feel "whole" inside. Your sense of self will be solid gold.

WHAT IS SELF-ESTEEM?

Self-esteem is what you think of yourself—your sense of self-value or, to put it another way, your reputation with yourself. People with high self-esteem believe in their hearts that they deserve to be happy, that they have the right to stand up for their needs. They trust in their ability to deal with the problems that come up in life. In short, people who have healthy self-esteem *love themselves*—not in a narcissistic way (to the exclusion of others), but in a healthy way. One way to think of it is that a person with high self-esteem treats him- or herself the way a well-balanced parent would treat a child: with unconditional love.

People who have low self-esteem, on the other hand, have a bad reputation with themselves. They believe in their hearts that they don't have the right or even the ability to be happy—and that they don't have the right to stand up for themselves. They have little confidence that they can cope with the problems that come up in life, and in fact, they often dislike, disrespect, or even hate themselves. Many people fall somewhere in the middle—they have neither very high nor very low self-esteem. But a lot of people fall below the middle. Those who fall into this category are not only very often hampered from achieving their goals, but they suffer great emotional pain on a daily basis.

You need a certain degree of self-esteem to believe that you are worthy of happiness and to be *motivated* to try to get what you really want out of life. Clearly, if you have low self-esteem, you may think that you are not worthy of achieving anything—and you can stop yourself from trying. In fact, should success or "good luck" happen along, a person with low self-esteem will often find a way to sabotage that success or find a way to sidestep the good luck.

Here's how it works. If you have low self-esteem, you will be afraid to try for two reasons. First, in your secret heart you'll feel too guilty about imagined shortcomings. You'll think that by daring to try for something, you'll expose yourself to the world. Others may notice you. If they do, they may discover that you are unworthy, inferior, damaged, inadequate, and even despicable. So why even try? "Keep a low profile," you tell yourself. "Better be careful. You don't want them to find out the truth about you." Second, you feel that if by some chance you should succeed, you'll know deep down in your heart that you are a fraud (the "impostor syndrome") and that you are really not worthy of the success you have achieved. Unconsciously, you may realize that the success will cause you to feel even more uncomfortable than you already feel. Those who dare to try for success, despite low self-esteem, secretly believe that it is only a matter of time before people discover that they are not worthy of the success they have achieved. They live in fear of "discovery."

So it is important to repair damaged self-esteem in order to free yourself to get excited, to dare to pursue your goals—and to enjoy the realization of those goals once you achieve them. It's critical to extinguish once and for all that nagging voice that would otherwise whisper, "And who do you think you are, anyway? How dare you? What makes you think you deserve a better life? Get back into your place before real trouble comes."

But how can you raise your self-esteem? How can you repair the damage? You can say aloud, to yourself and others, "I am a good person. People like me. I love myself," from now until next New Year's. But if you have low self-esteem, it will remain low, and what's more, you'll feel like a fool in your own eyes. What you need to do to raise your self-esteem is to change your reputation with yourself—to change *what you think of yourself*—and the only way you're going to do that is first by realizing that the images you formed of yourself were distorted or erroneous, or due to circumstances over which you had no control. Then you must take specific actions that will help to raise your self-esteem. First, let's talk about how your self-image was formed.

HOW YOUR SELF-IMAGE IS FORMED

As a child your caretakers had total power over what you thought of yourself. Their "opinions" of you were not opinions to you, but the word of God—your only choice, the only game in town. So if your caretaker continually called you stupid, or sloppy, or lazy, or inept, you had little choice but eventually to learn the lesson they were teaching you—and to believe those things about yourself.

Let's go back to when you were five years old and look at a typical example in childhood where self-image is affected. If one day you had an "accident" and wet your pants, and if you told your mother about it, and she reacted as if it were a normal thing, you thought little of it. You went about your business and resumed your play. Probably the next time you had an "accident," you had no hesitation in telling your mother. This process went on until eventually your bladder matured to the point where you no longer had "accidents." End of drama. No damage done.

But if, on the other hand, your mother said, "Shame on you. Big girls (or boys) don't wet their pants. What a baby you are," you probably felt ashamed and vowed never again to have an "accident."

Even so, it happened again, and this time your mother got really angry. "What's wrong with you?" she shouted. Don't I have enough work to do without you adding to it? Maybe I should put you in diapers again." At this point you experienced doubt about your "okayness" as a person. You felt anger at yourself for not being able to control wetting your pants, and guilt for making your mother angry, and fear or loss of your mother's love, and with it, shame as you imagined yourself being publicly humiliated by having to wear diapers once again.

I use the above example to make a point not about wetting the pants, but for a slew of other events that occur in the course of normal child-parent relationships. Many well-meaning parents treat children in a way that causes them, at an early age, to form a fractured image of themselves. Sometimes normal childhood mistakes, perhaps better viewed as attempts to grow up, draw harsh criticisms such as, "You're a baby," "You're clumsy," "You're sneaky," "You're stupid," "You're mean," "You're bad." As children, we interpret it all to mean: "I am not good or lovable." As time goes on, we form an image of ourselves as not okay, not okay at all. In fact, we begin to believe that we are inferior to other people.

Let's take it a step further. What happens if our parents beat and otherwise abuse us, and we learn to accept this as our due? We think, "I'm not lovable. I deserve to be punished. I'm bad, I'm inferior." And later we seek out abusive relationships—and in fact feel relieved when find them because, unconsciously, it is only when we are being abused that the our inner world makes sense. It's the only subliminal logic we know. And so it goes, until we challenge the whole system.

Another reason many of us have low self-esteem is due to the unwillingness of our parents to be truthful with us when we were children. For example, if a child overhears a mother and father screaming at each other (while the child is supposed to be sleeping) and the next day the child asks, "What were you and Daddy fighting about?" and the mother says, "We weren't fighting. We were only kidding," or "You imagined it, you must have been dreaming," the child, over time, begins to doubt his or her ability to perceive reality. This undermines a child's feeling of being able to "read" and judge the world, and chips away at the child's self-esteem at a most vulnerable age.

I'd like to help you reevaluate your self-image, and to build your self-esteem, whether you need just a little help or a lot. For starters, thankfully, most of us have formed some good images of ourselves. Most of us heard some positive things from even the most critical parents, or others who have influenced the way we think about ourselves, such as teachers, grandparents, and other relatives, also said some positive things. You might have heard, "How pretty you are," "How fast you did that," "What a nice drawing," "That was a funny joke," and so on. Those positive statements, even though they may have been "crumbs" in the big picture, were enough to help you to see that you were not "all bad." That is probably why you were able to get as far in life as you've gotten despite the negative input of your world when your self-image was forming.

And if you think about it, wherever you are today, whatever you have managed to make of your life, given what you may have had working against you, you should probably pat yourself on the back. You were fighting with one hand tied behind you, and yet you managed to do rather well. How so? You're here and you're still sane, and what's more, you're striving for self-actualization.

But you've accomplished other things, both great and small. Let's use those things as a foundation to build on. Stop for a moment to think about it. Make a list of all the things that you have already accomplished in your life— despite the odds. Did you graduate from high school? Are you self-supporting? Did you marry and have children? Did you have the courage to get out of a bad marriage? Did you get back on your feet after a painful divorce? Did you win any awards or prizes? Do you have any friends? (Yes. If you have friends, it indicates that you took the time to develop a relationship with another human being—who, in turn, is responding to you.) Do you have any skills? Do you have any hobbies? Have you read any books? Are you an expert on any subject? Do you have any talents that have ever been rewarded or recognized, or even talents that have never been recognized or rewarded by others yet you know are there? Are you good in any sport?

Make a list of things of which you are proud—nothing is silly and nothing is too humble to mention. And don't feel as if you are bragging—and don't be embarrassed to write it down. Anyway, this is your book and no one will see it unless you let them see it.

THINGS I'VE ACCOMPLISHED IN MY LIFE
IN SPITE OF THE ODDS

1.

2.

3.

4.

5.

Don't stop here. Feel free to add as many accomplishments as you choose.

Our self-image is also formed by the way we measure up—not the way we really measure up, because there is no actual "standard of perfection" out there that we must achieve, but the way we measure ourselves against others. This self-measuring against others is often fueled by parents, relatives, teachers, and acquaintances in our early childhood years. In many cases it's a brother or sister who is put up to us as the ideal. "Billy is so responsible—he takes after his father. I wonder where you got *your* genes?" or "Paula learned to read so quickly. What's wrong with you?"

My own mother admits to having used this method—and why not? Chances are she herself was raised that way. When I was born, psychology was in many ways a young science. It was certainly unknown to laypeople, at any rate.

It is small wonder that we judge ourselves against others, behaving as if there exists—somewhere out there—"the perfect person." We constantly and erroneously ask ourselves, "Do I measure up?" Measure up to what? Measure up to whom? The answer is clear: to the "ideals" of the ones we love and admire—the parental figures.

CREATE YOUR OWN STANDARD AND LIVE UP TO IT

Now you can challenge the negative image of yourself that you developed as you were growing up. You can realize that the reason you feel you are stupid, or lazy, or slow is due to words that were spoken to you when you couldn't argue back. You can realize that as a child, you were probably being asked to measure up to impossible standards half the time, and to other people's standards the rest of the time.

Some of us fought this practice. "I don't want to be like everybody else," we cried. And we became rebels. But why should you have to become a rebel just to be yourself? Now that you understand what has happened, you can create your own standard for yourself, and you don't have to feel like a rebel because you do it. You can joyfully and peacefully and, in fact, with sheer, unthreatened calm, work on being yourself. Now that you are an adult, no one is stopping you anymore. Finally, no one is stopping you from finding out what you should be. No one is preventing you from creating your own standard and living up to that standard alone.

Once you've started living by your own standard, your self-esteem will increase to levels you've never before enjoyed. People will begin to recognize and validate your true "self," and your self-esteem will grow even further. Why? Because you'll realize that your worth is not dependent upon what others think, and that, ironically, people seem to respect and approve of you when you dare to be yourself. This knowledge will cause you to be less and less afraid to take chances, to act upon your own hunches and intuitions. In fact, in time, as you continue to take chances and to live up to your own standard, you will become as bold as a lion!

TWELVE SPECIFIC THINGS YOU CAN DO TO RAISE YOUR SELF-ESTEEM

There are certain actions that we can take that will net us an almost instant and permanent boost of self-esteem. In and of themselves, each suggestion in this chapter will help, but cumulatively they are a sure-fire way of achieving a more positive self-image. In putting into practice the suggestions below, you will gain a clearer sense of who you are, a more lucid "sense of self," and this will contribute greatly to your self-esteem.

1. FACE THE MUSIC AND DANCE

This is an old expression that I love: "Let's face the music and dance." If you want to build self-esteem, whenever you are confronted with a problem in life, no matter how unpleasant, rather than burying your head in the sand, whitewashing it, trying to cover it over, confront the problem head on. Admit the truth to yourself, no matter how painful it may be, and search for ways to solve the problem.

This is not always easy. For example, if a mother notices that her six-year-old son is unusually cruel to animals, she may at first deny the problem. She may think, "No. It can't be happening. Not my son. If my son is cruel, it would mean that I'm not a good mother." Rather than paying strict attention to her son's conduct, she glosses over numerous incidents, attributing them to "boyish" behavior, and in fact defends her son's behavior when others point it out. She'd rather not "know" the truth because that truth is too painful to face. But what is she really doing? She's sparing her own emotions, at the expense of her child's well-being, and on some level she knows this—and she loses respect for herself. In short, she lowers her own self-esteem.

In addition, she has probably reinforced a hurtful way to cope with problems that come up in life. She has learned that by magical thinking (if I ignore it or wish it were not so, it will go away), she can make everything all right. The more she "wishes away" problems rather than dealing with them, the more "chickens will come home to roost" and haunt her. For example, if her child grows up and hurts or kills someone, and is arrested, she is confronted with the "truth" that has apparently risen from the dead (the sand in which it was buried). And the less she will trust herself in the future.

But what if, as painful as it may be, this mother faced the music and danced—the moment she realized her son had a problem. Suppose she took him to a psychologist and got at the root of the problem, and began to see her son flourish. What lesson would she have learned about herself? "I have the courage to face reality, even when reality is painful, and when I do, I can solve problems," she would think. She would have cemented into the foundation of her being self-respect, the feeling of competence, the belief that she is a capable person who need not shield herself from truth. She would have improved her reputation with herself. She would have built self-esteem.

Many people avoid "the music," and refuse to "dance," in other ways. They have a strange lump or skin lesion, and rather than go to the doctor and face the possibilities head on, they avoid the issue. All the time, a nagging doubt is allowed to fester. Had they gone to the doctor, they would have found out exactly what was going on, and felt better about themselves—empowered, capable—aside from the very real possibility that such action could have saved their lives.

Another way of facing the music and dancing has to do with standing up for what you know is right in spite of the fact that it may be inconvenient or scary to do so. For example, if a mother sees a father mistreating her child, if she steps in and refuses to allow such behavior to go on—even though it may cost the peace and tranquility of her relationship with her husband—she builds self-esteem. She learns to respect herself because she was true to her values. She has maintained her integrity. There is no contradiction between her thoughts and actions.

If, on the other hand, a mother stands by and allows her husband to mistreat her child, telling herself, "I have to keep the marriage together," she lowers her self-esteem. How so? On a deeper level, such a mother "knows" that she not only has betrayed her child, but she has betrayed her "self," and because of her hypocrisy, she loses respect for herself.

What, then, should you do if you haven't made it a habit to face the music and dance? You can begin to do it now. The next time you see something that is wrong, instead of brushing the thought aside, do what is needed to right the wrong—in spite of the discomfort and temporary pain it may cause you. In my opinion, it is the only way to live— to live consciously rather than unconsciously.

2. TAKE ACTION: GET UP AND DO SOMETHING

The lazy person, the lethargic person, the "spectator," the person who wiles away his spare time or even his life watching things (such as TV, sports events, movies), never feels as good about himself or herself as someone who is always participating in things. As a matter of fact, a sure-fire formula for low self-esteem is not to do anything. Just sit around and waste time, and if, God forbid, you are forced to do something, put as little effort into it as possible. Not only will this modus operandi lower your esteem, it will also lower your income.

Why do we lose our self-esteem when we are not active? Human beings were not meant to vegetate or sit by help-lessly. We are natural experimenters with our environment. We were meant to engage in goal-oriented behavior. Goal-oriented behavior is easy and automatic during times when survival is the first and foremost objective, such as it was in the days of the caveman. I can hardly picture a caveman or cavewoman having low self-esteem due to boredom and depression. He was too busy hunting for food and securing the safety of his home. She was too busy bearing children and making sure they survived, and taking care of her difficult charge of cooking for the family. When we are busy surviving, we don't have time to spare. Thankfully, civilization has given us that luxury, and we must find something productive to do with that time or we get bored and may eventually lose respect for ourselves.

No matter what your job is or what your life is like, chances are you have found yourself in the position of feeling depressed because you sense that you are just "vegetating" during your spare time—or even in your job or in your relationship. You find yourself just going through the motions at work, or moving through a humdrum routine with your partner, or sitting in front of the TV, hour after hour, day after day, wiling away the hours of your life when you know you should be doing something more productive. But what?

Start with small things. For example, instead of lying around, get up and clean the house. Fix that broken outlet. Answer the mail. Make that annoying phone call to check on something you ordered. When you accomplish something, you feel much better about yourself than when you sit and do nothing.

Take it a step farther. Think. What is it that you could do—something you love to do but just don't have time for? Pursue an interest, something you've thought about doing. For example, you could take a course in self-defense, or better, a course in the martial arts, such as judo, jujitsu, or karate. The martial arts can help you to call upon and develop inner strength and with it, self-esteem. They teach discipline and respect. They teach you to center your energy and concentration. They teach self-control.

The beautiful thing about pursuing your own interests is that you don't have to depend upon anyone else. You can do it alone, and this further builds your self-esteem. You feel in control. For example, you go to your martial arts class yourself every week. Sure, when you get there you deal with other people. But you go alone. You're not depending upon someone else's mood to dictate whether or not you go to class. You realize that in order to be happy, you don't always need someone else. Whether it is working out, reading books of interest to you, or learning new vocabulary words (we'll talk about this later in this chapter), you'll be delighted to know that you don't have to depend upon anyone else to do it, and this knowledge, in and of itself, will help you to feel more powerful, more in control, and it will increase self-esteem.

But where will you find the time to pursue interests and activities? Well, you can do it during some of that time you used to waste watching TV. For example, right now, sit down and honestly calculate how many hours a week you spend watching TV. If it is twenty hours a week, make a compromise. Divide it in half and decide what "action" you will take for ten of those twenty hours—hours when you will be doing something, making something happen, instead of watching something.

Who knows? What starts out as a hobby or an interest may lead to an income or even a new career. For example, one woman wrote to me and said that she started out taking jewelry-making. When the course ended she bought materials to continue her hobby, and each evening and on the weekends she continued to make jewelry. She wore the jewelry to her job as a telephone operator, and soon people began asking how much she would charge to make them a pretty parrot, dog, flower, or some such pin. Before you know it, she was making quite a bit of money on that hobby, and eventually she decided to go into her own business. Now she makes jewelry full time.

3. Find Something Small and Succeed in It

The feeling of being successful and capable builds self-esteem. When you take on a challenge and overcome it you feel better about yourself than you did when you first started.

Start with a small success that would help you in your daily life. For example, I know so many people who hunt and peck away at the computer keyboard or typewriter when a simple typing course taken evenings or on the weekends would have them speeding away at eighty words a minute in a matter of weeks. How great these people would feel if they took action, if they picked up the phone and called their local business school and found out what was being offered when and for how much. How great they would feel if they figured out their schedule, signed up, and began the course. Soon they would have accomplished something that would remind them on a daily basis, as it made their life run more smoothly, that they had taken action. In short, they would have taken a small but important step in bolstering their self-esteem. They would think, "I am in control. I can make my life better. I can succeed when I make up my mind to do so."

Another example of small successes leading to big rewards in self-esteem: You may know how to use the DOS system on your computer, but you may not know how to use the Windows program, even though your boss has offered you the option of switching to it, and in fact has implied that soon you will have no choice. You've always been curious, but a part of you pulls back because, like me, you're a creature of habit, and have to be dragged kicking and screaming to make changes, or because you're just lazy, and you know you don't really have to do it yet.

Take the challenge. Call your local computer store and ask if they give courses in Windows. If they are too expensive, check your local community college. If that is too much for you, buy one of the "dummy" books and start working on your own. In one or two three-hour class sessions or a few days of reading, you'll learn all you need to know to begin using the Windows program, and what's more, you'll feel proud of yourself. This little feeling of pride raises your self-esteem.

You may be afraid of public speaking. My daughter felt that way, and in fact was terrified to speak to an audience. She was in her last year in college, had some room in her schedule for an elective course, and asked my opinion on what she should take. When I suggested public speaking, she was at first appalled. "How could you say that? You know I hate public speaking." "That's just why you should take it," I replied. "You may be able to expand your borders—overcome your fear." She thought about it and decided to give it a try.

When her first speech was due, she was terrified. She went over and over her speech in her mind while she pictured herself making a fool of herself by standing paralyzed in front of the room. But armed with a card outlining her speech, and with fear and trembling, she got up in front of the room. Five minutes later, when it was all over, she wondered what the big deal was, and in fact felt very comforted by the fact that thirty other students felt the same way she did—and also gave their speeches and lived. In fact, her presentation was complimented by more than one student. In addition, she found that instead of laughing at those people who did forget what they were going to say, the audience was quite supportive and helped the speaker along with questions and uplifting comments.

In any case, she discovered that going up in front of a group to speak was not the equivalent of going before a firing squad, and that she did live to tell about the experience. "I'm proud of myself," she said when she finished the course. "I can't believe I did it." And after that, although she still does not thrill to the idea of public speaking, she is no longer terrified of it, and in fact has confidence that she can handle the challenge if she's ever called upon to do so.

Why do we feel proud of ourselves when we pick something small and succeed in it? We expand ourselves—we
stretch ourselves. In short, we grow, and the human organ-
ism is meant to grow, not to stagnate. Our self-esteem rises
when we are being true to our nature.

I'll use myself as an example. When I first took up ballroom dancing, I didn't know a fox-trot from a waltz. But I always loved ballroom dancing and fantasized about doing the
tango, a romantic dance that had always appealed to me.

I decided to take a challenge. I found a conveniently located dancing school and signed up. Now, a year later, I
can do every ballroom dance, both smooth and Latin, and
in fact, I'm quite good at some dances. In fact, if I compare
myself to myself, I'm great. I have it all on video, in living
color. When I look at myself, my body, moving to the
music in graceful form—keeping my head in the right position, my body just so as I perform the dips and steps in
rhythm with my partner—I am amazed. "Is that me?" I ask
myself. I can't believe what I've accomplished in a year.

But I never had a time frame in mind. I just took it up as
a challenge. And look what I have to show for it a year
later. I think of it this way: If I hadn't taken up ballroom
dancing, by now a year would have gone by anyway, only
I wouldn't know how to dance. Now I do. And now I can
go out dancing (and there are quite a few places where
you can ballroom dance), and I can calmly say yes to any
man who asks me to do any dance or ask a man to dance
myself. (And I have done so, and do so whenever I get the
inclination.) And mind you, you're talking to me—a
woman who couldn't tell the difference between a skip and
a gallop in kindergarten, and formerly condemned herself
as a hopeless "klutz" because of it. So my small accomplishment, ballroom dancing, certainly did raise my self-esteem. It changed my opinion of myself from worse to
better.

Think of something small that you might want to try to
accomplish. It could be something as simple as getting a

recipe book and cooking a meal, following the directions exactly and seeing the wonder of the tasty finished product. It could be getting a kit and building something. It could be painting or wallpapering a room in your house, or reupholstering a chair, after having read a how-to book on it. It could be studying for and passing an exam that will qualify you for a job. It could be getting a book that you've been meaning to get, and reading that book.

Think of some things that you would like to do, some things that you would like to accomplish. Anything—great or small. List them here. You don't have to do them now, just write them down as something to think about, and then one day, when you're in the mood, you'll find yourself doing one and then another and then another on the list.

THINGS I WOULD LIKE TO DO

1.

2.

3.

4.

5.

4. CHALLENGE YOUR NEGATIVE THINKING
ABOUT YOURSELF

When you make a mistake in front of people, why do you call yourself a dummy? You want to say it before other people say it first, right? But then why do you call yourself a dummy out loud, even when no one else is around? We do it because it becomes such a habit. Maybe it started when we were children, and our parents called us dummies every time we made a mistake. Then we started calling it to ourselves in front of our parents.

Sadly, I saw this with my own daughter. One day, when she was about four years old, she piled her toys so high that the stack fell down with a very loud bang. I was standing there getting ready to yell at her, but before I could say a word, she cast me a glance and said, "I don't know what's wrong with me." Then quickly she turned to a fallen pile and began restacking.

Needless to say, I felt sad, even pained. How many times had I said to her, "What's wrong with you?" when she spilled her milk, dropped something, or had been clumsy? How sad. How pitiful that so many of us, without ever realizing it, hammer away at the self-esteem of our own children on a daily basis. If I—who was well versed in psychology and striving not to do to my child what was done to me by my parents—could do this, how much do most human beings assault their children's self-esteem on a regular basis? But let's not despair. At least if we become aware of our common mistakes we have hope of correcting them.

Getting back to my story, I was tempted to condemn myself and go away depressed, but instead I called my daughter into the kitchen and hugged her. "I love you," I said. "Nothing is wrong with you. You're only a little girl who is learning new things every day. You're doing a great job at it, too—like a little scientist experimenting and figuring out the best way to do things."

The next time I slipped and started to say "I don't know what's wrong with you," I stopped myself and said, "But I do know what's right with you," and she continued, "I'm a scientist." We laughed and hugged each other with glee.

But what happens if a mother never checks herself and continues to criticize and call her child names throughout the childhood and teen years? Quite naturally, such individuals, even as adults, call themselves names every time they make a mistake. But even if this happened to you, the good news is, you can change your self-talk now that you know better. Every time you catch yourself saying out loud or to yourself, "Stupid. How could you do that? What's wrong with you?" instead say, "Whoops. I made a mistake. I guess I'm human." Believe it or not, even that simple correction will go a long way in bolstering your self-esteem. In time you will stop condemning yourself every time you make a mistake, and instead will forgive yourself—give yourself some breathing room to be human and fallible.

That the self-image is extremely malleable can be demonstrated in an experiment I performed with a group of third-graders I taught. I was an elementary schoolteacher in a notorious "ghetto" area in Harlem, in New York City. In those days the classes were unabashedly grouped according to academic-achievement levels and intelligence tests. I was a new teacher, and had been assigned what was known, off the record, as the "dumb" class.

I decided to try to raise the performance level and, I hoped, the self-esteem of these children. I told them that because of prejudice against the "dumb" kids the principal didn't want to identify who the slow ones were, but that this class was really the smartest. I then began an all-out campaign to change the self-image of a group of thirty elementary schoolchildren who had been told all their lives that they were stupid. My first effort was to give them a list of three vocabulary words per week, "big" words that would impress any adult who heard them, who would immediately suspect that the child uttering them was precocious. I taught them how to bandy these words about in any and every possible context. In short order, I had them using words like *tenacious, arduous, portly, astute, altruistic,* and *martinet.*

I then had each member read a book of his or her choice every week, and required each of them to stand up in front of the class and tell what the author was trying to say about life. The "reporter" would then open up the session for questions and opinions. Each member of the class would also be required to find one positive thing to say about the report, including a way in which the report aided his or her education. I backed this up with a regular dose of praise any time a class member reported having learned something.

By the time the year ended, almost every child's reading level had increased by more than two years. And each and every one had changed in attitude so much that it even showed up in their posture. As a class, we would walk down the halls with heads high. But more than that happened. When promotion time came around, one-third of the class ended up in the section that really was the smartest section for fourth grade, and all but three students advanced their academic standing.

I tried a similar experiment with my own daughter. In the fifth grade, she began having big trouble in math. Her math teacher, an elderly man who was about to retire and who had obviously lost patience for struggling students such as my daughter, called her "obtuse" to her face. He pulled me aside and told me, "Marthe will never be good in math. Don't expect too much."

So taking his advice, I found myself ready to say to Marthe, when she asked me for help, "Don't feel bad. I was the same way as you." But instead, I caught myself and said, "You know, you're really good in math. You take after your Auntie Barbara" (who really is a math whiz). "Your teacher admitted to me that he sees your talent, but he's getting too grouchy to teach. He told me to get you a tutor to bring out your talent." Smiling with delight, she said, "Really?"

I then proceeded to hire a tutor, who, in a matter of weeks, had her doing work on her level—and higher. She ended up in honors math in high school—and in fact, in college, scored higher in math than in English on her Graduate Record Exams!

What would have happened to my daughter's math career if I had told her that her teacher was right, that she just couldn't understand math? She probably would have believed it, and done poorly.

Okay. All well and good. It's great that you know this, and wouldn't it have been wonderful if someone had taken the trouble to tell you that you were really talented or great, or some such thing. But they didn't. So why am I telling you these things? Surely not to tease you with something that can no longer help you. No, you can do something about it now: (1) You can challenge ideas that were given to you about your own abilities, and give yourself a good reputation to live up to, identifying with positive models. (For example, if you think of yourself as uncoordinated, claim to yourself that you really take after Uncle Joe, a damned good athlete, instead of your dad, who couldn't hit a ball, and so on. Realize that what you were told had a lot to do with the way you turned out, but now you can "claim" a better model and, in time, get better results. And why not? Who can prove who you "really" take after anyway?); (2) You can do to others what you wish had been done to you. Start using this methodology on your own children and other loved ones.

So the next time you get negative thoughts about yourself, don't just accept them. Challenge these thoughts. Within reason, brag about yourself to yourself: "I'm intelligent and creative. I have a strong mind. I am warm, loving, and compassionate. I'm generous. I'm adventurous, I'm fun to be with. I make a good friend, I'm loyal, I never give up." To break the power of negative self-talk and negative "reputations" you've been given, make a list of the traits and qualities that you've assigned to yourself—and refute them. Then draw a line through each of them and write the word No next to them. Then write a sentence claiming the opposite quality. I'll do number one for you to show you how it works. If you've been told that you take after a family member in some negative way, name him or her and X out that person's name, and write the name of someone who has the opposite quality.

NEGATIVE TRAITS AND QUALITIES
I'VE BEEN "ASSIGNED"

1. Uncle Tom: Stupid, slow to catch on. No. Cousin Brian. Intelligent and quick.

2.

3.

4.

5.

5. UNDERSTAND YOUR "DARKER MOODS"

There are many reasons for "lows," the times when dark clouds seem to fill our field of vision. In fact, some of the greatest minds in history have been plagued by dark moods of depression. Winston Churchill is a case in point. In fact, I remember reading that he even gave his depression a name, calling it his "black dog." The renowned writer William Styron suffered with this malady, calling his depression "darkness visible."[1]

Dark moods and depression come for a variety of reasons, too many to give fair treatment to here. But for now it is important to know that many times we become depressed because we expect too much of ourselves or others, then get angry when we are disappointed. Since we can't really keep attacking the self, or others, we eventually begin to hold in our feelings of anger, and we become depressed.

I suspect that is why so many great minds have battled with despair. These people have wonderful, but not perfect minds, and probably, like most of us, they have less than perfect relationships. But perhaps they hold themselves up to an unrealistically high standard, thinking that they "ought to" have fewer shortcomings and more ideal relationships.

I believe that when we see shortcomings in ourselves and our relationships, we get depressed, unless we realize that it's okay to be imperfect. We are not God. It isn't fair to expect ourselves or others to be perfect. We all fall short of our goals sometimes. We all make mistakes—and plenty of them.

The next time you feel depressed, you may discover that your reason for feeling down is due to a mistake or a "failure" on your part. But if you then say, "Okay, so what! I'm human," and loosen the choke hold you have on yourself, you may find that you are once again able to breathe, and the dark cloud of depression and gloom lifts or at least lessens.

I remember a time in my own life when I felt very depressed. It wasn't because of a failing in my own life, but rather because of a sorrow and loss—the death of my father. "What's it all about? Why go on?" I asked. "We're all going to die in the long run." But then a very strong thought came to mind: "If I ended my life now, who knows what I could have done with my life—something that could have helped others." Then I thought of a stanza from a poem I loved in my college years, when I was often stricken with dark moods. I remembered that the author was Robert Frost, I looked it up and reread it, and it gave me great comfort and the determination to go on. In his famous poem Frost talks about the woods being lovely and dark and deep, and having promises to keep.

I thought about my father and how he had so much hope for me, how he always encouraged me never to give up no matter how tough the going, how he urged me to develop my potential. He believed that I had a gift to give the world. How could I let him—and myself—down? How could I quit? Even though the dark cloud of despair was heavy upon me and at times it felt tantalizing to give up, how could I walk into the dark, deep woods and end it all?

No. I couldn't do that. I had promises to keep, promises to my father and to myself. I had a "job" to do—I dared not end my own life. I was thirty-four years old then. I did not have one book published yet. I had not begun to make my contribution to helping others through the printed word.

I'm glad that with the help of God I was able to resist the temptation to succumb to my darker mood. But more important, I want to encourage you to realize that no matter how bad things seem today, doing something drastic would not be the answer. You have a gift to give the world.

6. GET YOURSELF IN SHAPE

Getting in shape affects your self-esteem because there is a chain reaction. Your body language—the way you walk, your sitting posture, your demeanor, what your body says to the world—is affected by the way your body looks, and this in turn affects what you think of yourself (your self-esteem).

If your body is strong and muscular and well proportioned, you carry yourself with your head up and your shoulders back. You walk with an energetic gait. Your body sends a message to your mind: "You are strong. You are capable. You are in control," and your mind agrees: "Yes. I am a worthy person. I deserve respect."

If your body is weak and flaccid or obese and misproportioned by storehouses of excess fat, you carry yourself with your head down and your shoulders slumped and you shuffle along with a dragging gait. Your body sends a message to your mind: "You are unsightly. You are incapable. You're not in control." And your mind agrees: "Yes. If people see me, I must apologize for myself. I deserve no respect."

But no matter how badly out of shape you are, a small or even a major part of you knows that "you," the *real* you, are strong, and worthy, and capable, and that in fact your out-of-shape body is *not* a reflection of your true soul. Yet here you are, carrying around this burdensome contradiction, and it weighs on you, not just in the obvious way—physically—but also psychologically, forcing you to battle for your self-esteem on a daily basis.

"I'm overweight," you might say, "but I don't feel weak and out of control. I feel that my body is a true reflection of my soul. I'm happy." If this is you, and your weight is remarkably not causing you health problems, great. You are very unusual. You can skip this section, because I'm not talking to you. If and only if you ever feel as if your body is getting in your way, if you find yourself spending creative time and energy worrying about your body that could be better spent on achieving goals, then come back to this section.

But chances are that if you are out of shape, your body is not a reflection of your true soul—and of your mind—and you know this because you are spending too much time obsessing about diets and you find yourself apologizing about your body to people who aren't even asking. For example, you'll say to a co-worker, "I'm so fat. I really have to go on a diet," or you'll say to your husband or boyfriend, or wife or girlfriend, "I really need to lose weight," hoping against hope that he (or she) will say, "Oh, you look great just the way you are."

So you really don't have a choice. You have to get in shape and get it out of the way so you can enjoy the peace of mind that comes from being "at one" with yourself. And the beautiful part is, no matter why you got fat and out of shape—whether it was neglect or frustration that you took out on eating, or sheer laziness—you have the power to do something about it. You can take systematic action that will cause your body to evolve slowly into the shape and weight that reflect the true you. And as you see your body change for the better from week to week, month to month, and yes, from year to year (my body is in better shape now, in my fifties, than it was in my twenties—and yours can be too), you will feel better about yourself. A lot better. In fact, your reputation with yourself will improve. You will think, "If I can make improvements in my body, I can make improvements in other areas of my life," and you'll take on other challenges and overcome them.

So let it be known here and now that getting in shape is not all about vanity. It's all about self-esteem. (See my latest fitness book, *Definition*, for a whole chapter on how I battled with obesity and won, and how you too can get in shape once and for all. See the bibliography in this book for a complete list of my fitness books.)

7. BE GENEROUS: CONTRIBUTE TO THE WORLD AROUND YOU

One of the best ways to raise self-esteem is to take a welcome vacation from yourself and focus on someone else. Instead of trying to help yourself, try to help someone else. You'll feel better almost immediately.

Did you ever notice how great you feel after you do something kind for someone? You feel physically elated. It's almost as if you took a mood-elevating substance. Being generous produces a natural high—but it's a very special high. It's a high that says directly to your "self," "What you just did was great. Bravo! I'm proud of you." But why does this high come about? It goes back partially to the vacation you took from yourself. In worrying about the troubles of others, in offering assistance to someone other than yourself, you are temporarily relieved of all worry or pity for yourself. What's more, you are given appreciation by the person you help. The positive energy being directed at you feels almost like love as the person beams at you, or thanks you with body language and/or words. For a moment in time you are a hero, and that gives you an almost physical thrill.

You can start small, experimenting with things that take only a moment of your time. Hold a door for someone. Ask an elderly or disabled person if you can assist him or her in crossing the street. Offer to pay the dime, quarter, or dollar that someone is short in the store. Even in such seemingly insignificant instances, you'll feel as if you have done something wonderful—and you'll get that "natural high" that seems to come from God, who may be saying, "Great. That's what I love to see."

Another way to be generous is with kind words. How many times do we see someone who could use an encouraging word, yet keep our mouths shut? On the other hand, have you ever given someone an honest compliment and seen their whole face light up? At such times, one wonders, "Isn't it amazing the power that we have to make others happy, and how this power crosses all barriers—race, religion and economic." For example, a millionaire's face will light up with delight when told that he is looking young and fit this morning, even if it is just the doorman who delivers the compliment!

Take your generosity a step farther. Even if you are struggling with financial problems, it's a good idea to make a habit of giving a small portion of your money to someone who is much worse off than you are. You can start in your own family, if you choose. Do you have a relative who needs something badly but is so tight for money that he or she can't or won't give themselves the luxury of buying it? It could be a small item, like a pair of gloves or a few pairs of socks, or something a little more expensive, like a household item. Surprise this person with a small gift and watch his or her face light up! Just say, "I was thinking about you today and I bought you something."

Another way to start practicing generosity is in tipping. Tipping has become a mandate, so most of us just calculate based on the bill. But what about when something tugs at your heart. You see a hard-working waitress—you notice the lines on her face. You see her running back and forth. She is so pleasant, despite the impossible workload. Something tells you, "She probably has three children to support, alone," and you think of leaving her a five-dollar tip, even though the bill was eight dollars. Then you start thinking, "But that's crazy. That would be more than a fifty percent tip. I can't do that."

Yes you can. Who says you can't? Don't let your mind get bogged down in going by the book. You *can* break the rules. You can do anything you want, if you dare to. Listen to your inner voice. Let that be your guide.

I do it all the time, and it's the most wonderful thing. When I get that feeling to give someone a generous tip, I check my inner voice to make sure. I say, "If I'm wrong, change my thinking. Otherwise I'm going to do it." I did it just the other day. En route to an important meeting, I was buying coffee to go. The clerk was a young man in his twenties, very busy and obviously new on the job. He quickly, but at the same time a bit too fastidiously, wrote up a check for the person before me, while his obviously critical boss stood behind him with arms folded, waiting for him to make a mistake.

While waiting for my order, I asked the clerk if he was new at the job. I could tell that he was about to deny it, but then he looked into my eyes, and after studying me a moment, he felt safe to say, "Well, sort of." I told him he was very efficient, and was doing a great job. He smiled guardedly, but kept moving. I got a strong urge to give him five dollars, but I had to figure out how to do it without getting him in trouble with his boss, so when he gave me the check and I paid it, I looked around to see if his boss was watching. Thankfully, he was at the other end of the counter, so I handed the clerk the money. "You're a very hard worker," I said. "I want you to have this." I said it with authority, not giving him the chance to argue with me. He thanked me and accepted the tip gratefully, quickly putting it into his pocket. I walked to my meeting with an extra swing in my gait.

But how far should we take this giving business? The Bible suggests that we give ten percent of our income to charity, and promises that we will get back more than we give. "Give and it shall be given unto you; good measure, pressed down, and shaken together, and running over, shall men give into your bosom. For with the same measure that ye mete withal it shall be measured to you again" (Luke 6:38).

Call it "what goes around comes around," call it the law of karma, call it whatever you will. It just seems to work that way. People who give seem to be blessed. But of course you don't want to do your giving with the idea of seeing how much you can get back. Give from your heart and leave it alone. Life itself will take care of you.

But how can I be generous, you say, at least with money, when I am so poor myself? Did you ever hear of a case where an extremely wealthy person was a very poor tipper? That's why you have to practice being generous now, when it hurts, or you won't want to do it when you are wealthy. In other words, you need to get into the habit of giving early, or you will not do it even if you become wealthy.

But many wealthy people do give—and give plenty. Why? In order to be happy, in order to feel good about themselves, for some seemingly strange reason, they need to make a contribution, to "give something back." Small wonder you often hear of famous movie stars who are multimillionaires donating time and money to charitable causes—and often hear them use these very words: "I want to give something back."

Who is it that the world honors anyway—after we die? Is it those of us who have lived only for ourselves? Or does it remember those who made a contribution to mankind? I think of the words of one of my favorite psychologists, Alfred Adler, who says:

> If we look around us today, at the heritage we
> have received from our ancestors, what do we
> see? All that survives of them is the *contributions*
> *they have made to human life*. We see cultivated
> ground; we see roadways and buildings. . . .
> These results have been left by men who con-
> tributed to human welfare. *What has happened to*
> *the others* . . . who asked only "What can I get out
> of life?" They have left no trace behind them. Not
> only were they dead; their whole lives were futile.
> It is as if our earth itself had spoken to them and
> said, "We don't need you. . . . There is no future
> for your aims and strivings. . . . Be off with you.
> You are not wanted. Die and disappear."[2] (Italics
> mine)

Yes. What has happened to the others? Could this be the
reason why so many wealthy patrons donate millions to
foundations such as universities, libraries, and museums
that will literally engrave their names in stone for the contribution?

I believe that it is written in our human nature to help
our fellows. But why is this so? The answer lies in the col-
lective survival instinct of the human race. Without this "altruistic" desire to be generous, to give something back, the
human race would not survive. We would all be totally, 100
percent "out for ourselves," and loving it—with no guilt or
compunction.

But thankfully, that is not the case. When we go out only
for ourselves to the total exclusion of others, many of us
experience unhappiness and loss of self-worth. In short,
we think less of ourselves. So we are compelled to do kind
things for others, and to make contributions to society. My
advice to you is, the next time you feel a generous urge, no

matter how small it may be, go with the flow. It will be a significant step in building your self-esteem.

8. GO TO THERAPY IF YOU'RE "STALLED" OR "BLOCKED"

A good therapist can be the key to building self-esteem. Here's how it works: By having an accepting, nonjudgmental attitude toward you, by listening to your feelings, a caring therapist helps you to do the same sooner or later. Once you are willing to accept yourself just the way you are, seemingly paradoxically you begin to change and grow—and to let go of the unhealthy psychological chains (your neurosis) that held you in bondage, perhaps all your life. What a wonderful gift to yourself.

Carl Rogers, in talking about the experience of the person in therapy, gives a picture of the evolution of the thought process that eventually allows the patient to heal. The patient, he says, thinks:

> But now that I've shared with him some of the bad side of me, he despises me. I'm sure of it, but it's strange I can find little evidence of it. Do you suppose what I've told him isn't so bad? Is it possible that I need not be ashamed of it as part of me? I no longer feel that he despises me. It makes me feel that I want to go further, exploring *me*, possibly expressing more of myself. I find him a sort of companion as I do this—he seems really to understand.[3]

My own experience in therapy confirms what Carl Rogers says. It is in fact quite true that when you sit in the chair across from the therapist, you almost literally cringe in expectation of the rejection and shame that will come after you have spoken. But you take the chance, because the therapist has assured you that nothing is shameful, and that you can tell him or her anything.

And it turns out to be true. Once you've revealed your "secret," instead of blaming and shaming you, the therapist helps you to see your thought process, why you behaved in such a manner. When you see that the therapist is working toward showing you a more effective way of dealing with such a situation next time, you say, "Wait a minute. She's not rejecting me. I can tell her more." And you spill your guts, telling the full details of how you felt at the time and why you think you did what you did. The result is the building of your self-esteem. And with each session, your self-esteem continues to grow, until you are strong enough to become your own therapist.

But how can you find the right therapist for you? My first advice is simply to pray. Ask God to have his will in the situation—and to lead you to the right therapist. He will not let you down. In the Bible, which I read frequently, Matthew 7:9 says that if you ask for bread, God will not give you a stone. In other words, if you ask for something that will sustain and nourish you (bread) he will not let you down by giving you something that will not nourish you (a stone). Having done this, take action, and remember that the saying "God helps those who help themselves" holds true. Now you begin your search.

Begin by asking friends and acquaintances if they can recommend someone who has helped them. If you don't know anyone to ask, look under "Mental Health" in your local telephone directory. If you are covered under a health plan, look in the plan's book, or call your health provider and ask for a list. Now pick three therapists and call them, leaving messages on their machines and listening to their voices. How do they strike you? If you like the sound of one better than the other, leave your number. If you're not sure, leave your number for all three and, after they call back, make an appointment with the one that feels best for you. If you get a secretary, ask to have the therapist call you back.

At your first appointment be sure to check the credentials of the therapist. If you don't see them displayed on the wall, ask, "Where did you go to school? What degree do you hold? How many years have you been in practice?" Then relax and let the therapist take the lead. By the end of the session you should feel better than you did when you walked in. You should feel "heard," and comforted. You should feel optimistic and hopeful. If you don't feel this way, or if you feel that something is wrong, trust that feeling. It's your inner voice telling you that this is not the therapist for you. Try the second therapist, and if necessary the third. If you're still in doubt, ask God again not to let you make a mistake. (For more detailed information on the various kinds of therapy and finding the right therapist, see pages 298–301 in *Get Rid of Him*—see bibliography for this book.)

9. STAND UP FOR YOUR RIGHTS

Your self-esteem suffers when you don't assert yourself, when you go along with something because you feel too embarrassed or too intimidated to take a stand and spell out what you really want.

A simple example can be seen in a sales-pitch situation. Some dancing schools, for example, are notorious for pressuring people to sign up for expensive "package deals" after the initial, low-priced, introductory lessons. If you have the money, and if you want to sign up for the high-priced package, great. No problem. But if you don't have the money, or if you don't want to commit a chunk of money to twenty-five or fifty dance lessons, then you need to be assertive and say, "No. I'm really not interested." Learn how to say no when you mean no and yes when you mean yes!

But how do you do this? Say for example, your trial lessons have run out and you are asked to come into the office of the owner for a conference, and the owner says, "Your lessons are finished. You're really doing great. I have a few possible deals. Here is package A and here is package B. Which do you prefer?" Both of them are way out of your budget, and you already know you don't want either. You feel embarrassed, and you start making excuses. "I'm really busy now," or "I love your school, but . . ." and before you know it you are apologizing for not signing up.

Don't do it. Why are you making excuses, anyway? It is because the owner of the school has a big desk that symbolizes authority? Is it because you are ashamed that you don't have the money? Is it because you don't want to make the owner mad at you? It can be a combination of these things. But who cares? It's your money. It's your life.

Instead of making excuses, look straight into the owner's eyes and pleasantly say, "I've really enjoyed the lessons (only if you did) but I don't wish to go any further. But thank you very much for your offer." Then get up and leave. Having dared to stand up for your rights in a seemingly small way, you'll walk out of there feeling great about yourself.

The difficulty of saying no when you mean no surfaces for many women in the area of sex. I am reminded of a story told to me by a nurse who was asked out by a handsome and powerful doctor, a man known to be quite a catch. They had flirted and exchanged numbers, and had talked on the phone a few times, and finally made a date. Since he lived about an hour's drive away, they agreed that he would come to her house and she would select a nearby restaurant.

At dinner, the conversation never lulled. "He's brilliant," she thought. "I wonder if he thinks I'm intelligent too?" The evening wore on, and by this time they had both had a few drinks. When they arrived at her house he asked her if he could sleep on the couch, since he didn't want to drive home. She felt uncomfortable with the idea, but said yes. (Mistake number one. She should have said, "I know a local hotel—I could call and make you a reservation—and I know of a reliable local cab service that would drive you there and back in the morning to pick up your car.")

Instead she invited him in and, after a nightcap, prepared for bed. "Could I sleep in your bed, not for sex, just to cuddle?" he asked. She felt very uncomfortable about this idea, but was too intimidated to say no ("I didn't want him to think I thought men were uncontrollable animals," she said). So she said okay. (Mistake number two. She should have said, "No. That would not be comfortable for me, but I'll make up the couch right now; I'm going to bed.")

Instead she let him get into bed and "cuddle." And as you might have guessed, in a short time, he made his move. He began to fondle and then to kiss and then to get on top of her to have sex. And just like the two times before, she wanted to say no, but she thought, "Oh well. After all, I let him into my bed. He'll really think I'm a jerk if I suddenly push him off of me." So mistake number three: She allowed him to have sex with her.

The next morning she was angry and couldn't wait for him to leave. After getting him out of there as quickly as possible she took a shower. "I felt dirty," she said, "and angry with him for manipulating me." But what's more, she felt angry with herself for letting herself be manipulated. When he called to go out again she felt repulsed and asked him not to call again.

What really happened here? When she could have stopped the action at any point, why did she allow herself to end up having sex with a man she barely knew, and for whom she had little sexual attraction? Clearly she felt intimidated by him; she felt that she dare not assert herself. She feared making him angry with her—and dreaded his possible rejection.

When we don't stand up for our rights, when we don't assert ourselves, sometimes it is because we are in conflict, and are not really sure what we want to do. More often it is because we don't want the person who's making the demand to get angry with us. What's more, we don't want the person to reject us. In reality, we are giving that person power that we need not give him or her. We can stop this fear of the wrath and rejection of others by refusing to give such power to others. We can do this by rational thinking. We can say to ourselves, "What's the worst thing that could happen?" Let's think about it for a moment. What if those to whom we stand up do get angry and reject us? What will really happen to us? Nothing.

Getting back to the dance-school owner, what would have happened if he got angry and said, "You fool. How stupid of you not to sign up for this package. Get out and never come back"? What would have happened if the doctor had said, "You inconsiderate woman. How dare you make me go to a hotel. I never want to see you again." Would the woman have died? Would she have lost something valuable? Of course not. In fact, in either case the person involved would have gained something valuable: a sense of competence and independence from others' power, and self-respect. Standing up for your rights may be uncomfortable at first, especially if you're not used to doing it, but practice makes perfect. And once you get the hang of it, trust me, it makes you feel great about yourself and is in fact a great way to empower yourself.

Be alert to opportunities to be assertive. The next time you find yourself apologizing for wanting to say no, the next time you find yourself making excuses, and are about to postpone the no, or to say yes when you mean no, stop dead in your mental tracks. "What am I doing?" ask yourself. And then think, "What do I really want to have happen here? Then say, no, and let the person to whom you say it deal with it. Your self-esteem and sense of your own power will grow each time you do it.

10. INCREASE YOUR VOCABULARY

When I was about ten years old, my father taught me a secret that has made all the difference in my life. He told me that one of the most important ways to succeed in life is to have a big vocabulary, not just to impress people (and impress people it does; studies show that people with big vocabularies are twice as likely to get the job as those who have limited vocabularies), but more, to expand your mind.

Each time you learn a new word, you increase your ability to think. As you reflect upon the nuances of the meaning of the word, your mind is able in a sense, to "go up a different trail," and as your thought pattern branches off in a direction it couldn't go before, your mind expands.

Words are tools for thought. The more words you know, the more precise your thoughts, the more explicit your ideas. In fact, when you increase your vocabulary, you become more intelligent. You don't just appear to be smarter; you *are* smarter. Small wonder that the major part of all intelligence tests consists of vocabulary.

But how does learning vocabulary words raise your self-esteem? When you know a vast number of words you can communicate with people from every walk of life, whether they be the intelligentsia or the uneducated. The words you need to express your idea will come to your mind, and, like a high-powered computer, your mind will quickly select the exact word to express the thought effectively. The person to whom you are speaking will react more positively to you. The more positive reactions you get from people, the better you feel about yourself.

Whenever you pick up a magazine, a newspaper, or a book, you'll be able to understand what you read. This will not only make you feel smart and in control, but it will encourage you to read more, and to learn more—and the more you read and learn, the more comfortable and in control you will feel. The more opportunities you will discover. You'll take on challenges that you might otherwise have avoided, such as starting conversations with people who might have previously intimidated you, taking a course in school that you might otherwise have avoided, and moving in the direction of a job or profession that previously seemed out of your reach.

You will have a much better chance of getting a job than the next person, who may have a limited vocabulary, because, as mentioned above, studies show that interviewers tend to choose people with large vocabularies. Your income may well go up too, because you will be more valuable to a boss than someone who can hardly speak or think. And when you ask for a raise, your boss may fear losing you.

But finally, and this is perhaps most important, you'll be able to get in closer touch with who you are, because you'll be able to think more precise thoughts about yourself, and to assist those thoughts by reading psychology, philosophy, and self-help books that you may previously have avoided because you were not able to understand them.

When you think about it, vocabulary is such a sure-fire way of making ourselves feel better about ourselves that you wonder why you didn't think of this before. It's really no mystery when you stop to consider it. Chances are that one too many well-meaning schoolteachers jammed vocabulary down your throat in the form of odious "lists of words" to be memorized for tests, taking away what could have been the joy of learning new words. Even the word *vocabulary* became a threat for many people, especially for those who were not good at memorizing meaningless lists (because that's what words are out of context: meaningless).

If this was you, it's time to take a new look at words. First of all, memorizing lists of vocabulary words is not the way to learn new words. Take it from me, a former English teacher. The only way you really learn and absorb new words so that they permanently become a part of your thinking is to come across the word in a life situation such as reading or listening. Whenever you encounter a word that is either completely foreign to you, or one that you know, but is even a bit fuzzy, you must get in the habit of looking it up and then rereading and rethinking the sentence with the word's meaning in mind. Let's take an example.

As you were reading the above paragraphs, you came across the word *odious*. Perhaps you've heard it before, and you have a vague idea that it means something unpleasant, but you're not exactly sure. But, clever gal or guy that you are, you guessed it from context and figured that that was all that was needed. You did this because your former teachers probably taught you this skill, a much-needed but much-misused one. You should try to guess the word's meaning from context for immediate use. But then you must, and I reiterate, *must*, make it your business to look up the exact word later and rethink the sentence that it originally appeared in, and see how your thoughts expand.

Getting back to the word *odious*, you thought it meant something unpleasant. Now you look up the word in the dictionary, and it says: "Deserving of hatred or repugnance, exacting distaste or aversion." Now you know that I meant that when you had to face those vocabulary lists, you didn't just think of them as unpleasant, you *hated* them. They were even repugnant to you.

Repugnant? But what exactly does that mean? "Opposed. Contradictory, Incompatible." "That doesn't make sense," you might say. "What does that have to do with hating the sight of a list of vocabulary words that must be memorized?" Well, if you stretch your imagination you could think of the list as contradictory or incompatible with what you feel like doing: relaxing instead of studying the list. But that's stretching it. Let's take a look at the second meaning listed in the dictionary: "Exciting distaste or aversion." Now this makes more sense. The thought of memorizing that list of words excites distaste. It makes you sick.

But what does *aversion* mean? You can decide to stop here or go even farther. For the fun of it, I'll take you to the end of the course. "Aversion: a feeling of repugnance towards something with a desire to avoid or turn from it." Ah ha! Now we have come full circle. The word *repugnance* has been repeated. But wait. There is some new information; the other part of the definition of *aversion* says: "with a desire to avoid or turn from it." Now we've really hit the nail on the head. When you looked at those long vocabulary lists to be memorized for tests, your first feeling was probably aversion. You had a desire to avoid or turn from them. See how looking up the word *odious* would help to expand your thought process?

Just how far do you have to go with this vocabulary business, anyway? Am I asking you to spend all of your waking moments looking up words in the dictionary? Of course not. I'm offering you a wonderful, fun way to expand your mind and to delight and comfort yourself with new shades of meaning. You can go as far as you want to go, depending on the time you have and the mood you are in when you first look up the word. Let me break down the method into a simple plan, so that you can make it a regular part of your life if you so choose.

1. Whenever you are reading anything, whether it be a book or a magazine or a newspaper, read with a pen or pencil in your hand.
2. If you encounter a word that you don't know, or see a word that you think you know but whose meaning is not sharp to you, underline it if you can, and keep the reading material until you get it home, or copy it down if you can't. If you have to copy, take the whole sentence with it.
3. Now you have three options, in order of most effort required to least effort required:
   a. In a special vocabulary notebook, copy the word and the sentence, and the dictionary definition. Be

sure to choose the definition that best suits the word. You will do this by rereading the sentence and comparing the various meanings offered in the dictionary to the sentence. Reread the sentence with the appropriate dictionary definition in mind. Take a moment to really think about the meaning of the word in the sentence now that you have a more precise definition.

b. Copy the dictionary definition right there in the margin of the book, magazine, or newspaper you are reading. (Of course this applies only if you own the reading material.) If it is a newspaper or magazine, tear out the page and place it in a folder. Reread the sentence with the appropriate dictionary definition in mind. Take a moment to think about the meaning of the word in the sentence now that you have a more precise definition.

c. Skip the above and just look up the word then and there, and after choosing the appropriate definition, reread the sentence with the appropriate dictionary definition in mind. Take a moment to think about the meaning of the word in the sentence now that you have a more precise definition.

If you choose methods a or b on a regular basis, you can really set the words in your mind because you can go back to your notebook or the original reading material from time to time and reread the words and their meanings. But even if you don't use methods a or b, and just look up a word every time you don't know it, after a while you'll know the word. (I can remember looking up a word three or four times—I even put a mark in the dictionary next to the word so I could say to myself, "Hello," the next time I looked up the word.)

Too much work? And what would you be doing with much of the time you used to look up the words? Watching TV? Take out the dictionary and look up the words with the

TV on. Soon you'll get caught up in the words and forget all about the TV. It will become background sound. You can't tell me that you don't have time to do it if you like this idea and you really want to do it. If there's a will, there's a way.

And think of this: There are just so many words in the English language. If you read a lot, and keep looking up words, sooner or later you'll have quite a vocabulary. You'll practically become a walking dictionary!

11. READ THE BIBLE AND INSPIRATIONAL BOOKS

You are what you think—what you read, what you see. Small wonder the Bible warns us to be careful of what we put in our minds. It tells us to fill our minds with the true, the honest, and the just. It tells us to think about things of "good report." It admonishes us to guard our minds against thoughts that would taint our thinking.

Scientists now know that everything we see, hear, or read, especially if it is related to something fearful, hostile, or important to us, can become a permanent part of our unconscious. For this reason, many people have night-mares after watching horror and other unsavory movies, videos or news reports, or even reading frightening mater-ial. You need to protect your mind from the "ugly" as well as from the negative. Playing violent video games or nega-tive board games such as Dungeons & Dragons, or even watching negative cartoons such as "Beavis and Butthead," fills your mind with unhealthy, destructive thoughts over time. Not a good idea if you care about your mind and your life. Not a good idea at all.

You can do yourself a big favor by filling your mind with inspirational literature. I have found the greatest help to be the Bible. Get yourself a modern translation (in any major bookstore) and begin with the book of wisdom: Proverbs. It will give you great insight into various life situations, and advice on how to conduct yourself in your own affairs. Next, read the comforting Psalms. They will help you to see that you are not alone in your sorrow, and will help you to realize that when you cry out to God, he hears you and will help you. Next, turn to the New Testament. Read the Gospels—Matthew, Mark, Luke, and John—where you'll discover the life and humanitarian teachings of Jesus Christ. You'll read the Sermon on the Mount, where Jesus explains how we should treat each other and ourselves, and find out how to get answers to prayers.

There's no other book in the world like the Bible. It's the most-read book in the English language, and also the most quoted. It has so much simple, down-to-earth, practical psychology and philosophy in it that if we had no other book at all we would have all we would need to live a happy and fulfilling life.

If you really want to take on a challenge, you could make it a goal to read the entire Bible. If you start in the beginning, with Genesis, and read three chapters a night (a chapter is only a half-page to a page in the Bible), in three years you would have read the entire Bible. Whether you choose to read the entire Bible, starting from Genesis, or just to read the above-mentioned books, I suggest that you keep the Bible by your bed and read a chapter or two each night just before you go to sleep. If you do this, you will fall asleep to wonderful, uplifting, inspirational thoughts that can heal you even as you dream.

Read other inspirational books. Read the old classics in the self-help field, and some of the newer ones: *The Power of Positive Thinking, Psychocybernetics, The Magic of Believing, The Road Less Traveled.* These books can go a long way in helping you to heal yourself, with the help of God.

Look in the back of this book under "Inspirational, Empowering, and Informative Books" and go down the line and read every one of them. Never be in a position where you are not reading a book. You can get most of the books listed in the bibliography in paperback in any major bookstore. I prefer that you do this rather than getting them from the library, not only because I want you to have them for vocabulary purposes, but much more than that. I want you to write in them and really absorb them.

Whenever you are reading a book, don't be a passive reader. Passive reading makes for dozing off. I want you to become actively involved with the author by having a pen in your hand and underlining things that strike you. I want you to go farther than that. I want you to write comments in the margin. Say "Yes" or "Right" when you agree with something, and "No way" when you disagree. Go farther than that. Write whole sentences—profound thoughts of your own when they come to mind, memories that come to the surface as a result of something you just read, and so on. By using this method, you'll really absorb the book. It will be with you forever.

If you develop a habit of doing this, in time the books you read can become reflections of your own thoughts. When you go back and skim them years later, you can see what you were thinking at the time—and see how you've grown since then. Your books will become treasures to you. If a book is so great that you want to lend it to a friend, you will instead buy one for him or her, knowing that you don't want to let your "personality-stamped" copy out of your hands for fear that it might get lost or because you might not want others to read your notes. (On the other hand you might want them to read your notes, and to gain insight into your thinking.)

Inspirational books are a wonderful way to improve your thinking and to raise your self-esteem—and what extraordinary allies they can be.

12. FOLLOW YOUR DREAM

This is the last category in building self-esteem because it is the most important. If you give up your dream, it is very hard to have self-esteem. How can you respect yourself if you feel as if you have permanently "sold out"? You may be off your course, feel you have married the wrong man or woman, gotten involved with the wrong boyfriend or girlfriend, staggered in to the wrong job, and so on. And for various reasons, you may not be ready to take action to get back on course yet. But never give up your dream. Never surrender the hope that you will someday be able to correct your course step by step.

Did you ever meet a man or a woman who had abandoned his or her dream, and knew it? Such people always appeared to be somewhat of a shell of themselves. There's a hollowness to them. It's really quite sad when you meet them. They are often intelligent, witty, and even talented people who somewhere along the line lost faith. They've given up, and they know it. "I could have been a contender," they say, in a manner of speaking. "I couldn't afford college so . . ." and on and on. But what stops them from taking some courses now? "I've had three children, so my body is . . ." they say. But what stops them from working on a plan to get in shape now?

Don't you see it? If you're still alive, there's a dream that you can follow now—even if you did go off course and lose out on former opportunities. That's the beautiful thing about life. As long as you're alive you can do something. It's really up to you.

"But half of my life is over," you might say. Don't let that stop you. You have the other half to live on your path; you have a chance to find and follow your dream. Don't give it up. If you still have a dream, if you're still striving, your self-esteem rises. You respect yourself. You feel good about yourself because you, the most important person in your life, have not abandoned yourself.

HIGH SELF-ESTEEM
MAKES A BETTER WORLD

Picture it. Would a person of high self-esteem become a thief and a murderer by trade? Could he or she go into a store and say to him- or herself, "I respect myself—I'm whacking this store owner on the head and taking his property"? Of course not. Only people who have low self-esteem, anger, and resentment at the world are capable of doing such things. Just think of it. Self-esteem makes for a better world. You owe it to yourself to build your self-esteem.

Key #2.   The power of self-esteem. Respect, value, and love yourself.

NOTES

1. William Styron, *Darkness Visible* (New York: Vintage Books, 1990), p. 5.

2. Alfred Adler, *What Life Should Mean to You*, ed., Alan Porter (New York: G. Putnam's Sons, Perigee Books, 1931), pp. 10–11.

3. Carl R. Rogers, *On Becoming a Person* (Boston: Houghton Mifflin, 1961), p. 67.

4

THE POWER OF
MOVING ON

In one way or another, most of us have had hard lives; the only difference is the kind of hardship and the degree. Thank God that success, happiness, and peace of mind do not depend upon the degree of luck we had growing up. Otherwise many of us would be doomed. The fact is, amazingly, that some of the people with the most difficult backgrounds have, in the end, become the most successful, productive, and indeed, the most fulfilled in the long run.

But why? Why is it that some people spend their adult lives "crying in their beer," complaining about their abusive childhoods, bad breaks, what society has done to them, while others, in a manner of speaking, bury the dead and move on? Could it be that these people have decided to move on, to grow up already?

GROW UP ALREADY

Grow up already! But why should we want to do that? The answer is simple. It is only when we allow ourselves to let go of the past—no matter how mildly hurtful or even horrific it was—that we can be free to thrive and flourish today.

You can analyze and figure from now until the end of time why you are unsuccessful, unhappy, unfulfilled, and that may be just what you have to do to come to the same conclusion I have come to. After all is said and done, you still have to make that decision to let go of the past and "grow up already."

THE BUCK STOPS HERE

When all is said and done, in the words of Harry Truman, "the buck stops here." The choice is yours. You've got to decide whether you are going to make a move—take action and get on with your life—or "pass the buck." But what does it mean to "pass the buck"?

The word *buck* comes from the card game poker: The buck is a marker that shows which player has to deal the cards next. But in poker, if you don't want to deal the cards, you have the option of "passing the buck" to the next player. (They usually used a silver dollar as a marker, and in fact, that's how the dollar came to be called a "buck.") In essence, if you don't feel like dealing, all you have to do is "pass the buck." But what would happen if every player "passed the buck"? The cards would never get dealt, right? The game would never go on.

So when I tell you "The buck stops here," I'm really saying that sooner or later, if you want the game of your life to move on, you'll have to deal the cards. You'll have to stop finding others to blame, no matter how blameworthy they are, because when all is said and done, it's your life—and you're the only one who has the right, and usually the power, to decide what happens to you. It's up to you to decide whether or not you will allow bitterness and resentment to cause you to waste one more minute of your precious life because of "what happened to you," be it ever so horrendous.

Okay. The buck stops here. But what can you do about your past history, about the pain in your life? Of course you should look at it and acknowledge it. Identify the source of your pain. Locate and name your "enemies," those who have wronged you. Acknowledge the "bad luck" that befall you when you didn't have a chance to defend yourself. But after that, take responsibility and move on so that you can have the wonderful, fulfilling life that you were intended to have with the time you have left. Finally, once and for all, let the sun come out in your life. In order to do this, you must take the first step: forgive.

FORGIVENESS: WHO, HOW, AND WHY?

Before you can forgive those who have wronged you, you must have a clear idea of who they are. Think about your life and those who you feel were responsible for causing you the psychological problems or other problems you have now. For many of us it is a parent. For others it is a sibling, an aunt, an uncle, or a cousin. For others it is a nonrelative, a friend of the family or even a "stranger." In some cases, it is ourselves. We have done something in the past that we simply cannot find a way to forgive ourselves for—and we are determined to beat ourselves over the head with it until the day we die. You'll find out more about how to deal with this problem in Chapter 5.

Psychological problems can also be the results of events. Perhaps your home was destroyed by a fire when you were a child, throwing your family into "unfair" hardship and poverty. As a result, your life has been more difficult than it would have been. Think hard about everyone and everything you blame for your problems and write the list here. In other words, name your enemies.

PEOPLE AND EVENTS THAT CAUSED ME WOE

1.

2.

3.

4.

5.

Now, next to the name of the person or event, write down what woe was caused to you. For example, if it is your mother who constantly compared you unfavorably to a sibling, and you feel that this caused you to feel inferior and stopped you from going to college, write that down. If it was an uncle who molested you in early childhood and caused you sexual difficulties and problems with self-esteem, write it down. If it was an event such as the death of your father at an early age that caused you to feel abandoned and now makes you feel needy and insecure, write it down.

Now, as simple as it may seem, I want you to go over the list, look at each and every person and event separately, and say, "I forgive you," and mean it. Then write *I forgive you* over that person's name or the event and sign your name.

You probably laughed when you read the last paragraph. "Ha. Are you kidding? Just like that, I'm supposed to forgive." Well, I don't blame you. I used to have that reaction too, until I learned what the word *forgiveness* really means. Like me, you probably thought that by forgiving the person or event, you would be saying "What you did was okay," to the person, or thinking "What happened is okay" about the event. But that's not what forgiveness is at all, and when you see what the actual meaning of forgiveness is, you'll be happy to realize that in fact, you can do it. It's not as hard as you thought.

THE SURPRISE MEANING
OF FORGIVENESS

According to the dictionary, the word *forgive* means "to give up resentment of or claim to requital for. To grant relief from payment." (*Merriam Webster's Collegiate Dictionary, Tenth Edition*). "To give up desire to punish; stop being angry with" (*Webster's New World Dictionary, Third College Edition*).

So if you forgive, all you are doing is giving up your resentment, anger, and desire to punish. But why should you give these things up? Because resentment and anger and the desire for revenge will hurt you more than they will hurt your enemy, and in fact can cause heart disease, cancer, and a host of other maladies. More subtly, and just as bad, resentment, anger, and revenge can control you. They can steal your creative energy and indeed your time and attention, so that you deviate from your path in life and end up going out of this world without having the opportunity to accomplish the purpose for which you were born. With this in mind, one becomes much more motivated to forgive. But your motivation will increase even further when you consider the following.

Notice that nowhere in the definition of forgiveness is there any indication that you must be happy about, condone, or approve of what happened to you. You can in fact disapprove of and hate what happened to you. All you have to do is let go of the resentment, anger, and the desire for revenge that, in fact, cannot change the past or help in the future.

"Ha! Easier said than done," you rightfully think. But here is some more motivation: There is justice in the universe, only, thank God, it's not your job to mete it out.

DON'T WORRY, EVERYONE PAYS DUES

In my view, in the long run, we can't get away with anything in life. Nothing at all. There is, it seems to me, an invisible law of nature that assures that somehow, in some way, in this life (and perhaps in the afterlife—we'll never be sure of this until we die, however) everyone gets what's coming to him or her.

An interesting psychological theory called "psychological determinism" introduced by Sigmund Freud proposes that each psychic event is determined by events that went before it. In other words, according to the theory, there is a psychological chain reaction to everything we do.[1] The way I see it, this chain reaction can play a part in causing those who have committed misdeeds sooner or later to attract to themselves a punishment of sorts—a payback.

The Bible talked about this very principle way before the word *psychology* was coined. It's called "reaping and sowing." When a farmer plants corn, he expects to have corn grow up. He "sows" or plants a given seed and, being intelligent, he naturally expects to "reap" corn. The biblical teaching of reaping and sowing is just that simple. It indicates that a person will, in time, get exactly what his or her behavior has merited. The biblical writer of Galatians 6:7 says: "Be not deceived; God is not mocked; for whatsoever a man soweth, that shall he also reap."

In short, there is a built-in, orderly system in life, says the biblical writer. Everyone will get what is coming to him or her in the long run. To quote Proverbs 26:27, "Whoso diggeth a pit shall fall therein; and he that rolleth a stone, it will return upon him." Had the person not dug the pit with the goal of causing someone else damage, he would be in no danger of falling into it himself. It is only because he took the action of digging the pit that he can possibly fall into it.

And he *will* fall into the pit, according to the proverb. But why? Probably because in his unconscious mind he feels guilt about having dug the pit with the intention of harming someone else. It may be that this guilt, demanding relief in the form of punishment, *causes* him to stumble into the pit himself, something like the impulse that prompts the criminal to return to the scene of the crime—and get caught.

The second part of the proverb is a repetition of the first, a reaffirmation of the idea of self-punishment caused by the unconscious guilt one has for misdeeds. If you roll a stone with the intention of hurting someone, the stone will eventually roll back on you. Drug dealers often die violently at the hands of other drug dealers in the process of committing a crime, or in jail. Those who physically, sexually, and/or mentally abuse others may suffer psychological torture all of their lives, and so on. You may wonder, "But what about those people who are hardened sociopaths, and seem to have no conscience? What about people who seem literally to get away with murder—and go on apparently to enjoy their lives?" My answer to that is clear: Things are not always what they seem. Such people, in my view, suffer mental torment that we may not be able to perceive. In addition, although they may indeed be enjoying life for the moment—at least to some extent—who knows what waits for them just a little farther up the road?

But why, exactly, does this self-punishing system work psychologically? Psychologists such as Franz Alexander believe that one hypnotizes oneself for punishment, so as to balance the scales. It is almost as if one cannot relax or breathe easy until those scales are balanced—despite the fact that balancing those scales must mean self-punishment. In other words, it may well be true that it is impossible to hurt others without hurting oneself. Alfred Adler uses the analogy of a prisoner in a chain-gang who cannot push another prisoner away without injuring himself.[2]

Could there be an unwritten law implanted within the mind of men and women, a law that insures justice? Wouldn't it be amazing if it were as simple as that? I believe it is. I believe that psychologists and biblical writers have hit the nail right on the head. The fact is that it is not your job to get revenge. Romans 12:19 says, "Vengeance is mine; I will repay, saith the Lord." What a liberating idea! We don't have to do the job. We can allow ourselves to be relieved from the burden of resentment and anger. Justice will be done—and we don't have to be the ones to mete it out.

No one gets away with "murder." Even criminals who, due to either "good luck" or clever manipulations by highly paid lawyers, walk out of a courtroom laughing and thinking they are now free and clear will be surprised to see that they are only beginning their jail terms. What goes around comes around. The mental torture begins and, in addition, sooner or later the wheel of fortune turns and what seems like "bad luck" suddenly falls upon someone who has planted a field of misdeeds. The "bad luck" is really just the seeds finally growing up.

This principle can also be seen with the idea of karma. When you take negative action, you incur a cosmic debt to the universe. Sooner or later the debt must be collected, and usually the debt is collected at a most inconvenient time—when one least expects it. When the fullness of time comes (when the universe has had its fill), karma rains down upon the person in payment for the misdeeds. In short, in the words of one of my favorite Willie Nelson songs, "There's a whole lot of karma goin' 'round."

Think of it spiritually, think of it psychologically, or think of it from a karmic point of view, but think of it: You don't have to waste your precious energy hating and holding grudges. It's much healthier and much more productive to let it go and to believe that there is a built-in justice in the universe. I believe that in the long run, everyone gets what is coming to him or her.

One more thing: If you are ever tempted to think revengeful thoughts about someone, just hold that person up to God in your mind and say, "I put him (or her) in your hands. You promise justice." You can even quote the Bible:

"Vengeance is mine; I will repay, saith the Lord." And then leave it at that.

All of the above said, one cannot help but wonder, "What about innocent babies who are born handicapped? What about a hero who dies a stupid death from a random mugger? What about millions of people killed in natural disasters—or worse, as a result of tyrannical governments? What did they do to deserve punishment?"

The principle of reaping and sowing, or the theory of "psychic determinism," cannot explain all things—only some things. There are still a myriad of disastrous things that happen to people that we cannot explain. I call these events "mysteries of the universe." To expect the principle to work for all things would be as ludicrous as making the mistake called "single cause" in logic. For example, if we make the statement, "People who ride in cars that go sixty miles an hour are moving fast," which is a true statement, we cannot say that all people who are going sixty miles an hour and are moving fast are riding in cars. There may be other causes for the speed. They may be riding in buses, trucks, motorcycles, and so on. So if we say, "People attract personal disaster because of their own actions," it does not necessarily hold that all personal disasters that come upon a person are due to that person's actions. Personal disasters may happen to people for a variety of other reasons, reasons that are, in my view, "mysteries of the universe."

STOP FOR A MOMENT
AND UNDERSTAND

There's something else that will help you to understand and forgive those people whom you hold responsible for your present troubles. Consider that this person had a whole set of misdeeds done to him or her, and is himself or herself the result of such treatment. They, too, had a problem.

I think of my own mother. As a young adult, I was very busy resenting her for "not understanding" me, for taking for granted what I thought of as my creativity, for not seeming to see "me," but rather someone who should follow the leader. Feeling guilty about my resentment, and even feeling what felt like hatred of her, I remember praying one day, "God, help me to give up my anger toward my mother." Then a few days later my mother was going through some old family photographs, and she showed me one of a large group of people, a church photograph. "Find me," she said. I looked and I looked, and for the life of me I couldn't find her. But I had made a mental note of the one forlorn, little, bedraggled girl sitting just off to the side of the group.

She had a tear-stained face, old, worn shoes, and a dress that was markedly homemade. She seemed to be biting her lips nervously. "How pitiful she looks," I thought. I wondered if she was an orphan.

"That's me," my mother said, pointing to the girl at the edge of the crowd as if nothing were wrong. "That's you?" I exclaimed in shock as a wave of sadness overtook me, and I found myself wanting to cry. Suddenly I could feel the pain of my mother's entire childhood in one fell swoop. I realized for the first time that my mother, the woman I had judged so severely, had had a pile of troubles of her own growing up, and was doing the best she could under the circumstances. Yet I never heard my mother utter a word of recrimination against her parents or the life that she led growing up with Russian immigrant parents. She never seemed to blame a father who had to work three jobs all his life and who, being a strict disciplinarian from the old school, made his children kneel on rice for hours when they misbehaved so that they literally had to pick it out with tweezers.

This understanding helped me to forgive my mother, who, by the way, still bites her lips when she is under pressure. I thought, "How did I expect my mother to behave as a psychologist to me when she obviously had her own very real sadness and woe growing up? How could she understand and accept me when she had not been given an opportunity to understand and accept herself?" So from that point on, I began to understand and accept my mother in spite of her lack of understanding and acceptance of me. I finally believe today that my mother does understand and accept me—and we've almost become pals—but I couldn't feel that understanding or know that acceptance, or feel that camaraderie until I forgave her. I was only able to do that by stopping for a moment and putting aside my own problems, shifting the focus from myself to her.

If you find yourself unable to forgive someone whom you resent, perhaps you can do what I did. Ask God to reveal to you something about the person that may help you to see him or her in a more compassionate light.

MISFORTUNE CAN BE GOOD FORTUNE

And here's a surprise: The difficulty and the problems that you have experienced in your life, although extremely painful at the time, may have been just what the doctor ordered for you to become the person you are today. Perhaps everything that happened is exactly what you needed to equip you to do the job you were called to do in life.

Without the troubles, without the problems, without the difficulties you've had to overcome in your life, you would not have the depth of character that you have. You would not have the capacity to understand the meaning of hardship and pain, the ability to have compassion and empathy.

LIFE FOR ME AIN'T BEEN NO CRYSTAL STAIR

That last comment certainly applies to me. As I told you before, I was born in the Bronx, in what we now call the ghetto. My earliest childhood memories are of standing in a playpen and watching my mother do piecework for a factory, making belts, hour after hour. I have flashbacks of myself waiting patiently for her to come and pick me up out of the playpen. I can almost feel myself craving for that contact, and being so relieved when it finally came—her arms reaching down, her hands touching me as she picked me up, and her body close to mine as she hugged me. I remember how joyful I would feel when I got that hug. But often I would have to wait a long time. It felt like hours and hours.

In the East Bronx schools, I was a minority White in a system populated with 99 percent Black and Puerto Rican students. I had lots of friends, and in fact was the ringleader when it came to getting into devilment. Today I recall lots of mischievous adventures. But I also remember with pain how every day it was a challenge to get home from school without getting beaten up by a group who did not know me. I learned to use my wit and intelligence to talk my way out of almost every beating. I had to talk fast— and I can still remember literally sweating it out.

Getting into my apartment safely was another feat. Those daily races past the drunk hiding beneath the stairwell culminated in checking to make sure that no one was lurking upstairs near the roof, waiting to make his move once I opened my door. The quick thrust of the key dangling from a chain on my neck became automatic. (My key hung beside the "dog tag" I had to wear in the fifties—in case the Russians "pushed the button" and there was a surprise nuclear war.) Finally I was in the house. Safe at last—at least for the moment. I would make myself a snack and turn to my homework or a book. We didn't have TV until I was in my teens.

Next there was the wait for my mother to come home from her night job as a telephone operator. I often worried that something bad would happen to her on the way home, and lay awake in bed to make sure she arrived, when I would breathe a sigh of relief.

I remember the battle that I eventually won to accept my father's presence when he came back to live with us—when I was nine years old. Ironically, he turned out to be *the most important* influence on me. A brilliant, loving man, he helped me recognize and use my potential to the fullest.

So I think it's fair to say that I know what it is to feel alone and unsafe. I know what it is to dream that someday I could be happy and secure, like the people in the "Dick and Jane" reader, the ones who lived in the pretty house with the white picket fence and the green grass, and the dog named Spot. I know how a difficult beginning and a hard life can combine to make you a stronger person.

Did I walk a straight and narrow path? Did I avoid all mischief and trouble? Of course not. I got into trouble with the law more than once at an early age for being in the wrong place at the wrong time. In fact, my mother had to get the minister from the church to implore the authorities not to "send me away" to a home. I was tempted by marijuana and heroin as I watched many a young man nod out, stoned out of his mind, and lost friends to overdoses. I remember, at such times, clinging to the words of my parents—"Drugs will destroy you; drugs are sure death—and somehow I was able to resist.

Although I didn't do drugs, I did go out with drug addicts. When I was fourteen, one of them invited me to a "party" that took place in what I now know to be a "shooting gallery." I was sitting in the living room with another girl when suddenly two men climbed through the window, badges in hand, shouting, "Police. Nobody move!" We were all carted off to jail. Thankfully, my father and the police believed me when I told them I had not taken drugs and had no knowledge of the goings-on. I remember thinking, "Thank God I don't have to stay here." The jail cell was dirty, crowded, and smelly. I decided then and there it was the last place I wanted to end up—ever. To this day I remember the grateful feeling I had as, late that night, I pulled my covers over my head and slept in my warm, cozy bed.

THE TURNING POINT

After that I was on probation. The parole officer, a pretty Native American woman, believed in me. She said I could accomplish something with my life. I knew that I was at a crossroads. I could either continue to hang out with drug addicts and get in trouble or pursue an education—maybe plan to go to college, maybe be somebody someday.

So step by step, with God's help and acts of will on my part, I got to where I am today. I'll talk more about how in Chapter 6, "The Power of Your Will." For now, suffice it to say that I had to realize I had a choice.

MAKING THE BEST OF YOUR "HAND"

I often think of what former president Eisenhower's mother told him when he was a child and he was ready to become bitter because of a hand he was dealt while playing a card game with his family. As Eisenhower recalls:

> Well, Mother was the dealer and the hand she had dealt me was completely impossible. I began to complain that with such a poor hand I had no chance at all. Finally Mother said, "Put down the cards, boys. I want to give you some advice. You are playing a friendly game here in your home with your mother and your brothers, all of whom love you. But out in the world, life will deal you plenty of bad hands and those involved may not love you at all. So the lesson is to take whatever hand is dealt you and with God's help, just play it out."[3]

We have a choice. We can take the reality of our situation—the pain that went into all of our history—and use it as a force to drive ahead and accomplish things, or we can put it around our neck and use it as an anchor to weigh us down till the day we die.

ACCIDENTS THAT ARE NOT

Many times I've heard someone say, "Oh, I can't believe my bad luck. Why did this have to happen to me?" I heard it once from a man I know who had just missed a plane—and it turned out that plane crashed, and everyone on it was killed. It was easy for him later to learn the lesson of "Why did this have to happen to me?" But for most of us, we have to take a closer look.

President Eisenhower was shooting for a career in football. But he had an injury that caused him to have to give up football forever, and with it, his dream of becoming a pro. But he became one of the best presidents in American history. I guess his "accident" was meant to happen.

The big key is to know how to stop and "listen" to the accident, the misfortune. I know a young man right now who is going through the same struggle that Eisenhower went through. He was billed for pro football—in fact, he was a senior in college and already signed up for a major team. But he had an accident and permanently damaged his back. Instead of absorbing the natural heartbreak and disappointment and getting on with his life, he's bartending, smoking pot, drinking beer, betting on football games in his spare time, and talking about how unfair life is.

Just today I noticed my neighbor coming home with her two-month-old baby. As I waved hello, she seemed extra happy, so I took a moment to ask her how things were going. "I got laid off my job," she said. Surprised, I asked, "Then why do you look so happy?" "Well, it was the best thing that could have happened to me. You see, I really hated to leave my baby with a sitter at this young age—and I was suffering every day. My husband and I can manage without my salary, but we wouldn't have chosen to do so. And now I decided to go back to school part time to finish my master's degree. I'm so excited, I can't tell you," she said.

Now the woman, who happens to be Hispanic, could have spent her time resenting her layoff, bemoaning the possible prejudice behind it. Instead, she took a moment to think, asking herself, "Why did this happen?" She told me that she went to church and asked God to help her to know what to do now that she was laid off, and the next thing you know, she realized that it was the best thing that could have happened to her. In fact, she added, "The courses I'm taking toward my master's degree will get me a promotion when I go back to work."

Bad luck. Poor breaks. We need to stop for a moment and ask, "What now?" Remember, you will not always get the answer as far as the big picture is concerned. President Eisenhower did not hear a voice from the sky saying, "Thou shalt become president!" But we can get a feeling, a sense of what to do next—and if we follow this feeling, we will see *later on* how it all worked together for the big picture.

I think of my own life. So many "accidents." I was an avid judo player. I had not written one book yet. I was planning to devote all of my spare time to judo. I wanted to make a name in that field. But one day someone landed on my knee and the cartilage was torn. I was forced to give up judo for a year—and during that time, while rehabilitating my knee in a fitness center, I seemingly by "luck" met body-builders who later taught me the secrets of getting in shape. I ended up writing books that have helped millions of women conquer their weight and get their fitness under control. But at the time of the accident I was very upset. Yet I had to move on to the next step, stay open to the future. That's what you must do every time some misfortune comes your way. Naturally you will need to grieve your loss, but then remember to look up and to ask, "What next?"

ANGER IS ENERGY

Anger is like electricity. You can use it to operate an appliance—or even to run a power plant, or you can use it to electrocute yourself. Instead of letting anger eat away at you and destroy your life, you can take control of it, harness it and use it as energy to achieve positive goals. You can use your anger to spur yourself on to success.

Nathan McCall, a young black man, was well on his way to destruction. He had fallen in with the wrong crowd, and was willfully doing drugs and committing violent acts. Eventually he ended up in prison. I'm sure he was very angry about his life, his lot, and his luck. He could have said, "See what I mean? Society is against me. What chance did I really have, living in the ghetto and all? And here I am in jail—and what kind of an education do they expect me to get here? I guess I'll learn everything I can from the criminals around me, and when I get out, I'll be the most dangerous of them all. I'll get even with them for ruining my life, for not giving me a chance."

But he didn't do that. Instead, he decided to channel his energy in a positive direction. He began educating himself even in prison, and eventually he got out and persisted until he ended up as a journalist for the *Washington Post*— and the best-selling author of his life story, *Makes Me Wanna Holler: A Young Black Man in America.*[4]

I think of another example of making the best of a bad situation. In this case, the worst imaginable: the Jews who survived Hitler's concentration camps. Wouldn't it have been tempting for these people to say, "There's no justice in the world. I give up, I quit." But instead of using what happened to them in Germany as an excuse to spend their lives getting revenge, being depressed, or worse, a great many made the most of the life they had left.

In fact, it is known that many Holocaust survivors not only resumed their lives, but became more successful than American Jews in their own age group who did not suffer that horrendous experience. Not only are many Holocaust survivors more successful financially, but they also have more stable marriages and are more likely to contribute to charitable causes.[5]

What was it that enabled them to succeed after having suffered such unjust punishment? Clearly, it was the will to live. But more than that, it was the decision to take the gift of life and use it to the fullest extent. Instead of using their most horrific and indeed unmerited mistreatment as a life-long weapon of blame, they channeled their energy in positive areas, such as getting an education, becoming successful in a profession, raising families, and donating time to charitable causes.

COUNT YOUR BLESSINGS— IT COULD BE WORSE

When you stop to think about it, you were not completely alone and misunderstood all your life. I'll bet you could come up with a positive influence, someone who was kind to you. This person must have served to strengthen and reaffirm your "self," a self that was just beginning to emerge and develop. That someone served to help you to see that you were not completely alone in your pain. He or she could validate your experiences by letting you know that what you were going through was not your imagination, that what was happening to you was real. You were able to see that you were not "crazy." You were also able to know that the suffering you endured was not okay, that someday you could have a better life.

Alice Miller talks about this in her book *The Untouched Key*. In discussing the most horrendous cases of child abuse, she asks why some abused children become serial killers or even Adolf Hitler, while others become productive citizens or even great philanthropists. She says:

> The question is why all battered children don't turn into monsters like Adolf Hitler, why some grow up to be brutal, unfeeling criminals and oth-

ers highly sensitive people, like painters and poets who are capable of expressing their suffering? I detected a presence . . . of a sympathetic and helpful witness who confirmed the child's perceptions, thus making it possible for him to recognize that he had been wronged . . . a particular witness helped the child experience his feelings to some degree.[6]

If you were severely abused as a child, think back. There was probably someone in your life who affirmed your feelings, validated your anger, and helped you to recognize that you were wronged, that it was not your imagination. Indeed, it was happening to you.

Think hard. Who was a light in the darkness for you in your childhood or early adult years? It could have been a grandparent, aunt or uncle, a teacher or friend of the family, or even a relative stranger with a kind and open heart. But someone affirmed you or, quite frankly, you probably would not be reading a book such as this. You might have given up on trying to better yourself, to struggle to become the person you have the potential to be, to become self-actualized.

Make a list of anyone who brings back even a flicker of positive memory from your early years.

PEOPLE WHO WERE A POSITIVE INFLUENCE IN MY LIFE

1.

2.

3.

Whenever I appear distraught about a seemingly disastrous situation, my daughter reminds me of a play entitled,

It Could Be Worse. In second grade she participated in this play, in which all of the characters were animals. She was the goat. The animals were all living on a farm, quite contented with their life, when suddenly a bad storm caused a shortage in the food supply—and their food rations were cut by one-fourth. Complaining bitterly, the animals lamented their bad luck, bemoaning the fact that now they would have less to eat. But the goat, my daughter, stood aside and pointed out that while sacrifice was tough, most of them were fat anyway, and that "it could be worse."

And sure enough, it got worse. The next thing you know, thunder and lightning struck the barn, and it fell on the animals, killing some of them and breaking up their coops and cages. Now the animals really had problems. They were forced to sleep on top of each other. But not having learned their lesson, the animals lamented their fate. "Why does this have to happen to us? Of all the farms around, our farm has to get hit with a thunderstorm, and of all the barns around, our barn has to fall down." And instead of working to rebuild the barn, the animals stood around complaining. Except for the wise old goat. He began working to repair the barn, all the time saying, "It could be worse."

The next thing you know came another disaster, and then another. Finally, the animals were left with no barn at all, and no food at all. But the goat, in the meantime, had rationed out his food, and had built himself a shelter—and was able to survive all of the disasters. And one by one, the animals joined him in helping to rebuild the barn and plant more seeds, making do with the crumbs of food that the goat was able to give them, until the crop of food the goat had planted grew up. Finally, the animals learned that no matter how bad it was, "it could be worse." They realized that the smartest thing one can do when trouble, and even tragedy, hits is to seek positive action to remedy the situation.

Yes. No matter what happened to you in your life, no matter how bad it was, it could be worse. Are you still alive? Do you have another day of sunshine in which to make the most of the life you have left on this earth? Even those with potentially fatal diseases such as cancer or AIDS have been known to choose to live fulfilling lives right up until their last day, becoming a blessing to those around them until they draw their last breath.

It could be worse. Count your blessings. Stop crying in your beer. Bury the dead and move on. Grow up already.

Make a list of all of the good things in your life. Think of your health, your looks, anyone you can call on for friendship or companionship, a roof over your head, an income, food to put on your table, a course in school that will lead to a brighter future, a talent that you have that you are developing, your intelligence, the beautiful view from your window, any lucky break that you have had in life, any time you were saved from near disaster. Anything. Anything at all. Count your blessings. Name them one by one. List them here.

MY BLESSINGS

1.

2.

3.

4.

5.

REFUSE TO HAVE THE TANTRUM

I remember it to this day. When my cousin Jeannie, who was about three years old, didn't get her way she would have a tantrum. She would fall on the floor and kick, and scream at the top of her lungs until she wore herself out. I would see her doing that, and would wonder why my aunt didn't do something to stop her, give her anything she wanted just to get her to stop screaming and kicking her legs like that. But, wisely, my aunt knew that such action would teach Jeannie the wrong lesson.

So instead, she let my cousin's tantrum burn itself out. And lo and behold, when it was over, Jeannie discovered that she still didn't get what she was demanding, whether it be more candy, her friend's new toy, or the right not to go to school if she didn't feel like it. She decided to give up having tantrums and instead to behave in a reasonable manner when she did not get her way. She had discovered that having a tantrum was not the way to get what she wanted and, indirectly, that having tantrums would not work to control people, and life in general. She would have to learn a more productive way to operate—and she did.

We all need to learn this lesson. We all need to realize that by allowing ourselves to spend our precious time and energy lamenting our bad luck for events that unfairly fell upon our heads, seething in hatred for those who have wronged us and constantly talking (in a manner of speaking, screaming at the top of our lungs) about how unfair life is (having a psychological tantrum), we will get exactly what my cousin Jeannie got: nothing but mental and physical exhaustion.

So why do we have tantrums if they don't work? Some of us learned the wrong lesson growing up. When we had a tantrum, our weary parents gave us what we wanted. Now we are quite confused when the world does not respond in the same way. Well, it's time to learn a hard lesson, and yes, to grow up already. The next time your mind starts taking you up a path of fury regarding your past treatment, say to yourself, "I'm not going to go there," and instead use your energy to make the best of the situation you are faced with—and use the life that you have in front of you, your reality and your possibilities, to the best of your ability.

I'M A VICTIM

I believe that Alcoholics Anonymous and other twelve-step programs are, for the most part, wonderful, helpful, and even life-saving. But in my view, there is one big mistake that many of them make. They ask people to label themselves according to their pathology. For example if I had a problem with alcohol, and I went into an Alcoholics Anonymous meeting, I would be required to say at each meeting, "My name is Joyce. I am an alcoholic." I believe that making such a statement about one's self is in many ways a bad idea.

You are not your disease, but rather the sum of many things: your genetic coding, your life experiences, the choices you have made, and so on. You are a mother, a father, a sister, a brother, a teacher, a salesman, an athlete, a skater, a tennis player, a loyal friend, and on and on. You are not merely "an alcoholic" (or whatever your problem or pathology may be). To claim to be your disease or pathology is to appropriate it as an integral part of yourself—and in a sense, to own it as a part of your being—for life.

As far as I'm concerned, when it comes to your pathology or your problem, don't claim it. You have already overcome many of the problems and diseases in your life, and you will overcome this one. Your name is _____. If alcohol is your problem, it's your problem. It is not you. You are not an alcoholic. You are beleaguered by the disease of alcoholism.

What should one say, then, about one's problem or pathology? "My name is _____. I have a problem with _____. It has been taking over my life. I don't like the feeling. I've decided to use my will to fight against this, and with God's help I'm going to overcome it."

Labeling oneself according to one's pathology can be seen all around us. Just look at the talk shows. Guest after guest will label themselves according to their misfortune. "I'm an incest survivor," or "I'm a rape victim." No. No. No. You are Mary Jones or Bill Smith—a woman or man with many life experiences and multiple strengths and talents.

Don't for one moment allow yourself to linger any longer than necessary on the negative things that have befallen you. Admit them: "I survived incest." "I survived rape." "But I'm much more than what happened to me." Deal with them, and then by all means, by the grace of God, move on.

Why do I feel so strongly about this subject? I believe that when people are encouraged to label themselves and in turn to think of themselves as their pathology, eventually they become their pathology and are forced to cling to it for the rest of their lives. They can't let go of it even if they wanted to, because they have now built their entire identification as a person around it.

The misdeeds that happened to you, the abuses you suffered, are *not you*. Instead they are battle wounds. Learn to wear them as a badge of courage rather than as a label to identify yourself.

In closing this subject, I must remind you of something I spoke about at the beginning of this chapter: the importance of forgiveness. Take the time to forgive those who were your abusers, those who wronged you in your early years. It can be a relief to let go of the bitterness you have felt toward those people for years. If you don't let go, whether you know it or not, you are allowing these people to remain important in your life—and to define your present self. If you forgive, you can release the pain and anger, let go, and forget, and although you can't change what happened in the past, you can at least deny them any further power over your life.

ENJOY YOUR LIFE:
STOP AND SMELL THE ROSES

Recently I decided to do some landscaping. One of the first things I did was to plant some yellow roses. It was late for planting roses, so all I could find were some bedraggled plants that were already half dead. But I planted them anyway. I was taking the gardener, who said they would bloom again in the spring, at his word. I planted them at the side of my house, which happened to be the only available space, so that if and when they did bloom, I would catch a glimpse of them when walking by.

Winter came and went, and I forgot all about the roses. It was well into spring, and one day I was returning from walking my dog. Out of the corner of my eye, I caught a glimpse of the roses. Abundant and yellow and exquisite, they were in full bloom. Why hadn't I noticed them before? Dave, my muscular English bulldog, was pulling to go in the house, and I was tempted to follow his lead. But then I thought, "No. I've been looking down a lot lately, worrying about the cares of life, while the roses were blooming. Now I'm going to stop and enjoy them." And with that, dragging reluctant Dave along, I went over to the rosebush, leaned over, and took a long, dizzying whiff.

As I write this paragraph, for the life of me, I can't remember the specific problems that kept my head down for much of the spring, but I can clearly remember the beauty and the delicate fragrance of those roses. Perhaps there is something after all to the saying, "Stop and smell the roses." Take time to acknowledge the beauty all around you.

Look at the sky. Watch the tide go out. Study the green grass, the trees as they wave in the gentle breeze, watch a squirrel as he races up a tree. Buy yourself a lilac plant and put it on your table. Look at its multiple shades of purple and think about life. Turn outward. In short, take time to be happy with your world. You owe it to yourself.

IT'S THE WAY YOU THINK ABOUT WHAT HAPPENS THAT COUNTS

You can't control what happens to you, but you can control how you think about what happens to you. This will determine your emotions and actions, which will in turn affect the outcome, making the outcome either better or worse for your life. Let me explain.

A. The event happens to you.
B. You tell yourself "such and such" about the event that has happened to you—and what you tell yourself results in
C. The emotions you feel, which in turn affect the way you behave.

In other words, it's not what actually happened to you, but the way you talk to yourself about what happened to you that causes you to be miserable and in a panic, or allows you to feel at peace and in control. Based upon that feeling—misery and panic, or peace and "in control"—you take actions that affect your life for better or for worse.

Suppose, for example, you are on a diet. You've been doing great for three days, and then the weekend came and even though you were careful to order a low-fat dinner in the restaurant, somehow you let down your guard and gave in, and ordered a very fatty piece of pie for dessert. After you finished the last delicious morsel, the guilt set in. You think, "What have I done? Why am I so stupid? I have no self-control. I knew it. Now I'll have to start over again on Monday." And you plan to eat like a pig all weekend, and you do so. In the process, you eat ten times more fat than was in that meager piece of pie, setting yourself back weeks in your weight loss plan.

You could have done something different. You could have thought about the event (eating the pie) in a different light, and that would have caused you to have different emotions, and to take different action. Let's look at this using the A,B,C structure.

A. The event happened (you ate the pie).

B. You told yourself, "This means I blew my diet. What a loser I am."

C. You feel depressed and disgusted with yourself, and you pig out all weekend.

But what would have happened if you had told yourself something different after having eaten the pie? For example, you could have told yourself, "Whoops, one small slip. No big deal." You would not have felt depressed but more determined, and instead of pigging out all weekend, you would have been that much more vigilant to keep on track.

The way you think about what happens to you, whether the event is of your own doing, such as a lapse of self-control when eating the pie, or not of your own doing, such as being laid off from your job, will determine your experience of happiness or misery.

Apply this idea to your own life right now. Think of something that is getting you down, that is making you feel sad, discouraged, or afraid. Write it down. Then identify the thoughts you are having about the event. Then identify how you have been behaving as a result of these thoughts. Now see if you can change the way you're thinking about the event—and see how much better you feel. And indeed, see how your behavior can also change:

A. The event happened to me.

B. I told myself "such and such" about the event that has happened to me.

C. Now I feel the following emotions: _____ and I am behaving this way: _____.

Now do your work. The event stays the same. Now change what you told yourself about the event by drawing a line through what you wrote down for B and writing in something more hopeful. You will *feel* more hopeful. You can now cross out what you wrote down for C and write in the new way you feel now, and the way you *will behave* now that you are thinking about the event in a different way.

DON'T LET UNMERITED GUILT CAUSE YOU TO PUNISH YOURSELF

Whether you know it or not, you may be allowing your past—the things that happened to you in your early life—to plunge you into self-punishment. I learned a lot about this idea when I was writing my doctoral dissertation, "Guilt and Atonement in the Novels of Bernard Malamud." As it turned out, each of the main characters in Bernard Malamud's novels was continually stumbling into "bad luck." However, on closer inspection, all of the characters had unconsciously set themselves up for the bad luck, because they felt in their hearts that they were unworthy. A careful analysis of the background of each character revealed that at an early age each and every one had suffered extreme mistreatment or misfortune through no fault of his or her own, and because of it, felt unworthy of a successful, happy life.

Literature is an imitation or even a mirror of life. The study of psychology reveals that self-punishment because of undeserved guilt is a pitfall that can be avoided once we identify the source of the undeserved guilt. Think for a moment about your own life. Who or what have you, up until now, unconsciously used against yourself, saying, "See? That proves you are unworthy. You don't deserve success."

For me, it was having an absent father, being extremely poor growing up, competing with a sister who was billed as smarter than I was, and a host of other things that are either too embarrassing or lengthy to mention.

But my early experiences also served to strengthen me. Looking back, although I would never have chosen some of the things that happened to me, it was indeed because of them that I was able to muster up the inner strength to overcome obstacles. In fact, because of the many stumbling blocks in my way, I learned to make it a habit to forge ahead in spite of the odds—and to keep going until I reached my goals. I believe in my deepest heart that difficulty can be the fuel to fire a life of success if it is used in a positive way.

You can help yourself to bury the dead of your unfortunate past and move on, by making a list right here of those things in your past that may have, up until now, been unconsciously causing you to think that you don't deserve success. List them here, and after realizing that these unhappy events may in fact have helped you to become the strong person you are today, negate them because they are no longer needed. They have served their purpose. You need not carry them on your back to weigh you down.

THINGS IN MY PAST THAT CAUSE ME
UNDESERVED GUILT

1.

2.

3.

4.

5.

Now, next to each one, write a comment. "I could not control that," "It was an accident," "It was a human error," "How could I have known any different." Then once and for all, liberate yourself and move on with your life, free and clear.

SOME THINGS WILL NEVER BE KNOWN

The fact is, there are some things that happened to us in the past that we will never figure out, no matter how much time we spend. Again, I call these events the "mysteries of the universe." If we refuse to allow ourselves permission to move on in our lives until we understand all about our past and why what happened to us happened, we will paint ourselves into a corner. The best we can do is "leave it as a mystery," and move on with the intelligence, creativity, energy, and life that we have left on this planet.

If there's something we cannot know, we must forget it, put it in God's hands. I think of a comforting song we used to sing in church: "By and by, when the morning comes, when the saints of God go marching in, we'll tell our story, how we've overcome, and we'll understand it better by and by." Yes. If all that I hope is true, someday we will all get to ask our questions—and finally understand all things. And yes, just like the ancient gospel song indicates, "we'll understand it better by and by."

Key #3. The power of letting go of the past and moving on. Liberate and free yourself.

NOTES

1. Charles Brenner, M.D., *An Elementary Textbook of Psychoanalysis,* 1st ed. (New York: International Universities Press, 1973), pp. 12–14.

2. Manes Sperber, *Masks of Loneliness: Alfred Adler in Perspective* (New York: Macmillan, 1974), p. 144.

3. Norman Vincent Peale, *The True Joy of Positive Thinking* (New York: Ballantine, 1984), p. 252.

4. Nathan McCall, *Makes Me Wanna Holler: A Young Black Man in America* (New York: Random House, 1994).

5. Daniel Goleman, "Holocaust Survivors Had Skills to Prosper," *New York Times* (October 6, 1992), Section C 1, pp. 1 and 4.

6. Alice Miller, *The Untouched Key* (New York: Doubleday, 1988), pp. 50–51.

5

THE POWER OF
ADMITTING IT

Confess! Own up! Admit it! Because until you acknowledge your wrongdoing, you won't get past your sticking point and grow, thrive, and mature. In other words, name it, admit it, accept your responsibility in it, and be free of it.

But what should we admit or confess? Clearly, it is those things we have done for which we feel guilt. I'm not talking about the unmerited guilt that we discussed in Chapter 4. That's the guilt we sometimes feel because of the blame others lay upon us. I'm talking about the guilt we feel when we willfully violate our own conscience. (Later in this chapter, I'll talk about why some people never feel guilt—and why this is disastrous to them.)

THE SIDE EFFECTS OF
UNRESOLVED GUILT

When we do something that violates our conscience, our own "inner law," the guilt we feel causes us to experience an internal imbalance, a psychological disruption that drains mental and physical energy. This energy could otherwise be used for creative thinking and productive living. The result is a less fulfilling life. In fact, those who struggle through life bearing a load of unremitted guilt will never know what they missed; they will never know what they could have accomplished had they faced their guilt, dealt with it, and moved on.

In short, we may think we get away with wrong deeds that have violated our own conscience—even acts that no one has yet discovered, or acts that may never be discovered. Yet we pay the devil for it, for as psychologists agree, when we violate our conscience it "registers" on our unconscious mind, as surely as if a ledger or a balance sheet were being kept.[1] In time, if we don't admit our wrongdoings and clear the slate, and learn the lessons from our errors by taking responsibility for them, those deeds will weigh us down just as surely as if a millstone were hung around our necks.

In thinking about this unconscious "register" or ledger, I am reminded of an image from Revelations 20:12 that so many religious leaders talk about, a book kept in heaven by God that records the deeds, both good and bad, of every individual, for a day of reckoning. Traditionally, fundamentalists have used this image to motivate people to behave properly, emphasizing the idea that even though you can't see God, he sees you and is recording your every deed. Interestingly, the religious leaders who put forth such ideas were not so far from the psychological truth. They were right on the money—if we exchange the image of the literal book in heaven for a blank slate in our own unconscious minds, where, as the medical and psychological professions agree, everything we see, hear, think, or do is indeed permanently recorded.

So we see, then, that religious leaders could have said the same thing differently, in psychological terms: There exists in our own minds a psychological system, a "book" that must be balanced if we are to enjoy a successful, peaceful life. In other words, we cannot really "get away with anything."

WHEN THE PSYCHOLOGICAL BOOKS ARE NOT BALANCED

What happens if the balancing of the books is neglected—if the psychological ledger is allowed to remain askew—and we refuse to deal with unresolved guilt? As psychologist Franz G. Alexander points out, we send ourselves an unconscious message that we do not deserve to succeed, and one way or another, if we find ourselves succeeding, we either prevent or later destroy that success—and sometimes ourselves—with it.[2]

In some cases, we stop ourselves from succeeding in the first place. Should success come knocking on our door, land on our heads from the sky, or even smack us in the face, we would do something to sidestep it at all costs, because if we allowed it to happen, we would not be able to bear the internal contradiction. It would cause us too great a discomfort. It would fly in the face of what we believe in our innermost beings: that we deserve punishment, and not reward.

Let's look at an example of how this works. Say you were offered a promotion on your job, one for which you were perfectly qualified, but you had to attend a meeting of the top bosses for a required interview. The meeting is just a technicality, but a necessary one. Although you rarely go out during the week, and rarely drink, for some seemingly strange reason, the night before the interview you go out and get drunk, and wake up late with an incredible hangover. You throw on wrinkled, mismatched clothing and show up for the interview "in a fog." You behave in a confused, incoherent manner, and the top bosses have second thoughts about promoting you. To let themselves off the hook, the next day they tell you that something unexpected came up within the organization and you will have to wait for the promotion. Of course you never get it.

I bet you can think of people you know who behave exactly this way, and perhaps, before you read this, you couldn't figure out why they seem to step on their own feet every time success is at hand.

Some people manage to succeed despite unresolved guilt. They become business tycoons, or successful doctors, lawyers, and so on. But a closer look will reveal that "no one gets away with murder," so to speak. Such people, in order to gain at least temporary comfort, may try to balance the psychological books by engaging in a variety of self-punishing activities, for example, masochistic and humiliating sexual acts.

How often I've wondered why it is that people from every walk of life, even highly successful people, can have the need to be beaten, humiliated, and even defecated upon in the privacy of their sexual lives. Psychologist Karen Horney discusses this phenomenon at length, and asserts that in such cases people behave this way because of unconscious, unresolved guilt. If the punishment that is needed and expected does not come from an outside source, the "guilty" person either inflicts it upon himself in a masochistic way, or asks someone else to do it for him or her.[3]

There is one final case to consider. What about people who succeed in a very big way, despite a cargo of unresolved guilt and internal messages that they do not deserve success? They can suffer disabling depression or anxiety, and may always worry about being "exposed," but can continue to do well for a lifetime.

On the other hand, I believe that often the answer to this question can be found in the tragic endings of the lives of so many of the celebrities who have died of overdoses of drugs or have perished by their own hand. These individuals, who had "the world on a string" and were seemingly headed for nothing but more success, were suddenly cut down at the height of their careers—by their own doing. Why? we ask.

Could it be that to such people, colossal success seemed like too much of a hypocrisy to bear, an enormous lie? Could it be that in time, the discomfort of bearing the burden of the contradiction between what they felt on the inside and what they appeared to be on the outside weighed them down—to the point where they could no longer endure the pressure? Could it be that in order to balance the internal books, they had to destroy themselves by taking the drugs that eventually snatched their lives, or in some cases, by taking the more direct route and putting a gun to their heads?

Thankfully, it doesn't have to end this way. A little introspection—as painful as it may be—can go a long, long way, even save your life.

BALANCING THE BOOKS: AT-ONE-MENT

The word *atonement* means "a return to the self, a return to one's right mind," or, if broken down further, "at-one-ment," or oneness with the self. It is a graphic description of what we must all do in order to have peace of mind, joy, and success in life. We must somehow balance the books.

But how can we achieve this end? We can do it by confronting our errors and hurtful behavior, feeling remorse for them, and resolving to do better in the future. In other words, we must repent.

Atonement in the Bible provides the "sinner" a way to pay for his or her sins symbolically and to correct the imbalance of the guilt, to connect the breach within the self (the conscience) and to become "at one" with the self once again. In the Old Testament, the provision for atonement was made through an animal sacrifice. The animal had to be an unblemished sheep or goat, who paid for the sin of the transgression with his life (represented by the blood pouring out upon the altar). By sacrificing the animal in place of the self, the transgressor was able to escape a much more severe self-punishment.

The idea of a blood sacrifice is carried through to the New Testament, where it now becomes symbolic. Jesus Christ takes the place of the unblemished animal and, once and for all, by the shedding of his blood on the cross, atones for the sins of the world, for anyone who will claim that sacrifice as his or her own, as atonement for sin.

A good therapist can function to help a person to become "at one" with the self. As a patient sits in the therapist's office and is gently coaxed into talking about even his or her most heinous behavior, and as the therapist listens and helps the patient to understand the reasons for that behavior, and to accept and then forgive himself or herself, the patient is able to believe that he or she can change, and indeed is not a "bad" person. The patient is then free to go on and live life with the belief that he or she can continue to learn and indeed do better in the future.

Clearly, both the psychological and religious communities are in some agreement that intense, hurtful feelings, specifically guilt, must be addressed. If we commit hurtful acts and other misdeeds that violate our own "inner law" or conscience, something must be done in order to free ourselves to go on and lead joyful, productive lives. Suggestions on how you can do this will be offered later in this chapter. But for now, let's talk about what it is that makes us feel so guilty, what it is that must be reconciled: "sins" against the conscience.

THE MEANING OF SIN

The word *sin* in the original Hebrew of the Bible means "to miss the mark." I like the analogy of the mark, because we can imagine ourselves shooting at a target, missing it, and clearly knowing that we did so. In other words, there is no way we can shoot and miss the mark, and not clearly see it. We know what we did. It is the same way with sin. When we do something wrong, we know it. Nobody has to tell us we did it. We feel it as clearly as if we saw ourselves shooting at a bull's-eye and missing it by a long shot. With this idea in mind, let's take a look at some "sins," both modest and grand.

Suppose you are asked by your boss to research the best deal for his travel arrangements. You fear this task might impinge on your lunch hour, so you make only one call and lie to your boss, telling him that you spent an hour calling around and got the best deal in town.

You get away with the deception free and clear, because your boss trusts you. But your "sin" lies clearly on your conscience. Not an enormous transgression, but clearly a sin, a missing of the mark. Your misdeed or failing is clear to you. It has been recorded on the negative side of the ledger in your unconscious mind. You were wrong and you know it.

There are greater trangressions. Suppose, for example, you are working for a company and are in charge of keeping the books. Your boss has no way of knowing how much you actually spend for certain items, and you can inflate things so that by the end of the week you end up with a hundred dollars extra in your pocket. You've been doing this for the three years you've worked there. You've gotten away with it, and chances are you will never get caught— at least not by your boss. But every penny you have stolen is as clear as day to you and is recorded in the "book" or your unconscious mind as a mark against you, weighing you down and making you think less of yourself.

There are bigger sins. You are married to someone or are in a committed relationship, but you have fallen in love with someone else. The new person has no money, while your present partner is wealthy enough to pay most of the bills. Because you would rather not risk the loss of the benefits of your present relationship, you decide to lead a double life, knowing that your partner will probably remain oblivious to what is going on and, chances are, will never find out. You continue this lifestyle for a year—and seem to be getting away with it quite well. But all the time you have a slightly uncomfortable feeling. It is as if there were an invisible finger pointing at your very soul. You know you are wrong— and you can see it in your mind's eye as graphically as if you were shooting at a target and missing the mark.

Most of us can't live with sin—at least not well. We can't prosper with it—at least not permanently. Literature such as Proverbs 28:13 in the Bible expresses it succinctly: "He who covereth his sins shall not prosper: but whoso confesseth and forsaketh them shall have mercy."

The message is clear. Those who live with unresolved guilt are under a certain stress that will prevent ultimate, peaceful success. But how do we face up to our wrongdoing?

WHY WE SIN:
MAKING ADMITTING IT EASIER

In order to own up to the fact of your wrongdoing, you may want to ask yourself what you were thinking at the time, what helped you to make that wrong decision. Psychologist Nathaniel Branden says: "Our actions are always related to our effort to survive, or to protect the self, or to nurture ourselves, or to grow."[4] I would like to add "or to gain momentary pleasure."

When you come to think about it, when you did the wrong thing you probably did it for one of the above reasons, and perhaps for the most forgivable reason of all: You did it because on some level, you thought you had to do it to survive. At the time of your misdeed, you probably gave quick thought to the immorality of your actions, but then brushed that idea aside and did it anyway. It was more convenient for you not to acknowledge the wrong of what you were about to do.

I can think back to a wrong action I took, something that may not seem so bad to someone else—after all, it wasn't against the law—but clearly it was against my inner law. I had planned and in fact initiated the idea of taking a trip to Florida with my sister Barbara and her husband. My ex-husband and I were all set to go, but one week before the trip, I found out about a deal where we could all go to Paris for just a few dollars more. I asked my sister to change her plans, but she didn't want to do it. She had no desire to go to Paris. But I wanted to go to Paris, so I convinced my ex-husband to go—and we left my sister and her husband in the lurch, to go to Florida by themselves. They ended up staying home. They didn't want to go alone. The whole idea was to go with us.

What was I thinking at the time? What made me choose to go to Paris and say, "The hell with my sister. Let her shift for herself"? I can clearly remember what it was. It was my desire to nurture myself, to fulfill my desire for adventure, and to do it with the same amount of money I would have spent on "boring old Florida!" I clearly remember thinking, "Am I crazy? Here I can go to Paris for the same price as Florida. Why shouldn't I take advantage of the opportunity? If Barbara is too stupid to see it, too bad for her."

But what was I really doing? My actions were understandable—and fully in accordance with Nathaniel Branden's explanation for why we do "wrong things," or why we sin: "Our actions are always related to our effort to survive, or to protect the self, or to nurture ourselves, or to grow." But I was also "missing the mark." I was violating my own conscience by choosing something that would (and here is my added explanation as to why we sin) give me the most momentary pleasure—at the expense of others.

Yes. I agree with Nathaniel Branden. My deed was understandable; I wanted to "grow." But I knew that in this case it would be at the expense of others. I didn't have to do it. *I chose to do it.* I *decided* to do it. I could have refused to do it. I could have done what I knew in my heart was the right thing: follow through on my plans with my sister. In fact, I clearly remember thinking, "This is wrong. I shouldn't do this." But I did it anyway. When thoughts about how unfair it was to Barbara came into my mind, I clearly remember rationalizing them away. "Too bad," I would say to myself. "It's not my fault if she's not spontaneous. It's her choice. She could go to Paris with us."

My sister never condemned me. She never said a mean word to me about it. But until I *admitted* to myself—some five years after the fact—that I had done the wrong thing, and then apologized to her, the guilt haunted me and even weighed me down. After admitting the wrongness of my actions—first to myself and then to Barbara, and then asking her forgiveness—I was finally, once and for all, free of the guilt.

I'm sure if you think back in your life right now, you can call up similar examples. Someone else may say, "Oh, so what. That's not so bad." But you remember those things, and to this day they bother you. If you have such things, I suggest that you think of them right now and write them down—then look at them and admit to yourself, "I was wrong." Then if it is possible, contact the party involved and make it right. (Also see the seven steps at the end of this chapter.)

CONFESSION IS GOOD FOR THE SOUL

There are a variety of ways to confess. Some people can, in the privacy of their own minds, admit that they did something wrong, feel remorse about it, and resolve to do better, and it ends right there. Others must get on their knees and pray to God, asking for forgiveness. Still others need to go to a church and confess to a priest. Others require a therapist. Some need to do a combination of the three. But there is a fourth way to find solace. We can confess our misdeeds to others—a friend or relative, or even a perfect stranger.

Some time ago, I conducted an experiment. I had read in a psychology book that most people have a deep, dark secret, some wrongdoing that they have been hiding but that they would love to confess so as to "get it off their chest." If given the opportunity to confess this deed, they would do it—even if it were to a perfect stranger—and in so doing, the person would be so relieved that his or her face would show an immediate change with the demeanor brightening up and the body language demonstrating relief from a burden.

The author suggested that we try an experiment the next time we were with perfect strangers. The idea was to ask each person in the group to confess something they had done, perhaps a long time ago, something they had never told anyone before, something that still bothered them or even haunted them.

I decided to try the experiment, and soon I was afforded the perfect opportunity. I was waiting for an acquaintance in a hotel restaurant-lounge and struck up a conversation with two people who were at the next table. When my acquaintance joined me, we all continued to talk, and finally agreed to join tables. After a couple of disinhibiting glasses of wine, I suggested that we all dare to confess a deep, dark secret to each other. After some coaxing and "you go firsts," we each told of something we had done, something we felt guilty about and had never told anyone else. The nature of the confessions ran the gamut from stealing to beating someone up, to infidelity, to breaking a promise, and even to a childhood act of revenge—the injuring of a neighbor's pet.

After we had all "confessed," the change of mood was dramatic. Suddenly everyone seemed relieved, joyful—indeed buoyant. There was a gaiety in the air, as if we had just received news that we were all to be the recipients of some good fortune. We were lighthearted and acted as if our burdens had been lifted. I ended the "session" by telling the "strangers" about my experiment. We all agreed that perhaps we had saved ourselves a few hundred dollars' worth of counseling.

Clearly, honest confession of any kind, even to perfect strangers, is a form of therapy. In fact many psychologists agree that if one shared one's "humanity" in this way and confessed one's misdeeds on a regular basis, whether it be to a friend, the clergy, or to attentive strangers, one might never need go to a professional therapist.[5]

Confessing one's sins to others is equivalent to judging oneself, equivalent to saying, "I did it. I am wrong. Don't you agree?" But with the admission of the wrong and the acknowledgment of the wrong by yourself and others comes another agreement: that you are worthy of forgiveness. The people hearing the "crime" will usually say something like, "Yes. What you did was wrong, but you're only human. You have to forgive yourself." In encouraging you to forgive yourself, they indicate that they too would forgive you—and you feel forgiven.

By confessing one's misdeeds, one relieves the psyche from the kind of stress that can cause many diseases. Interestingly, a biblical writer in Psalms 31:10 seems to describe a cancerlike disease that was alleviated once he confessed his sin:

> When I kept silent, my bones wasted away in my
> groaning all the day. For the day and night thy
> hand was heavy upon me: my marrow dried up
> as in a summer drought. I acknowledged my sin
> to thee and my iniquity I did not hide. I said "I
> will confess my transgressions to the Lord," and
> thou didst forgive the iniquity of my sins."

The imagery of wasted bones and dried marrow are graphic demonstrations of the effect of guilt on the body as well as the psyche.

REFUSING TO OWN UP:
PEOPLE WITHOUT A CONSCIENCE

Actually, guilt is a good thing. It was created, I believe, to point us in the right direction. What would happen, after all, if you never felt guilt for any wrong deed you committed? You would not have the motivation to correct your actions. In fact, you would be dangerous to society, a sociopath.

But how do some people become "conscienceless" or even sociopaths? I believe they do it by convincing themselves that ethical behavior does not apply to them. Some cause themselves to believe that there is no such thing as "wrong" by continually refusing to admit, even to themselves, that they have done wrong—until the time eventually comes when they can no longer feel guilt. They behave in a deplorable manner, without compunction. Such people end up with calluses on their consciences, calluses so thick that they are literally unable to tell the difference between right and wrong.

Perhaps it was just this kind of thing that Jesus was talking about in Luke 12:10 when he discussed the sin against the "holy spirit," the "unforgivable sin." Could Jesus have meant that if one continually hardens one's heart, refusing to admit and feel sorry for one's wrongdoing, that eventually one would no longer feel the urge to repent, because one could no longer feel guilty?

Think about it for a moment. Haven't we all wondered from time to time, when reading the paper, how certain serial killers, torturers, and other sociopaths are able to sit during interviews with a smiling face and place the blame for their outrages on everyone but themselves? They truly seem to believe in their deepest heart that they have done no wrong.

Psychologist Erich Fromm, in line with this thinking, states:

Every evil act tends to harden man's heart, that is, to deaden it. Every good act tends to soften it, to make it more alive. The more man's heart hardens, the less freedom does he have to change; the more determined already by previous action. But there comes a point of no return, when man's heart has become so hardened and so deadened that he has lost the possibility of freedom, when he is forced to go on and on until the unavoidable end which is, in the last analysis, his own physical destruction.[6]

"He is forced to go on," as Erich Fromm puts it. He has set up a momentum that cannot be interrupted. And what is the result of this momentum? Both Erich Fromm and the biblical proverb agree: physical destruction. We cannot ignore the mind-body connection. If we refuse to allow the mind or the conscience to direct our lives, eventually our physical body will be destroyed, either by disease, as is implied by Erich Fromm, or by being in the wrong place at the right time, as is implied by Ecclesiastes 7:17: "Be not overmuch wicked. . . . Why shouldest thou die before thy time?"

What, then, should we do if we have "sinned," brushing aside the voice of our conscience that tried to shout at us, "No, no, no"? The first thing we need to do is to refuse to engage in rationalizations such as "I really had no choice" or "Anybody would have done the same." Instead, admit that you did it—and let yourself feel sorry. If possible, take action to make it right and resolve to do better in the future.

FACING YOUR DARKER SIDE

While we are on the subject of rationalizations and avoidance, I think it is very important for me to point out that we must, and I stress *must,* face our darker side—early in the game, before the time comes when it may be too late. I think of the many men who beat and abuse women—and eventually commit murder. These men (and the women they abused and killed) may have been saved from such an end had they dared to admit to themselves and face head on, in the early stages, the darker side of their behavior. What could they have done to save themselves? They could have sought out help in the many available counseling facilities.

The same principle holds true no matter what your "darker side" may be. It's always very important to admit to and face your darker side rather than rationalize it away. Think hard. Is there something about yourself that scares you? If there is, don't try to pretend it isn't there or talk yourself out of it. Instead, do the courageous thing. Speak to a qualified counselor about it (see p. 72–73 on choosing a therapist). In the long run, it will save you much anxiety—and it may even rescue your life.

INTEGRITY

I've always loved the word *integrity*. It means "the integration of convictions, standards, and beliefs with our behavior; to be undivided." In other words, a person with integrity behaves in accordance with his or her beliefs. There is no contradiction between the two. People of integrity are at one with themselves and, as a result, have peace of mind.

But more than that, people of integrity are admired and remembered by others. For example, I'll bet you could think of someone right now who stands out in your mind like a shining light for demonstrating integrity. My ex-husband comes to mind immediately. He knows his values, and he would not compromise them for anything or anyone. He behaves in accordance with his beliefs. He would be embarrassed to read this, but I must say it. To this day I have never met a person with more integrity than Charles J. Vedral.

The first step toward achieving integrity is to face up to our wrongdoing and to clear the slate, to face the negative side of the ledger. Then, every time we are ready to do something that would violate our values, our internal law, instead of brushing it aside or outshouting it, we will be able to think of how we will feel later, after the compromising deed is done, as opposed to how we will feel if we do what we know in our innermost being is right. In fact, take it a step farther. Imagine how you will feel ten years from now if you yield to temptation and take the road of immediate convenience, and compromise your values for temporary gain, as opposed to how you will feel ten years from now if you take the high road and do the more difficult, but right, thing, suffering temporary loss in order to remain true to what you know in your heart is right.

I was recently put to the test myself when I was in the process of getting myself booked on talk shows for the paperback edition of my book *Get Rid of Him*. Naturally, my publicist and I tried first to get me booked on *Oprah,* who by far has the highest ratings of all the talk shows. We waited three weeks, hoping that the producers would call, but they didn't, so we sent out the invitation to all the talk shows, and finally the *Maury Povich* show called. The producer was a lovely woman who worked diligently with me to set up a show, as well as booking a panel of women to come in from various parts of the United States for an agreed-upon tape date.

Then two days before the show I got a call from the producers of *Oprah*. They needed an expert on the exact topic of my book. I would be the only expert, and they would feature my book throughout the show. But there was only one catch: The taping was on the same day as *Maury Povich*. I couldn't ask *Oprah* to change their air date because, number one, they don't do that for anyone, and number two, Oprah insists on an exclusive "first" booking when you do her show. In fact, neither *Oprah* nor *Maury Povich* would have agreed to play second fiddle to the other.

What to do? Everyone knows that getting on *Oprah* could mean being number one on the best-seller list. Everyone knows that ten times more people watch *Oprah* than any other talk show. And everyone knows that you would have to be out of your mind to turn down *Oprah*.

I was tempted. I was pained. I was in agony. But not for long. You see, I know how it feels to do the wrong thing and then to have to look in the mirror. I know how it feels to have to live with an unbalanced psychological ledger and how it feels to try to rationalize away wrong decisions—and the price you pay in self-respect. And I know that in the long run, it just isn't worth it, no matter how glittering the prize being dangled in front of you seems at the moment. But I didn't just snap my fingers and come to my decision. I still had to go through the wrestling match with my conscience.

I thought of the hardworking producer of the *Maury Povich* show. I thought of the position I would be putting her in, how she would have to explain to her superiors and then desperately scurry about trying to put together another show for that studio time—and with just two days' notice. I thought of the many women flying in from all over the country and how they had probably rearranged their lives to appear on that show on that date.

Then I thought about my options. How could I pull this off if I did want to do *Oprah?* I could lie to the producer of the *Maury Povich* show, telling her that there was a death in the family or some such thing—and run off to Chicago to do *Oprah*. Perhaps the *Maury Povich* show would never find out—and might even be willing to rebook the taping. Then I could have both, and if they did find out my ploy, it would be too late—both shows would have been taped and would air. But even the thought of that made me sick. A blank wall rose in my mind when I thought of making that call, a clear dead-end road in my conscience. I couldn't do that. It was wrong.

But I could tell her the truth. After all, she would understand why no author in his or her right mind would want to pass up *Oprah*. But when I thought of doing that, I had a simultaneous vision of myself on *Oprah* expounding on being true to one's values (a major theme of *Get Rid of Him*). I would probably not be a very dynamic guest that day because I would feel like a phony, a hypocrite.

I then thought the reverse. Suppose I could pull it off, and in fact manage to do well on *Oprah*—be my usual self—and suppose everyone ran out and bought my book, and it made number one on the best-seller list, and stayed there for a full year—and I made a million dollars. Would it be worth it then? I thought about how I would feel ten years from now if I did the right thing and turned down the show, as opposed to how I would feel if I did the wrong thing and compromised my values, and realized that even if I netted the most unimagined success, I would regret it later—and that it wouldn't be worth it.

So the next day I did the right thing. I called the producer of *Oprah* and told her that I had made another commitment and would have to pass on this show. Do I regret it? Not one bit. I may have lost that show but I cemented another solid block of integrity right into the center of my being. You can't put a price on that!

But here is the amazing punch line to the story. As it turned out, the *Oprah* show that I missed doing was aired on the day of former President Nixon's funeral, and was preempted in most markets by that event. Had I done the show in violation of my conscience, I can just imagine how I would have felt having "sold out," only to *be* sold out. At least *Maury Povich* aired in all markets—and my book was exposed to a certain amount of viewers. I'm sure, under the circumstances, that it was exposed to more viewers than saw the *Oprah* show I would have appeared on.

It's interesting to consider how many times we do the right thing and think we paid a price, when in reality, we may have been rewarded instead. Had I not taken the trouble to find out when the *Oprah* show that I missed aired, I would never have known that indeed, I was lucky to have chosen to follow my conscience.

YOU DID HAVE A CHOICE

It never ceases to amaze me—and it always makes me sick—when I hear criminals who have committed even the most heinous crimes say, "I had no choice. It was because of the drugs, the alcohol, my abusive parents, my wife, society . . ." and on and on. Or when I hear talk-show guests who have neglected their children, committed incest, engaged in swindles and scams say, "I couldn't help it. I'm a victim of . . ."

The answer that always shouts out in my mind is: "No. Stop lying to yourself. You're not a total victim." I'm sorry to disillusion you. If you think about it, there is a role you played in your wrongdoing. You did something to contribute to the problem. Find your part in it and accept responsibility. Until you do this, you will never be free of the guilt and you will never be able to move on. As Proverbs 26:2 says, "As the bird by wandering, as the swallow by flying, so the curse, causeless shall not come."

If you've become addicted to anything—cigarettes, alcohol, drugs—nobody held a gun to your head and forced you to take the first, second, and third drag, drink, or dose. You chose to do it and now you are paying the price. The "curse," the addiction, "causeless did not come." It came because you wandered away from right thinking. You did the wrong thing.

As you by now know, my ex-husband was a minister. During the time when he was pastor at a church on the Lower East Side of Manhattan, I was able to talk to hundreds of drug addicts, and each of them told stories of how they got hooked. Many of them revealed to me that in the early stages of their addiction, each time they would be ready to take the drug, an "alarm system" would go off in their heads, warning them not to do it. Later, as the habit progressed, the alarm system seemed to dim, and eventually they were able to do the drugs without much thought.

After encountering our church group, and being given a reminder that it is never too late to make a clean start, many of these drug addicts chose to engage in the battle that would lead to the end of their addiction. Others chose to continue doing the drugs until they eventually died of overdoses.

What caused one drug addict to be free of drugs and live a clean life, and another drug addict to continue to do drugs and die? Did these drug addicts have choices even in the midst of their addiction? I believe they did. In fact, I believe that where there is life, there is a will, and there's hope and there are choices. We have the choice to change our ways. But the first step is owning up, admitting it. Every drug addict who became clean had to take the first step and admit that he or she was an addict, that he or she had chosen to do the drugs, and then had to decide that he or she no longer wanted to walk that path. The addict had to determine to change his or her ways.

Yes, we all have choices. It is one thing to make wrong choices. That is a failing in itself, but a forgivable one, understandable, and indeed fixable. It is quite another thing to pretend to ourselves that we had no choice at all—and that everything we did just "happened to us," that we share no responsibility in any wrongdoing in our lives. That kind of thinking is not forgivable, and in fact leads to the "unforgivable sin," as discussed in the above paragraphs: the point where one cannot admit one's wrongdoing and change because one is no longer capable of feeling guilt.

So it behooves us once and for all to take a hard and even painful look at ourselves and to own up and say, "Yes. I did have a choice. And I still have a choice. I have a choice right now."

THE STEPS TO REPENTANCE

After all is said and done, what can we do to insure that we admit and deal with our wrongdoing, so that the energy of our lives can flow unimpeded toward the purpose for which we were born?

There are six simple *R*s, steps that will lead to the big Seventh *R*: Rightness with the self, a feeling of having integrity.

1. RECOGNIZING

Name your offense and admit that you did it. Say it out loud: "I did _____."

2. REALIZING

Figure out why you did it. Ask yourself what you were thinking at the time. What were the circumstances surrounding the misdeed that led to the decision you made?

3. RESPONSIBILITY

Identify your choice in the situation. Look back and see where you could have made a different decision. Write down what better choice you could have made but didn't.

4. REPENTING

Ask for forgiveness of God and of yourself, then accept that forgiveness.

5. REPAIRING

If others were involved and are still available, apologize to them, and if possible, offer to do something to make amends.

6. RESOLVING

Resolve to do better in the future, to be alert to your conscience, and hook this decision into your will.

And now the prize:

7. RIGHTNESS

You have earned the inner feeling of oneness, of integrity, the freedom to be who you are and to go on in the world with untied hands and an unburdened conscience. Breathe easy as you accomplish the purpose for which you were born.

⚷ **Key #4**. The power of admitting it—owning up and taking responsibility. Mature yourself.

NOTES

1. Karen Horney, *New Ways in Psychoanalysis* (New York: W. W. Norton & Company, 1935), p. 237. Franz G. Alexander and Sheldon T. Selsnick, M.D., *The History Of Psychiatry* (New York: Harper and Row, 1966), pp. 299–300. Abraham Maslow, *Toward a Psychology of Being,* 2nd ed. (New York: Van Nostrand), p. 5.

2. Franz G. Alexander, M.D., *Fundamentals of Psychoanalysis* (New York, W. W. Norton & Company, Inc, 1963), p. 124.

3. Horney, *op. cit.,* p. 232.

4. Nathaniel Branden, *How to Raise Your Self-Esteem* (New York: Bantam Books, 1987), p. 79.

5. Manes Sperber, *Masks Of Loneliness: Alfred Adler in Perspective* (New York: Macmillan Publishing Company, Inc., 1974), p. 129.

6. Erich Fromm, *You Shall Be as Gods,* (Connecticut: Fawcett Premier, 1966), pp. 80–81.

6

THE POWER OF
YOUR WILL

We've all heard the word *will*. Sayings such as "Where there's a will there's a way" have been with us for years, and in fact, have been quoted to most of us in our early years, either by parents or teachers, or both. But what does the word *will* really mean—and how can we strengthen ourselves by learning to use our will? This chapter is going to dig deep into the idea behind that word and, in the end, help you to use your will to enable you to improve your life.

The dictionary definition of the word *will* is: "the power of making a reasoned choice or decision, or controlling one's own actions." I believe that every adult human being has a will of his or her own, the power to make a reasoned choice or decision—and the power to control his or her actions—the power, I might add, to refuse to accept helplessness.

You can get a "feel" for your own will by thinking back right now to a time when you "decided" to do something. Was it yesterday, when you "decided" to stop off and buy some food item before you went home—even though you really didn't feel like stopping for the food? Perhaps it was a bigger use of will—when you "decided" to ask for a promotion on a job, even though you were embarrassed to do so. Maybe it was when you "decided" to go to work even though you felt like calling in sick. In fact, if you wanted to, you could probably list ten times you used your will in the last week—and you could do it in less than five minutes. The truth is, we all have a will, and we all use our wills all the time.

But if we have a will, then why do we so often feel as if we are victims—that we have no choices? This feeling stems from a time when we may have indeed been victims, either as infants or children, at which time we did not have a free will because our power to make choices and control our actions was very limited. But *now we can choose*. Now, as adults, we have a will of our own. And by acts of will, one act at a time, we can, in most circumstances, virtually change our own destiny.

WHERE THERE'S A WILL THERE'S A WAY

I used to teach high-school English, and I remember one experience from those days very clearly. One day I asked my students to read one chapter a day in a given book, so that we could finish the book by the end of two weeks. Time dragged on, and only about one-third of the class was keeping up with the reading. When I confronted the class about their lax attitude, they said things like, "We have other things to do: homework for other classes, after-school jobs, responsibilities at home. And anyway, the book is boring!"

Then I asked, "If I pay you a thousand dollars for every chapter you read, and all you have to do is to answer simple questions to prove you read the chapter, would you do it?" Every single hand went up. It was amazing how suddenly reading the chapter was no problem.

"Where there's a will, there's a way." What is needed then, is the will or, better put, what is needed is motivation, something to spark the will. Obviously, I did not inject each and every student with a "will drug" to get them to agree to read the chapter. All I had to do was spark their will with an offer of giving them a thousand dollars per chapter read. In the end, I got the students to read ahead by giving them Fridays off—we watched movies. The students were willing to work harder during the week in order to "earn" the day of relaxation. But I must say, not *every* student was motivated by this lesser reward.

It is clear, then, that motivation is the spark that ignites the will. And that's what this book, and specifically this chapter, is meant to do for you, to be the spark that ignites your motivation to use your will.

THE POWER OF THE HUMAN WILL

People do all sorts of impossible things when they are motivated to do them. In his book *The Knack of Using Your Subconscious Mind,* John K. Williams says:

> *The New York Times* recently carried the story of a man who had been confined to a hospital bed for five years, unable to move himself in any way because of complete paralysis. The hospital patient in the next bed suddenly became insane and started to attack the paralytic. The man, who for five years had been unable to move his body or walk, pulled himself loose and, without stopping, ran up three flights of stairs.[1]

What gave the paralytic the sudden ability to rise from his bed and not only walk, but run up three flights of stairs?

Obviously, when he realized that his life was in danger, he ordered his body to get going.

I can just see him now: His mind "telling" his body, "Get up. I command you to get up! Move it or you'll die," and his body, his creaking bones and weak, atrophied muscles, in response to the powerful order of the mind, somehow getting up and propelling his body out of the bed, away. from the attacker and up the stairs.

Mr. Williams tells of another seemingly miraculous event:

> Eight patients, all helpless paralytics, were con-
> fined to a ward in Equador. One day a giant boa
> constrictor visited the paralytic ward by way of an
> open window. In less than ten seconds the snake
> was the sole occupant of the ward. Every patient
> was suddenly and completely cured. One patient,
> who had not left his bed in two years, jumped
> from a window six feet from the ground and
> rapidly crossed the hospital yard.[2]

We all have a will, a powerhouse located in the center of our being that can be sparked to cause the body to do the seemingly impossible under certain circumstances. If this is so under extreme conditions where life and limb are threatened, why can't it be so under less dire circumstances? The good news is, it can.

Let's think about it. Have you ever had a feeling of being incapable of doing something, and suddenly your will was sparked and you performed the seemingly. impossible?

I see it all the time in dating situations. Think of your own dating life. Was there not a time when you were crazy about a certain person? You were settled in for the evening, too lazy even to get up and clear the dishes from the dinner table. Your friend calls and asks you to go to a movie. "Are you kidding?" you say. "I'm vegging out tonight." Then the phone rings again, and it is the person you've been hoping would call all week. "I'm passing right by your house in about an hour. Could I stop by and take you out for a drive?" he or she asks.

Suddenly your adrenaline soars. You have all kinds of energy. Your mind starts wheeling around. "I could be ready in half an hour if I start right now," you think. "Why of course. I'm just hanging out," you say. And then you fly around the house looking for clothing, taking a shower, fixing your hair, and so on. Rising from your couch of ease is no problem now, but when your friend asked you to go to the movies it was a big problem. Something very specific sparked your will—and your will drove your body to get dressed and be ready for the date.

WHAT MOTIVATES US TO USE OUR WILL?

What is it that sparks the will? We already know from the hospital examples given above that the survival instinct (safety) can motivate and energize us to use it, and from the student examples, that money can stimulate us to use it, and from the last example, that romance or love can inspire us to use it. In fact, these three things can cause most people to move mountains. But there's yet another spark that will energize most people to use their will, and that is the promise of self-actualization.

But what is self-actualization? It is the fulfilling of your potential, becoming all that you can become, using your talent, your ability to the utmost. The feeling that one gets when one is on performing a self-actualizing activity, or is on a path that will lead to self-actualization, can be described as a natural high, but that feeling is better than a high, which is temporary. The pursuit of self-actualization provides a steady high—and that high is the fuel that keeps the will going.

To understand this concept better, let's take a look at some things that make us feel as if we are being self-actualized. We feel self-actualized when we study something we are interested in, and become knowledgeable, and can speak intelligently about that subject. For example, if you have always been interested in and curious about nutrition and you take a course and learn all about it, and find yourself talking about it to your friends, and even being called upon by them to give advice, you experience a feeling of self-worth and importance, and this feeling energizes you to take the time to give the advice being asked for.

Using another example, if you have always been interested in art, and you read some books, and visit some museums, and become a self-made expert, you feel great about yourself when you recognize a certain painting. Why? You are using your innate talent. Experiences such as these spark your will to study more about art. You determine to take a course in it. You think, "Maybe I'll even teach art someday." You are on the road to becoming self-actualized in a given area of your life.

We feel self-actualized when we develop and use a talent—such as singing, public speaking, or playing a sport well—and are often "tickled pink" when we are acknowledged for it. For example, if you have a great singing voice and someone asks you to sing at their wedding, you feel exhilarated when everyone compliments you on your wonderful voice. You may say to yourself, "Maybe I'll pursue a singing career." You are motivated to take possible action.

Self-actualization also happens when we start getting into good physical shape. If your body is weak and fat and out of shape, and you start seeing it slowly evolve into the you that you are inside, you begin to feel self-actualized in a certain way. And the more you see your body being transformed, the more motivated you are to keep going, the more willing you are to use your will when temptations not to work out assail you. Why? Because the reward of self-actualization has sparked your will.

The drive toward self-actualization, which is ultimately your "self" becoming what you were born to become, can spark your will and fuel it to make you do what previously seemed impossible.

YOU CAN USE YOUR WILL TO CHOOSE THE LIGHT

We know that the will is sparked by the need for safety, food, love, and self-actualization. Now I want to talk about using your will to strain toward the light, the "right road" for your life. Your will can help you refuse to be defeated—in spite of how easy it would be just to slip right onto that wrong road.

I've always been fascinated by the fact that two people who share the same difficult backgrounds—childhood, teen, and early adult years—can so often end up doing "opposite" things with their lives. One person takes the high road and ends up leading a productive, happy life, while the other person, it seems to me, chooses the low road and ends up leading a destructive, miserable life.

As a former high-school teacher in the inner city, I've been able to observe this phenomenon time and again. Some of my students, in spite of the most seemingly impossible odds, managed to resist drugs, stay out of jail, go to college, and later pursue successful careers, while others with equally dismal backgrounds become drug addicts, career criminals, and even murderers.

This story told by psychologist and author Scott Peck in his book *The Road Less Traveled* sheds some light on this enigma. Dr. Peck tells us about a thirty-five-year-old, exceptionally successful businessman who came to see him because of a mild neurosis. The man was born out of wedlock and raised until early childhood by a deaf and dumb mother. Then suddenly he was plucked from the custody of his mother because the state believed that due to her impediments, she was unfit to raise him. He then went from one foster home to another, where he was routinely mistreated and ignored. Dr. Peck explains:

> At sixteen he left his final set of foster parents and began living by himself. Predictably, at the age of seventeen he was jailed for a peculiarly meaningless assault. He received no psychiatric treatment in jail. Upon his release, after six months of boring confinement, the authorities got him a job as a menial stock-room clerk in a rather ordinary company. No psychiatrist or social worker in the world would have foreseen his future as anything but grim. Within three years, however, he had become the youngest department head in the history of the company. In five years, after marrying another executive, he left the company and eventually succeeded in his own business, becoming a relatively wealthy man.[3]

Peck goes on to tell about how the young man then became a loving and effective father, a self-educated intellectual, a community leader, and an accomplished artist. He then asks the question, the one I ask you today, "How, when, why, where did all this come about?"[4]

It wasn't difficult, Scott points out, using traditional therapy methods, to figure out the source and even the cure for the man's mild neurosis, but it was impossible to figure out the source of his success.

I believe I have figured out the source of his success (and indeed, that of so many other seemingly miraculous successes). I believe it was his will that ultimately saved him. The way I see it, he _decided_ not to go under. At some point during his unfortunate early life, at one of the many crossroads that he faced, he realized that he didn't have to keep slipping into the abyss, that he could make a choice, that he could will himself to strain toward the light. In short, at some point he chose to do what he clearly knew (and what we all clearly know at many crossroads) was the positive, the productive, the life-giving, the "right" thing. He chose to follow the road toward self-actualization.

In this case, apparently, when the young man got the menial job, rather than seeking opportunities to steal from his boss or finding ways to lighten his workload and still get paid, he decided to do his best to prove to his superiors that he was worthy of a promotion—and it worked. When he was promoted, I'm sure that inspired him to use his creative talent on the job, until finally the boss promoted him to the very top. As his self-esteem rose, he thought enough of himself to date a woman who was now an "equal," another executive. Once they were married, he probably felt loved and strengthened still further and perhaps, backed up and encouraged by his wife, gained the confidence he needed to go into his own business.

But what was it that turned his life around? Clearly, at some point, the man made a decision to take the right road, the more difficult road, to stop the direction of his life, which I'm sure he felt was the easy road. In fact, because of the weight of previous negative experiences, he may well have felt that there was almost a magnetic force pulling him into the abyss. I cannot tell you exactly when this young man used his will to break the momentum and change the direction of his life, but I believe it is clear that he did it. And once he did it, he began to experience self-actualization, which created a new force, a force that strengthened his "life force," his "will" to live and love and make a difference, and in essence, to choose to go in a positive direction.

DO WE HAVE CHOICES?

Looking back at your life, think of a crossroads where you had a choice. You used your will to make the best decision, albeit perhaps the more difficult choice, the choice that would lead to improving your life. Now think of a crossroads at which you know you made the wrong choice, a choice based upon laziness, selfishness, anger, or unwillingness to extend yourself. In short, you can ask yourself the question, "Did I have choices?" And then answer it yourself.

I believe that no matter what the circumstances of your upbringing and your life situation, you did have many choices in your life. In some situations you chose the low road—you chose not to use your will—and in other situations you fought for your integrity and your life—you used your will to choose "not to go under," and you chose the high road. In fact, choosing to read a book such as this is an indication that you are straining toward the light, searching for the high road for your life right now.

DID I HAVE A CHOICE?

I was having a discussion with a friend, a brilliant scientist who is so smart that in fact he's in the top 1 percent of the population in intelligence. He was holding forth the argument that we really can't judge anyone at all, no matter how horrendous their deeds, because what happens to us depends totally on environment. "In fact," he glibly asserted, "you never know what you would have become if you hadn't had the luck of a White middle-class upbringing."

If you've read up until this point, especially Chapters 3 and 5, you already know that I certainly did not have the typical "White middle-class" upbringing, and that my environment was anything but conducive to developing the person I have become today. I hesitated for a moment, uneager to dig up the disturbing details of my past. But my curiosity got the better of me. What would this brilliant man say to my situation? Perhaps he could straighten out my own thinking. Perhaps there was something I had missed.

I gave him a brief summary of my early life: the ghetto, the rat- and-roach-infested furnished room, being left alone for hours, father not there, mother struggling to support us, drug raids and drug-addict friends, and so on. I was careful not to say, "Look at me. I chose . . ." Instead I humbly and sincerely said, "Then please tell me this. How do you account for my success? Do I get any credit?"

There was a brief silence, very unusual since my friend's verbal ability usually runs in tandem with his quick mind. "You should be given a lot of credit," he said. "Well, then, does all success stem from a middle-class or better environment?" I asked. "No. I guess not," he said, his voice a little soft. "I'll have to think about that." And then we moved on to talking about ballroom dancing, which is where we met.

But when our conversation ended, I started to think. What were the points in my life where I had to use my will to save me? What were the points where I literally had to "decide" not to go under?

WRONG ROAD, RIGHT ROAD: I DECIDED NOT TO GO UNDER

It was not until the fifth grade that I think I became aware of myself as having choices. I remember a clear choice, one where to this day I still recall an inner voice shouting at me, "No, no. Trouble. Don't do it." But I chose to do it anyway.

One of the girls in my class had an uncle who owned a candy store. She asked me and another friend to help divert her uncle's attention while she stole money from the cash register—something she routinely did. Only on this particular day, her usual group of friends was not around. Our reward would be to go on a spending spree with the money.

I clearly remember thinking of the "wrongness of it," then about the chances of getting caught, and then about the goodies that we could buy with the money. The lust for the delicious candy was the deciding factor in my agreeing to go along. So we went to the store and, according to plan, my best friend Celestine knocked over a rack of newspapers while I stood by—my heart beating a thousand miles a minute—feeling as guilty as sin.

Hours later, after completing a twenty-dollar spending spree and returning to school, we were all ordered to the principal's office. The police were present. In a matter of minutes we all confessed to our part in the crime. I ended up in court and narrowly escaped a juvenile detention home.

There were many other incidents. Had I continued, I would have fallen into more and more trouble. But at one point, when I was in the seventh grade, I made a choice that I now know began a change in the direction of my life. I clearly remember it. An announcement was made that they were looking for volunteers who would like to learn an instrument and join the school band. It would mean having to maintain high academic grades and, in addition, committing to daily practice sessions after school and at home. All interested were to speak to a certain teacher.

"Ah, why bother," I thought. It will only mean more work—and I may look stupid carrying my instrument to school every day. I was tempted to wave it off as a dumb idea. But something inside me kept saying, "Try it. You might like it—it will be exciting. Don't be lazy. You can do it."

So I joined the band. And it was indeed a turning point in my young life. In short order, I became third, then second, then first clarinetist in our junior high school band. The band leader, a jazz buff, taught us to play wonderful songs, like "Summertime," "Ain't Nobody's Business but My Own," and "Porgy and Bess." We were regularly invited to play in neighboring schools where we—specifically, the clarinet section—would receive standing ovations when we would rise from our seats and play our solos.

What a feeling. What a high. What a wonderful sense of worth and accomplishment I can recall—and I can almost bring back the physical thrill even now. I can still remember my thoughts: "Wow. This is what life is meant to be, and all this time I never knew it. Everyone should get to experience this. If I had known this, I would have done it a long time ago." It was that moment when I became hooked on accomplishment and, with it, experienced the joy of recognition.

But even on the right course, there were many points where I could have quit (and indeed was tempted to): when I had my baby and now had to work, be a mother, and go to school; when my father died and I wrestled with what my life was all about; when after my divorce I fell in love with a man whose psychological problems aggravated my own and I became enmeshed in a love-hate relationship and stopped going for my Ph.D. for three years, temporarily surrendering everything I had to the relationship—including my goals. But always, with the help of God and with the force of my inner voice, and most of all, with the feeling of how much better it felt to be moving in a positive direction, I was able to continue to use my will to do what was best for my life—to make the right choices. And those choices are what brought me to this point. Those choices are what made me the person I am today. Not an accident. Not "luck." Not some break. But choices I made. I used my will to make choices, and you can too.

BUT . . .

I'm not implying that everyone had the choices I had. Some of you reading this have had a harder life than I've had. Some of you have not had the opportunities I've had. But that is not the point. You are alive and mentally intact enough to be reading this book, right here and now. I am concerned not with what you did about the choices you had to make in the past, because we can never go back, but what you are going to do now—right here and right now—with the rest of your life. You need to think about the choices you have to make, and how you can use your will to decide to make the best possible choices, even if those choices involve temporary or even extended discomfort. You need to decide what path will, in the end, help you to fulfill the purposes for which you were put on this earth, so that, in the end, you will not have to face death with "empty hands."

SYNCHRONICITY GOES TO WORK ONCE YOU USE YOUR WILL

As the great philosopher Ralph Waldo Emerson once said, "Beware of what you want, for you will get it." I wish to take the saying a step further to say, "Beware of what you will, for you will get it." It seems that once we make a decision to do something, especially the right thing, we set in force a magnetism in the universe. In a minute I will disucss this force in conjunction with the idea of synchronicity.

Looking back in my life, I consider it almost uncanny how even twenty years ago I had been crying out to the universe, declaring my goals. I can see this when I skim through the old self-help books in my personal library. Time and again I had written in the margins as my goals:

Write books, go on TV. I can also see it in an old card I discovered, one that I had made up when I was in my thirties, thinking it was a joke at the time. It reads, *Joyce Vedral: Star of Stage, Screen, and Radio.*

Little did I know (or did I know?) that I wasn't kidding. When you will something, you key both your conscious and your subconscious mind to that goal, you set off a "process," and everything within you strives toward that goal. And when that happens, something else is set in motion. Many seeming coincidences begin to occur to help you to achieve that goal. But are these events really coincidences? I think not. I think it is your psychic energy that serves as a magnet to draw you to the places, persons, and situations that will ultimately help to move you toward your goal.

Carl G. Jung had a name for this unconscious process. He called it synchronicity. Jung became fascinated by the fact that when many of his patients were struggling with certain issues, they would seemingly stumble into experiences in their lives that would help them to resolve these issues. What appeared on the surface to be mere "good luck" was, Jung concluded, the result of the subconscious of the person, drawing these seemingly lucky events into his or her life.

Synchronicity works not only to further psychological development, but to help you to move toward the path that you were meant to travel—and to use your potential to the fullest, to give your gift to the world before you say goodbye.

Looking back at my own life, I can recall many incidents that I could now label examples of synchronicity, seeming coincidences that offered me an opportunity that, in turn, led me a step farther down my "path." But I am even more impressed with the synchronicity experienced by so many of the women who have written to me about my book *Get Rid of Him.*

Time and again, women have written to tell me how they "happened" on my work. "I was browsing through the bookstore," one reader writes, "and I was looking in the cooking section, and for some strange reason, there was your book, misplaced into that section. I picked it up, and as I began to skim it, I realized that you were talking to me. I was struggling with the very issues you discussed, and had gone to therapy and read every book you could imagine, but it was your book that gave me the strength to take action." Or "I was about to purchase a book on relationships—in fact, I had it in my hand, ready to bring to the checkout counter—when on the bottom shelf, I spotted your book. I was in a hurry, and at first tried to fight the strong impulse to pick it up and look through it. But I gave in, and five minutes later, I found myself at the counter with your book instead of the other—and it confirmed everything my inner voice was telling me."

All of the women who wrote to me were in life-draining relationships that they knew in their hearts were killing them—if not in body, then in spirit. Everything they read in the book confirmed what they already knew: that they must get out. Each told me that after reading the book she was able to find the inner strength to do what friends and a host of self-help books had already recommended: get into therapy and get out of the relationship. Each of these ladies agreed that it was not an accident, not just sheer luck, that they "happened onto my book" when they did. It was because, unconsciously, they were crying out for help in this direction. They were, in a sense, unconsciously "willing" to move to the next stage of their lives, and in order to do so they had to be free of the life-draining relationship.

In a way, synchronicity reminds me of the statements of Jesus when he said in one breath, "Ask and it shall be given unto you," and then, in the next breath, "Seek and ye shall find." One first "asks" (wills, cries out to the universe) and then "seeks" (takes action). Note that each of the women seemed to be crying out to the universe for help (asking) and then each took action, based upon an inner voice that impelled her to do so.

FIVE WAYS TO STRENGTHEN YOUR WILL

We already know that physical exercise can strengthen and energize the body. Well, the good news is, there are also ways to strengthen and awaken the will. In the following sections, you will find five suggestions to get your will activated.

1. LOCATE YOUR HUNGER

To use your will, to be really motivated, you have to remind yourself that you are *hungry*. You have to tell yourself that you are so hungry that it would be more painful *not* to act than to act. Looking back at my life, I can identify many challenges I was afraid to take. In fact I was so afraid to take them that it was almost physically painful. But when I thought about not going for the challenge, I realized how starved I was to get what I had in mind, and I realized that it would be even more painful not to use my will—not at least to take a stab at it—even if at the time it felt like a long shot.

For example, when I was thinking about going for a Ph.D. in English Literature, I did the research and found out what a long road it would be: the Graduate Record Exams just to be accepted, plus a grueling six-hour exam and a three-hour interview, and then up to ten years of courses. I would also have to write a book-length dissertation that had to be original research, ending with a three-hour exam where I would be eliminated if I failed to defend my dissertation properly.

I clearly remember tossing it around, time and again. "Am I crazy? Why am I doing this? I already have a great job that I love—teaching. A Ph.D. will not add to my salary—not a cent. Why am I torturing myself?" I'd ask. And I tried to rationalize it away. But try as I would, when the dust of my rationalizing thoughts settled, I was always left with the cold, raw hunger in the center of my soul: I wanted to see how far I could push my mind; I wanted, in a sense, to run a marathon of the mind, to see if I could go to the end of the road in academic education. If I didn't do it, I would always be jealous of any woman I met who had a Ph.D. But if I did try and failed, I would not be angry at myself for not trying.

So every time I thought of not going for it, I got a sick feeling in the center of my being. It made me see that, sink or swim, I had to try. It gave me the will to take the first step, and then the next, and then the next, because each time I was tempted to quit, I willfully located my hunger— and that was enough to spark my will to plow through to the next step.

What about you? What is your hunger at this very moment? It may not be as time-consuming and intellectually demanding as getting a Ph.D. It may be something that people make light of, but that is important to you. Do you want a promotion in your job, perhaps one that requires you to pass a test? Are you afraid that after spending a year studying for the exam, you may not pass it after all, and it will all have been a waste of time? Don't let that kind of thinking trick you into letting your will go to sleep. Instead, spark your will to "go for it." How? Locate your hunger. How badly do you want this promotion? How will it make you feel about yourself when you are working at the job of your dreams? How much easier will your life be when that extra money comes in every week? Imagine it. Imagine all of it. Dare to dream.

Yes. You want it. You see that you really want it. See how excited you got just thinking about it, when just for a moment you imagined how you would feel once you achieved that desire? (In Chapter 8 I will give you specific instructions on how to visualize in order to spark your hunger further.)

Now think of how you will feel if you just call the whole thing off right now and forget it. Do you feel sad, kind of empty, depressed? Then the hunger is there. There's no getting around it. It will probably always be there unless you satisfy it.

I used getting a promotion and going for a degree as examples, but this method applies to anything you might want to achieve in your life—anything that will bring you to the right road in your life. For you it may be taking the steps necessary to change jobs or even careers, finding ways to save enough money for a trip or an important purchase, and on and on. No matter what you want, if you locate your hunger, you will find that you can spark your will to take the next step, and then the next, and then the next—until finally, seemingly miraculously, you achieve your goal.

2. RECYCLE YOUR FAILURE

In Chapter 4 I talked about how anger is energy, and how it can be channeled into positive areas to achieve goals. Now I want to tell you how to correct and recycle failure and turn it into the energy to succeed.

I hate to say it, because it sounds too bizarre to be true, but in some cases, the more times you have failed to reach your goal, the better, because the more frustration energy will be available for recycling now. That's right. Think of your specific goal. Now think of how many times you tried to achieve it, and failed, either because you gave up midway or because you tried a wrong method that turned out to be ineffective in helping you to achieve your goal.

Let's use the example of learning a new sport. Suppose you tried more than once to learn to play tennis or golf. You have friends who play the game, and you would really like to join them, but each time you tried to play, you ended up calling yourself uncoordinated and did not try again for months. Then the next time you tried, and kept missing the ball, you decided that you just don't have good hand-eye coordination, and vowed never to try again. "This game is not for me," you told yourself.

But you just can't get it out of your mind. You have so many friends who play the game, and you're missing out on the fun. You think of trying again. This time you say, "Maybe I'll look in my telephone directory and see if there are any tennis (or golf) coaches listed." But then you re-member your long history of failure when it comes to ball sports (even in high school, you almost always caused the volleyball team to lose a point). You feel disgusted, and then depressed. You tell yourself, "Forget it. It's just not for you."

Stop the music. You need to think differently. You need to recycle your failure. Instead of letting your past history of failure depress you and put your will to sleep, turn it around and use it to energize you. Think hard about your failure and get mad—get hopping mad—mad enough to say, "Hey. Wait a minute. This is ridiculous. What do I mean by saying I can't achieve this? Other people less co-ordinated than I have done it—even physically handi-capped people have been able to be taught to improve their skills and even to play ball sports. Why should I limit myself this way? If they can do it, I can do it too."

Say to yourself, "I'm sick and tired of telling myself I can't do it. I'm fed up with the feeling of weakness that holds me back. I'm not going to crawl away like a defeated dog, with my tail between my legs. I don't care what it takes. If it means I have to call a number of coaches until I find the one who is patient enough and enthusiastic enough to help me, I'll do it." Take your feeling of disgust with yourself and turn it into energy to reverse the failure. Learn to land your punches while you're on the ropes.

Think of it. Have you ever seen a boxing match where it looked as if a fighter were finished—he was against the ropes, being pummeled mercilessly, and he looked as if he were about to slide to the floor and go for the eight count—but then suddenly, something within him, something that seemed to rise from nowhere, took over and—boom, he started punching like a madman, and before you know it, he's knocked out his opponent. I've seen such fights, bouts where a fighter was not only against the ropes, but had been beaten in every round, and would have lost the fight by a unanimous decision but suddenly came back, seemingly from the dead.

Don't write yourself off. Get angry. Recycle your anger into energy, energy that will spark your will to go and keep going until you achieve your goal.

3. REMEMBER THE TORTOISE AND THE HARE

I really love this will-strengthener because it has been the secret of my life, a secret told to me by my father, the late David Yellin. My father would tell me this story, using my sister and me as the characters in the story, every time I was discouraged. I, of course, was the tortoise in the story, and my sister was the hare. (Growing up, I was continually compared unfavorably to my sister. This pained my father, and he gently tried to undo the damage by reiterating this fable every time I seemed defeated.)

As my father told it, the tortoise challenged the hare to a race one day because he was tired of being mocked for his lack of speed. The quick hare mocked the tortoise for even dreaming that his slow body could win over him, but because he was bored and had nothing better to do that day, the hare agreed.

As expected, when the starting gun was fired, the hare quickly gained a substantial lead, one big enough to give him the idea that he could take a nap and still win the race. In the meantime, focusing on his own business, the tortoise just kept plodding away, refusing to think about the hare at all, but instead tending to the purposeful action of putting one foot in front of the other, and all the time keeping his mind's eye on the finish line. Finally, the tortoise plodded right over the finish line, but the hare was nowhere in sight. He was just waking up from his nap.

The race is not always to the swift, but to the determined. If anything is true about my life, if there is any principle that I can say has been a constant strengthener to my will when I am tempted to give up on something, it is this one: the idea of not looking at the odds against you but aiming toward the mark. This practice has caused me, time and again, to achieve success where success was seemingly impossible.

I am reminded of how I got my first book published. I was a high-school English teacher, and noticed that the students were lacking in self-confidence, and in the ability to use psychology in dealing with people. I searched for such a book for teens but none was written, so I decided to write one myself. I did, and called it *I Dare You.*

When the other teachers heard that I had written a book and was in the process of looking for a publisher, they literally laughed in my face. "Do you know how hard it is to get published?" they asked. And as it turns out they were right: It was hard, but not impossible. I sent the book out to over 100 publishers—and was rejected by all of them— over a period of two years. Finally, I got a catch, and the book was published by Holt, Rinehart and Winston in hardcover, and later by Ballantine in paperback. After that I wrote seven other teen books, and two for parents.

I remember how during that two-year period I was tempted to stop sending out the manuscript. But the story of the tortoise and the hare stayed in the back of my mind.

I believed in my project, and I said to myself, "If I keep going, sooner or later I'll reach my goal. Someone will see the value of this book and publish it."

Whenever you are tempted to quit something, whenever you look at the long road ahead, remember the story of the tortoise and the hare. Remember the saying, "A journey of a thousand miles begins with a single step." Remember that getting in shape starts with the first repetition that you do and the first day of eating right, and *is won* by the daily, seemingly tedious movements, up and down with the dumbbell, and the daily low-fat menus, until one day, just like the tortoise, you reach your goal. You are in shape, while the hares sleeping lazily (those people who were fooled by quick weight-loss liquid diets and fad shape-up devices) gain back all the weight they lost and are not in shape in the long run. Anyway, it feels great to overcome a tendency to fail.

The Value of Discipline

The story of the tortoise and the hare teaches us yet another lesson, and that is the precious value of discipline and perseverence. It isn't the one burst of effort that wins the day in the long run, but the daily discipline of plodding, refusing to give in to the mood, the weather, the weariness. In short, the obstacle that may tempt us to say, "Oh, just for today I'll give myself a break," and that "just for today" leads into "just one more day," until the goal is lost.

The more I think about it, the more I've come to realize that in fact, it's a very lucky thing to be a tortoise. A tortoise has no choice but to develop discipline. A tortoise doesn't get 95 on a test without studying, and breeze through college skipping most classes and still getting *A*'s and *B*'s on the exams. He has to put in the effort. He develops the habit of extending himself, which carries over later to putting in a day's work for a day's pay. The tortoise is the coveted employee in the real world—because he's reliable. He does his job. The hare, on the other hand, can get the surprise of his life when he graduates from college. He may find out that in the real world, the way of a hare will not work. The boss is not likely to be impressed with how little effort he can put in and still "get over." It is the tortoise and not the hare who learns the right lesson for a successful life.

I don't care how old you are. I don't care how smart you are. I don't care how tired you are. You can learn the lesson now. You can get that tortoise action going.

4. CONQUER SOMETHING SMALL—DO IT NOW

In Chapter 3 I talked about how succeeding in something small helps to build self-esteem. Now I'm going to tell you how to do it.

One of the ways to strengthen your will is to pick some odious chore—something you just don't want to do—and then, by an act of will, face it head on and do it. I'll use myself as an example.

I can get up on a given Saturday morning and just feel plain old lethargic. Although I have a mountain of unpleasant chores to do, I'm already planning not to do them. I'm sitting at the kitchen table having my coffee and I think, "Ugh. Look at those bills that have to be made out—where is my checkbook anyway?" And I go look into my desk drawer, and ugh, the drawer is so full of papers and old receipts that have to be filed and other junk and I already have a headache. Walking back to the kitchen, I remember I have to pick up my clothes from the cleaners—and I also notice that the house is a mess, and I really should clean it today. I'm sitting at the table and, to add to my woes, I realize that I still haven't returned three phone calls I've been putting off until the weekend.

I go back to my coffee. While I'm sitting there, I think, "I'll make a list." I always like to write things down—it makes me feel more in control. I know I'm not committing myself to doing anything yet; I just want to see how it looks on paper. I start writing them down, one thing after the other—and already I feel better. While I'm writing, I think of a few more things I would really like to accomplish today. I add them to the list:

1. Make out bills
2. File papers in desk drawer
3. Return phone calls: Carol, Edna, Nancy
4. Clean house
5. Pick up clothes from cleaners
6. Get new curling iron
7. Pick up book from bookstore

I look at the list, and all of a sudden I feel more in control already, and this gives me energy. I decide to attack the file drawer. I take my coffee into my office and pull out all the contents of the drawer, and begin making piles. I then place each pile in its appropriate folder in the filing cabinet. All the charge accounts, all the canceled checks, all the telephone-bill receipts, and so on and so on, and before you know it, I look in the desk drawer and it is neat and clean and organized.

Suddenly I have energy. I feel more powerful. The act of attacking that one, small, odious chore has given me positive feedback and has in turn sparked my will. Now I say to myself, "I think I'll make out the bills," and I do it with gusto. With that accomplished, I get a happy feeling, and as I look at my list I realize I can cross off two items. I do it and somehow the very act of drawing that line through them makes me feel strong. I think, "What can I attack now?" I realize that if I get dressed and go out, I can kill three birds with one stone. I can pick up my clothes from the cleaner's, stop off and get a new curling iron, and pick up some books I ordered on my way home. Energized by the thought of crossing those three items off my list, I dress quickly and go to it, and in an hour or two, it's all done.

I get home and relax, and while I'm relaxing, I look at my list. I **X** out those three items, and see that the only two left are to clean the house and return phone calls. I'm feeling lazy and mellow. It wouldn't take much effort to talk on the phone while I'm sitting here. I make the calls, one after another. That wasn't so painful! With that done, I cross it off my list and see that only one item remains: *Clean the house.* This is a big one. I'm really feeling lethargic, but I think, "Wouldn't it feel great to look at that list and see every single item checked off?" I think, "How long will it take to clean the house? An hour. What time is it, anyway? Six-thirty. If I start now I'll be finished by seven-thirty. Then I can sit and relax with my food and watch TV with no guilt. I'll do it." And I do. And later I mark off the final thing on the list. And guess what? I'm so energized that after I watch TV for an hour, I decide to put in a couple of hours on a book I'm writing—even though I was planning to wait until Sunday to do that.

See what I mean? By an act of will, if you attack one small unpleasant chore, it will energize you and spark your will to attack another thing, and then another, and before you know it, you've accomplished more than you dreamed you could in a day.

If you make it a practice to exercise your will this way, it becomes easier and easier to perform that first act of will, to get the chain reaction going. In a sense, your will, just like the muscles in your body, becomes stronger, and more agile. After a while, you don't feel as if you're trying to wake the dead when you call your will into action.

I use this method all the time, and now it is second nature. Just this week I was faced with making three unpleasant phone calls. I had to arrange to dig up my old oil lines and replace them. I had to make preparations for the spring cleanup. And I had to schedule a bath for Dave, my bulldog, which is always a battle royal. Every time I thought of making those calls and then dealing with the people when they came to my house, I wanted to procrastinate. "I'll do it after I come back to town next week," I told myself. But then I thought, "But then I'll have to deal with it when I come back, and who knows what new devilment will await me then?"

So by an act of will I did it "now." I picked up the phone and called the oil company, and in a matter of minutes had an appointment. Energized by how easy that was, I called the gardener and the dog groomer, who agreed to my schedule. By the end of the week, I had gotten three burdensome tasks out of the way, by acts of will and by telling myself, "Do it now," and picking up the phone and making that first call.

5. Do Something You're Afraid Of

This one takes a wild act of will, a definite feeling of "Damn the torpedoes, full speed ahead." I'll never forget what I read in G. Gordon Liddy's book, *Will*. He said that in order to prove to himself that he had the will, he thought of the most disgusting thing he could do, something that would test his will to the utmost. He realized that for him, it would be to eat a rat. So he did it.

My father once did something that took an enormous act of will. When he was in his early twenties, he used to travel cross-country by hopping freight trains, and one day, when being chased by a conductor as the train was going through the Mojave Desert, my father fell between the cars. His leg was nearly severed from just below the knee. The train went on and he was left to die.

Realizing that his only chance was to cut off the leg and crawl for help, he took out his pocket knife and, by an act of will, cut off his crushed leg and buried it. He then tied his torn T-shirt around the stump as a tourniquet to prevent himself from bleeding to death. In a second act that took a continuous force of will, be began to crawl toward the nearest town. Luckily, before he could bleed to death, and after about an hour, a car came by and picked him up and brought him to a hospital.

After that my father not only recovered, but fought in the Golden Gloves boxing tournament with an artificial limb.

Those are enormous acts of will; the first, Gordon Liddy's, by choice (he didn't have to eat the rat to save his life) the second, my father's, by necessity (he had to either cut off his remaining limb and tie the stump in a tourniquet, or die). But I'm hoping you won't have to ask yourself to do something so extreme—either by choice or by necessity. You can start small, where you are now. But for you, small will be big enough of a challenge. Think of something you are afraid of. List three things here. At the end of the chapter, go back and choose one to conquer by an act of will.

THINGS I'M AFRAID OF

1.

2.

3.

No matter what you choose to do, when you pick something you're afraid of, and face it head on, and just do it, and let the devil take the hindmost, when you come out still alive and breathing, your will is permanently strengthened, and it carries over for the next and the next and the next time.

YOU ALWAYS HAVE A CHOICE

You almost always have a choice. Why, then, do we so often say, "I had no choice but to . . . ?" Probably because, as children, we really didn't have a choice most of the time. When your parents said, "We're going to Grandma's house," you went to Grandma's house. When your parents said, "We're moving to another state," you moved to another state. That was that. You didn't have a choice. But now that you're an adult, you do have a choice. You don't have to follow the leader; you don't have to wallow in your situation. There are lots of things you can do about your situation if you'll only use your will.

Stop telling yourself, "I'll never succeed," "Society is against me," "I'm not as smart as _____," "I'll never be rich," "I'll always be fat. It's in my genes," and so on. It's not what you've got, but what you do with what you've got that counts. And what you do with what you've got is your choice—it's up to you.

NOT DECIDING IS DECIDING

If you don't make a decision, you are "choosing" not to make a decision. You are choosing not to use your will. As discussed in Chapter 2, I chose not to use my will to call off my wedding, even though my inner voice was screaming at me. I took the path of least resistance because I feared humiliation, and I was loath to confront the pain in my husband-to-be's face if I told him that I had changed my mind. Because of it, I suffered years off my path. I eventually found my path, I believe, because God is good, and he works all things together for the best, no matter how many mistakes we make. But I'll never know what I missed by not daring to exert my will, to crash through the fear and humiliation and take a stand on my own behalf to save years of my life.

I've learned many things the hard way. Now I'm writing these words in the hope that no matter what you've done or not done up until this point, you will become more bold in using your will to make even the most difficult decisions.

YOU CAN DO IT ALONE, JUST BY DECIDING TO DO SO

The power of the human will can be seen when we observe how many people break addictions alone, without the help of support groups, therapy, or any other assisting party. They just decide to do so. (This of course, is not to diminish the importance of support groups. They have helped millions of people.) For example, according to the American Cancer Society, 95 percent of the people who quit smoking do it just by deciding to quit.[5]

In fact, I saw this happen with my own daughter. She had developed a cough and realized that her lungs were beginning to be affected by the smoke. She decided then and there to quit smoking and did so—on the spot. If you are not a smoker, this may not be the area where you can exercise your will to do a difficult thing alone. But I'll bet you could think of something difficult that you could do without the help of anyone—just because you decide to do it. Think of something and try it.

FIRST THE WILL, THEN THE HABIT

Thankfully, once we use our will to break a habit or start a new routine, we don't have to exert as much effort, because eventually the new behavior becomes a habit. After that, we are called upon to reassert our will only once in a while.

For example, if you use your will to break through the daily temptation of not smoking, eventually the temptation weakens, until finally you think about smoking only once a year—and, after a time, perhaps never. If you've started a workout program, and have been battling the daily temptation to skip your workout, as time goes on you have to exert less and less will to force yourself to work out. After a while, you only have to cope with an occasional battle of the will, to remind your body who is boss. In fact, after putting a workout routine into your daily regimen, take my word for it, it becomes just about as "set in" as brushing your teeth or taking a shower—and yes, some days we do have to fight ourselves to take a shower. But, thankfully, things like brushing your teeth and bathing are generally no longer daily battles, and so it will eventually be with any new habit you are trying to establish, or with any old habit you are trying to break.

WHAT DRUGS WILL DO TO THE WILL

Whether it be medication or social drugs, when you ingest chemicals into your body you anesthetize your will. For example, if you smoke enough marijuana you'll be about as capable of using your will as is someone under anesthesia. I have seen hundreds of young people who smoke marijuana lull away their lives as they convinced themselves that the drug is "not harmful or addictive," and that it was useful for just "mellowing out" while they waited for the right opportunity to come knocking on their drug-dazed brain's doors. Every one of these smokers was, according to him- or herself, not addicted. They only smoked occasionally! In the meantime, the best years of their lives have slipped away, and some of these people—now in their thirties and forties—are still "mellowing out."

Why do people smoke marijuana or do drugs of any kind in the first place? They want to ease the pain of life. They don't want to feel upset. But the way I see it, there is an appropriate time in your life to feel upset, and in fact, it is just that feeling that sparks the will into action, that motivates you to make changes. You get upset. You get revved up. You say to yourself, "I've had it. I'm not taking this anymore." And you use your will to do something about your situation. But if you're doing drugs, you don't. If you're doing drugs, instead you say to yourself, "Oh, this problem is not so bad. It will pass." And you do nothing about it, as you watch your life slip by.

If there is anything that will deplete you of all motivation, all direction, it is drugs.

DAMN THE TORPEDOES
—FULL SPEED AHEAD

In conclusion, when it comes time to use our will, we need to say, "Damn the torpedoes—full speed ahead." There's *nothing* that can stop the totally committed will. I think we should all wake up every morning to the words of the first stanza of the theme song from the United States Air Force:

> *Off we go, into the wild blue yonder,*
> *Climbing high, into the sun;*
> *Here they come, zooming to meet our thunder,*
> *At 'em boys, give 'er the gun!*
> *Down we dive, spouting our flame from under,*
> *Off with one hell-uv-a roar!*
> *We live in fame, or go down in flame,*
> *Nothing will stop the U.S. Air Force!*

That's it. You got it right. At 'em boys (gals), give 'em the gun!

ᦂ Key #5.   The power of your will: strengthen yourself.

NOTES

1. John K. Williams, *The Knack of Using Your Subconscious Mind* (New Jersey, Prentice-Hall, 1980), p. 39.

2. Ibid., p. 40.

3. M. Scott Peck, M.D., *The Road Less Traveled* (New York: Simon & Schuster, 1978), p. 237.

4. Ibid., p. 237.

5. Stan J. Katz and Aimee E. Liu, *Codependency Conspiracy* (New York: Warner Books, 1991), p. 3.

7

THE POWER OF
DOING IT ALONE

People often ask me, "Why are you so focused? Where do you get your energy? How do you stay so motivated? What is your secret?" When I think about it, much of my power comes from the fact that I have learned to be completely happy alone. I can go places, do things, and just "be" alone and be blissfully content, and in fact, a good portion of the time I prefer it that way. When I think about it, the ability to *be* and *do* things alone is probably one of the biggest secrets of my success.

In this chapter I'm going to help you to see the self-empowerment of learning to "do" and "be" alone; in other words, I'm going to help you to see the advantage of autonomy.

Autonomy means being able to function independently, without the help or control of others. It does not mean being "forced" to function independently, and it does not mean that you suddenly become a hermit. Of course there will always be a time and place for others in your life, but your center of power will come from you. When you have autonomy, you will not feel as if you can't do something that is important to you unless you have someone else to do it with. When you have autonomy, rather than feeling uncomfortable or hesitant going places and doing or accomplishing things alone—or just being by yourself to think, read, or relax—you begin to relish those opportunities and in fact seek them out. You come to realize that time alone can be used to help clear your mind, gather your forces, and achieve your goals.

WHY IS DOING THINGS ALONE IMPORTANT?

Just think about it: If you don't have to depend on anyone but yourself to do something, there's nothing stopping you from doing it (but yourself, of course). Whether it's taking a vacation to a place you've always wanted to visit, going to a movie, concert, or play, or taking a walk, if you're not dependent on anyone, if you're perfectly content to do it alone—in fact, if the idea of doing it alone makes you happy—then if you decide to do it, you're not at the mercy of someone else's availability, wishes, or life circumstances. You don't have to wait until someone else is in the mood to work out, you don't have to compromise where you would really like to go for a vacation, and there is nothing stopping you from seeing a particular movie, concert, sports event, or play—and seeing it on exactly the day *you* want to see it. It's all up to you. Think of the power in that. You can avoid the frustration of having your wishes thwarted by someone else. You're in control of your own life to a much greater extent than you would be otherwise, and in turn, in as great control as you possibly could be of your own destiny.

CHALLENGE YOUR NEGATIVE
THOUGHTS

If you were feeling uncomfortable just reading the above paragraph, if the mere thought of *doing* and *being* alone makes you nervous, let's try to find out why. In order to do this, I want you to ask yourself, for example, what emotion you feel when you think of going on a vacation alone. Is your immediate reaction a combination of fear and shame?

Whatever the emotion, the next question to ask yourself is, "What thought triggered that emotion?" Let's use the fear/shame combination as an example. Suppose when you imagined yourself going on a vacation alone, you felt the mixed emotion of fear and shame. Now ask yourself what thought went through your mind that caused you to feel fear and shame when you pictured yourself going on a vacation alone. You realize that you were afraid that people would notice that you were alone and wonder about you.

Let's take the mixed "fear/shame" emotion and follow it through with what is called "cognitive self-help therapy," a method of self-analysis that will teach you how to get to the bottom of, and indeed dispel, paralyzing emotions so that you will ultimately be free to take actions that you were previously afraid to dare. Here is a theoretical situation, and a series of questions to ask yourelf about it.

You imagine yourself going to a vacation place alone, and immediately get an awful feeling. Ask yourself (a) "What am I feeling?" (Identify the emotion.) You decide it's fear and shame. Now ask yourself (b) "What thoughts triggered that fear and shame?" You decide that you had the fear because you thought that people would notice that you were alone and seem to stare at you, and think, "Look at that woman. She's all by herself. Poor thing—I guess she has no man in her life," or "Look at that poor man, all by himself. What's wrong with him? I'll bet he has no friends," and you imagined yourself feeling ashamed.

Next, ask yourself (c) "What will happen if someone notices that I am alone, and in fact thinks exactly as above?" Think of all the possible ways you might react (reread b). Here are some possibilities:

1. I may be so embarrassed that I'll never come out of my house again.
2. They may in fact ask me what's so wrong with me that I am alone.
3. I will look at the person who stares at me and quickly look away.
4. I will stare back at the person until he or she looks away.
5. I'll strike up a conversation with the person and tell him or her that this is my first vacation alone.
6. I may tell the person off, ask, "What are *you* staring at?"
7. I may get depressed and hide in my room for the entire vacation.
8. I may get on the next plane and go home.
9. I may feel lonely and dependent—and incapable of managing my own trip.

Now challenge each statement on your list (c, above) with rational thinking. Ask yourself (d) "Do I really believe that? How likely is it that it will actually happen that way?" Then place a number next to each statement, using a scale of one to ten, where 0 equals no probability that it will happen and 10 equals one hundred percent probability. For example:

1. I may be so embarrassed that I'll never come out of my house again.   0
2. They may in fact ask me what's so wrong with me that I am alone.   1
3. I will look at the person who stares at me and will quickly look away.   9

4. I will stare back at the person until he or she looks away.   5
5. I'll strike up a conversation with the person and say that this is my first vacation alone.   5
6. I may tell the person off, ask, "What are *you* staring at?"   2
7. I may get depressed and hide in my room for the entire vacation.   1
8. I may get on the next plane and go home.   0
9. I may feel lonely and dependent—and incapable of managing my own trip.   5

Now cancel out the things on your list that have zero possibility for you. Out go *I may be so embarrassed that I'll never come out of my house again* and *I may get on the next plane and go home.*

Now look at each item on your list and say to yourself (f) "What will happen if that comes about?" Then answer the question each time—even if you have decided that the chances of it happening are as low as a 1. Then answer the question for each item listed. I'll do it for you here as an example.

They may in fact ask me what's so wrong with me that I am alone.

I'll say, "I'm happy to be alone," and I'll feel glad that I'm independent.

I will look at the person who stares at me and quickly look away.

Great. The person will go on about his or her business.

I will stare back at the person until he or she looks away.

He or she will realize that staring is rude.

I'll strike up a conversation with the person and tell him or her that this is my first vacation alone.

The person will invite me to see a show or offer an encouraging word.

I may tell the person off, ask, "What are *you* staring at?"	The person may say, "I'm sorry, I wasn't looking at you."
I may get depressed and hide in my room for the entire vacation.	I'll refuse to do such a dumb thing. For what?
I may feel lonely and dependent—and incapable of managing my own trip.	I'll realize that I've been able to manage many things in my life, and remember also that people have liked me for *me*.

Finally, ask yourself (g) "Are the things that cause me fear and shame ultimately capable of destroying me?" You will immediately see that they are magnified by your imagination—and are in fact incapable of harming you at all.

When you come to think of it, as a matter of fact, you are lucky if most people think about you for more than ten seconds, and this holds true even of celebrities. (We are only interested even in celebrity scandals for fifteen minutes, so to speak—the proverbial "Fifteen minutes of fame"—and then we get on to other things of real importance to us.)

The fact is, most people are more concerned about a pimple on their nose than they are about a million people who were just swallowed up in an earthquake. So don't worry so much what people think, and go on about your business and be free to do what you want to do—and do it alone whenever you feel like it. It will be to your advantage.

But before we leave this subject of what people are thinking when they seem to be staring at you, let's look at the other side of the coin. Since most people are reluctant to travel alone, maybe the person staring at you (if that person is indeed staring at you) is admiring you for your courage or your freedom. That person may be thinking, "I wish *I* had the nerve to go places by myself," or "I wish *I* didn't have my nagging husband along," or "If only *I* had come here without my demanding friend."

No matter what emotion you feel about doing something alone, you can learn to challenge your emotions by figuring out what thought triggered that emotion, and then asking, "What is the likelihood that it will happen?" and then thinking, "What will happen if that comes about?" Then, when you see that nothing tragic will happen and that your fears are just self-created monsters that can be dispelled when you turn on the light of rational thinking, you will untie your mind and your feet and will be free to do things you've never before done alone.

TRY IT IN SPITE OF YOUR FEARS

After you've challenged your negative thoughts, you may still feel a significant amount of fear and hesitation to do something alone. At this point, you'll have to do it by an act of will, as discussed in Chapter 6. In fact, I want you to choose specific things from the ten choices found later on in this chapter to help you get started in being able to enjoy the power of *doing* and *being* alone.

THE ALLURE OF SURROUNDING YOURSELF WITH PEOPLE

It can be very seductive always to have people around us. We feel safe when we are with people. After all, if something happens, at least we will not have to face it alone. But there's more to it than that. Many of us like to be with someone all the time because we are uncomfortable being alone with ourselves, with our own thoughts. How many times have I heard someone say, "When I'm alone, I think too much." What do they mean by that statement? How is it ever possible to think too much? Are they afraid that they may think so much that their brain will explode? Are they afraid that they may eventually discover the cure for cancer? I don't think that's what they are worried about.

I think such people are afraid of their own thoughts. I believe that they are afraid that if they are alone, and if they start thinking, they may realize that they are not happy with their lives—and may realize that some changes are in order. Since it is much easier to stick to the status quo, they would rather not be confronted with such ideas, ideas that would ask them to make choices that would cause temporary discomfort, but choices that would change the direction of their lives. So they fill their lives with noise—the noise of people—always around, buzzing in their ears, so they don't have to ever stop and think, "Am I really happy? Am I on the right path for my life? Should I dare to make a change?"

GETTING PAST THE DISCOMFORT OF BEING ALONE

Being alone, for some people who have always been surrounded by people, can at first feel uncomfortable. You don't know exactly what to do with yourself. If you're home alone, for example, and you refuse to turn on the television (okay, I'll make it easier on you—the television is broken), what do you do? Rule out calling someone on the phone. (That would involve communicating with another person. I want this to be strictly "alone.")

At first you feel a bit on edge. It's like being in a slightly too cool room. You're too cool to fall asleep the way you would if the room were warm and toasty. Your slight discomfort makes you alert. "What can I do?" you wonder, and you look around and realize that you want to accomplish a chore you've been putting off, like fixing a household item or sewing something that has torn, and while you're working on this miniproject, thoughts are floating through your mind. You're thinking in a relaxed sort of way. Later, you may pick up a book you've started. And as you read, various thoughts go through your mind. Later, you may just sit and plain old—dare I say it?—think.

When you are comfortable alone, you learn to be comfortable with your own thoughts. You begin to feel fine, and in fact begin to enjoy the thoughts that drift through your mind. Soon you begin to gather those thoughts and to solidify them, and, in a sense, to "center" yourself.

In other words, while being alone can be a discomfort at first, it turns out to be a positive discomfort, because it leaves you with no choice but to become acquainted with the one person who has been with you since your birth, has never left your side, and is the only one guaranteed to be—and who will be—with you the day you die: yourself. You start thinking about what is going on in your life, and what you like and don't like about it. You start thinking about ways to improve your lot. You become creative. You begin to take more control over your life. You make it more likely that you will not drift from one TV show to another until the grim reaper comes to call. You increase your chances of accomplishing what you were put on this earth to accomplish, and of not going out of this world with empty hands.

YOU HATE BEING ALONE—
YOU DIDN'T CHOOSE IT

Suppose you are recently divorced, or you have recently broken up with someone with whom you've spent most of your time for many years. You're alone not by choice, but by circumstance. Up until now you've been very unhappy about it. In fact, you may have resented it, or have even felt sorry for yourself. But when you come to learn the value of solitude, you may begin to treasure your time alone, and in time, you may be very reluctant to give up your precious, unthreatened solitude.

It is difficult enough to cope with change we have chosen, but it is even more upsetting to deal with change that has been thrust upon us, especially if that change requires that we learn a new way of living and even thinking. But when it comes to change regarding divorces or breakups, there's good news. In time, many people, even though threatened by change in the beginning, later find that the change was better for them. And, in fact, once they get used to the change, when they think of going back to the way it was before, they are horrified. When asked if they would marry again, or live with someone, many of the women who have kept in touch with me after their divorces or breakups say, "Are you kidding? I would never want to give up my freedom again."

I hear this all the time from women who wrote to me after having read *Get Rid of Him,* and who left unhappy marriages and relationships of up to twenty or even thirty years. They talk about the initial trauma and fear of being alone, and how, in time, they developed their own interests and hobbies, and how, in addition, they learned to relish guaranteed solitude, not always being "called upon," not being disturbed, being allowed to do things at their own pace—to linger at the morning coffee and the paper. They relish the freedom to decide when to take the dog for a walk, to decide to clean or not to clean the messy kitchen, to put on makeup on a Saturday and look pretty or lounge around the house frumpy and happy all day. These women tell me that doing exactly what they want to do and when they want to do it turns out to be a wonderful bonus of living alone.

Many of these women tell me that because of time alone, they were able to think and just daydream for the first time in their lives—and in so doing they realized that they wanted to do things they had never allowed themselves to think about or even dream about before. For example, one woman just called and left me a message on my answering machine: "I'm going to my condo in the Dominican Republic. I'll be back in a month." This same woman was so attached to her unhappy marriage that she had written to me a year ago expressing sheer terror of being alone once her husband decided to end the marriage of twenty-some years, against her protests. After one year of divorce, not only did this woman learn to relish her freedom, she bought herself a condo and was using it as a regular retreat, a place where she could go alone to think, read, and venture out and have some fun if the mood hit her.

Other women write to me and tell me how now, for the first time in their lives, they can read a book without the din of the television in the background, write in a journal without someone asking intrusive questions, and just sit and think about life. They talk of impulsively taking a ride to the country on a weekend afternoon, visiting an art gallery, taking a walk along the shoreline of the beach, and so on. "Where have I been all my life?" they ask. But when I question them, they all admit that they would never have chosen this solitude, which was first experienced as terror, but now translated in their lives as freedom.

One insightful woman put it this way: "My being so scared of being without someone around reminds me of how I felt when I was three years old. Even though my mother was abusive and neglectful, whenever she would be gone for hours, I would be terrified, and when she would come home, I was glad, even though I knew that I would probably get a beating for something I had done. Having her there was still a relief—I felt safe. The most horrible thought in my mind then was that she would leave forever—abandon me. I realize now that that's exactly what I was thinking about with my husband—even though he was a nightmare, ˉ feared his leaving with such terror—and I realize now that   was equating him to my mother."

This is a perfect analogy. The woman put her finger right on the issue. When we were infants or young children, we had good reason to ᶜear abandonment. Clearly, we would

have perished had our caretakers left us alone permanently. But not so now that we are adults. We are fully capable of feeding and clothing ourselves, of taking care of
ourselves. We will not die. The feeling of terror we have is
merely a throwback to the time when that terror represented a real threat. But now, as so many women tell me,
not only do they not die, but they live and thrive and can
find other compatible persons or interests. They find that
they are much better off without that person whom they
clung to for dear life.

So even if you are recently "abandoned" by a husband or
lover, and if you feel scared and insecure, and even filled
with terror, realize that these are feelings that stem from
childhood—and that once you settle in and see that you do
not die when you are alone, but instead survive and even
thrive, you will be happier than you were before. I have
letters from hundreds of women who tell me that they are
now not only totally independent from former boyfriends
and husbands, but are loving their independence and freedom so much that they would probably never give it up—
unless they could meet someone equally independent who
would be compatible to their new sense of self.

BE CAREFUL OF
THE COMPANY YOU KEEP

We need to be careful of the company we keep. People
can drain our energy, steal our time, and divert our center
of strength so that we are weakened in our focus toward
our goals. For example, if you have a friend who makes
you feel "off center" every time you leave his or her presence, you may be a lot better off not spending so much
time, or even any time, with that friend. The simple truth is,
not every friend or acquaintance we have should remain a
significant part of our lives forever. We do outgrow certain

friends and acquaintances, and we need not feel ashamed or guilty about this. In fact, it is a good idea to reevaluate friendships every once in a while, and ask yourself if they are still working for your best interests.

Carl Jung talks about this very issue as he discusses his own experience regarding friends whom he had to let go.

> For some people, I was continually present and close to them *so long as they were related to my inner world;* but then it might happen that I was no longer with them, because *there was nothing left which would link me to them. . . .*[1] (Italics mine)

What did Jung mean by saying, "So long as they were related to my inner world"? I think he meant that as long as these people were in tune with his soul, with his purpose, with his goals, as long as these people were not a drain on his life, he continued to spend time with them. But once he found that they were no longer in tune with him, that they could no longer relate to his thoughts, ideas, and purposes, he realized that "there was nothing left which would link me to them." In other words, he realized that the initial reasons for the friendship had disappeared, he faced the truth of that—and he let them go. In the end, he had to do what was right for his soul. I believe we must learn to do the same.

BIRDS OF A FEATHER

On the other side of the coin, people do tend to choose friends and acquaintances who are of like mind. In fact, even in mental institutions it has been noted that mental patients with similar psychological problems will seek each other out. Scott Peck says:

> The stale adage, "Birds of a feather flock together," is still a lively principle of psychiatry. In

psychiatric hospitals, for instance, one of the best ways of assessing the severity of a patient's illness is by the company he or she keeps. There is a profound tendency for the most ill patients to hang out with others who are most ill, while the least disturbed generally associate with the other least disturbed. . . . The pattern of choice is as predictable as it is unconscious.[2]

CREATIVE THOUGHTS NEED SOLITUDE

When you have a creative idea, it is important to keep it to yourself, at least until the idea has been fully developed in your own mind; otherwise you may never see the idea through to its potential development.

When I have an idea for a new book, for example, I begin jotting down ideas, and soon I start to develop a table of contents. If I'm on a plane, writing a mile a minute, and someone looks over my shoulder and asks, "What are you writing?" and I say, "I have this great idea for a new book," and then allow the person to draw me into a conversation about the book, before you know it, I dissipate my own idea. This is because as I talk, that person asks questions and puts his "two cents" in and I respond, and before you know it, the force of my original idea is gone, and I have scattered my thinking. I would have allowed him, like a bird, to have pecked up newly planted seeds, whereas I should have planted those seeds deep within the ground and not exposed them to anyone until the seedlings had popped through the earth.

The same holds true with projects and goals. It isn't a good idea to tell the world about what we are doing too soon. For example, suppose you have read a workout book and are very excited about starting the regimen. You are, say, sixty pounds overweight, and are planning to have a sexy, defined body in one year. You've marked your goal date on your calendar and your start date, which is three days from now. You've bought your dumbbells and you have even purchased a bench.

You are visiting your sister's house. The whole family is there, and after dinner you're all sitting around talking. You're very excited about your workout, because tomorrow is the day you start, so you say, "I'm so excited. Tomorrow is the day I start working out, and one year from now, look out, I'm going to be gorgeous."

Immediately, your brother-in-law starts to laugh. "How many times have I heard that before," he says. You explain the program and why you're so enthusiastic, and your sister says, "Oh, that won't work. You're much better off with . . ." Then someone else puts in their two cents. Before you know it, you are feeling a bit down, and by the time you get home, you're second-guessing yourself and thinking, "I wonder if I'm fooling myself with this goal?" Then you imagine the embarrassment and humiliation when you see your family at the next occasion (about three weeks away) if you don't show major improvement. Now instead of feeling relaxed and excited about your plan, you feel pressure, pressure you put on yourself by exposing your plans to others too soon. Resenting this pressure, you say to yourself, "Let's call the whole thing off."

See how much better it would be to keep your workout goal a secret? If they don't know what you're doing, you are not under pressure from anyone else. You are your only boss. There is no one to look at you and comment on your progress, no one to ask you questions about the workout and drain your energy.

When should you tell people what you are doing? After you've made enough progress to feel confident that no one could take away your driving force. In a workout program, it will probably be three to six weeks before you should start talking about it. It all depends upon you. You'll know when it's time to expose your plan to the air.

TEN THINGS YOU CAN DO ALONE

Now it's time to experiment with doing things alone. The following paragraphs offer ten things you can do alone. They are not presented in order of difficulty, because what is most difficult for one person can be easier for another. Read through the list, and then choose something that seems to excite you, that feels like just the right amount of challenge for where you are psychologically at the moment, and then make your plans and do it. After you've conquered one "alone" challenge, choose another, and then another, until you've accomplished at least eight out of ten. If you do that, you will be well on your way to learning to love *doing* and *being* alone.

1. WORK OUT ALONE

Many people ask me, "Do you work out alone or with a partner?" I work out alone because I would never want to be at the mercy of someone else's schedule, moods, or life situations. In addition, when I work out, I need to be alone because I feel as if someone else's energy will divert my concentration and weaken my efforts. Working out alone makes me feel centered and strong.

I want you to try becoming your own workout partner, your own faithful accomplice who will never let you down. Why? Because I get letters from women telling me, "My friend and I used to work out together but she became pregnant, so I don't have a partner anymore, and I haven't worked out in weeks," or "My friend changed her job so she couldn't work out with me, so I have to wait until I find a new partner."

Depending on a partner to work out is a tricky business. I'm not saying it can't be successful. In fact, I must admit that many women tell me that when they work out with a friend, they find that they have more energy, and that the workout seems to go faster. If this is true for you, fine, but even if you do have a workout friend, you should develop the ability to work out alone, and get used to working out alone so you don't have to put anything on hold if and when you are forced to do so.

2. GO ON A VACATION ALONE

Going on a vacation alone can be the most wonderful gift you can give yourself. Getting on a plane, crossing water—alone, as your mind wanders—is one of the most exhilarating experiences you can imagine.

When you vacation alone you meet more people than you would meet if you vacationed with a friend. Inevitably, you talk to people. Even if you are the shy type, sooner or later you find yourself asking someone a question, or making a comment to someone about something. Before you know it you make new acquaintances, and some of them become future friends.

My first trip alone was to Africa. I had gotten hold of a brochure on exotic trips, and decided to go on a combination African safari and mountain-climbing expedition. I tried to get various people to go with me, but since I was a teacher at the time and off in the summer, and the trip was four weeks in duration, no one was available.

I found myself faced with a choice: Either go alone, or don't go at all. So I decided to go alone. And since I was going alone, I realized that I could add another excursion to the trip. Why not visit Israel while I was at it? Why not also visit Greece? At the last minute, I changed my mind about Greece, but it was no problem because I was going alone—I had no one to take into consideration but myself.

Needless to say, I was not totally alone during my travels. Although most of the people who turned up for the mountain-climbing trip were in couples, either two same-sex friends or opposite-sex couples, once we started "trekking" we became one big network of survivors—with the common goal of reaching the top of the mountain.

The only time I was alone was at night in my tent, and that was perfect for me. I loved hearing the jungle sounds, smelling the river, and feeling the cool of the morning breeze as I woke up to the sounds of the rustling of the pots as the cook prepared breakfast. "This is the life," I would think.

After that trip, I felt as if I could travel anywhere in the world alone. I took a trip all around Italy, and traveled to various parts of Europe. Later I decided to opt for more leisurely trips. I visited several Caribbean islands. And although I traveled alone, I never remained alone. I always met a variety of people—single men, single women, couples and local residents.

Later I tried quite a few Club Med vacations (a perfect place to start for anyone who may be reluctant to travel alone, since many people go there alone; and in addition, you can request a roommate).

I've gone to health spas and taken adventure trips all over this country. At times I did ask myself, "What have I gotten myself into?" but the feeling invariably passed, and I always had a good time, and in fact, looking back, there is not one trip I wouldn't have taken if I had it to do over again. Each trip was a treasure in and of itself, and I was able to experience the trip completely in my own way, without someone buzzing in my ear unless I chose to have someone buzz in my ear.

In fact, I got so used to traveling alone that I'd forgotten how it would be to travel with someone else. (Aside from the trips I would take with my daughter, I hadn't taken a trip with a friend, male or female, in years.) Lately I have a friend who likes to travel and we've taken several vacations together, which I find enjoyable in a different way.

When I'm with my friend, we mainly experience each other, our ideas and reactions to things and the environment. We compromise to each other's desires to go here or there, and have a lot of laughs, and because we like each other, the trip is always fun. But I would never give up those excursions I take alone, because they are times when I can visit with myself in a very special way—and in addition, if I choose to, I get to meet so many more people than I meet when I'm preoccupied with talking to my friend.

3. GO TO THE THEATER, A CONCERT, THE BALLET, OR ANY LIVE SHOW ALONE

Think about a live performance that you would like to attend, a play that you've been wanting to see, a concert that you would really enjoy, a ballet, any live show. I don't want you to get the ticket too much in advance or you will have time to second-guess yourself and build up a dread of going alone. Go on the spur of the moment. Single tickets are often readily available.

While you're getting dressed to go to the show, imagine yourself feeling relaxed and peaceful in the audience. Picture yourself watching the performance undisturbed by anyone's potential comments. As you arrive at the performance, think about the hour or so in front of you, a time when you can totally relax and indulge in the performance. Think of it as sheer pleasure.

Once the performance has gotten under way and you have settled in, you'll wonder what the big deal was about going alone. You'll feel relaxed in a special way. After the performance, on your way home, you'll feel empowered by having been able to do what you wanted to do and having done it alone, without the crutch of a comrade. If you don't like the performance, you can get up and leave—without having to worry about what your companion wants to do or about what the people around you will think.

In any case, you'll feel great about having done what you wanted to do when you wanted to do it, and may even be tempted to make a weekly or monthly "date" with yourself to attend events of interest to you.

4. Go to a Restaurant Alone

Many people dread going to restaurants alone. In fact, some people would rather eat lunch alone in their office than go out to lunch alone where people can see them. Why do they feel this way? They imagine that people are looking at them and wondering why they are eating alone. They think people feel sorry for them. Some people say they feel lonely dining by themselves.

If you are reluctant to go to a restaurant alone, you can break the ice with yourself in this way. Try going to a local restaurant for lunch, armed with a newspaper or a book. Then make up your mind to look around and just think and relax. To your amazement, you'll find that no one is thinking about you, and that you can enjoy your meal alone, while at the same time thinking, people-watching, or just daydreaming.

If you vacation alone, chances are you will find it easy to have dinner alone in a fine restaurant. Instead of apologizing for your presence with your body language (head down, eyes diverted), walk with your head up and a bright smile on your face. When seated, after looking at the menu, watch the other guests. Think about who you see. How many families are present? How many men are dining alone? How many single women are there? You can learn a lot if you do this often enough.

If you feel like talking, you can engage the waiter in a conversation, asking him about things to do in the area. But beware: He may keep coming back to talk, and that may disturb the tranquillity of your meal.

If you're even tempted to be embarrassed about dining alone, remember one thing: The management of the restaurant is very happy to have you. To the management, your money is just as green as is the money of couples or groups, and they would much rather see the table occupied by one person than see it empty.

5. Go to a Beach or Park Alone

Pick a lovely afternoon or early evening, put on comfortable clothing, and take a long, leisurely walk along the shoreline of the beach, or through a lush park. You can use this time just to let your mind run free and think about life.

Enjoy the grandeur of creation. If you're at the beach, look at the vast ocean and the gleaming, endless sandy shore. Think about the wonder of the force behind such a creation. Look up in the sky and soak in the endless blue of the heavens. Watch the feathery clouds float by. Realize that whatever problem you may have at the moment is a speck in the universe. Putting your life into this perspective will help to lighten your burden no matter what has been troubling you.

If you are in a forest, listen to the trees as they whisper in the wind. Look at the thick trunks and imagine how many years they've been there—and what they've seen in all of that time. Look at the yellow wildflowers, the scurrying squirrels, the chirping birds. Think about how happy they are, how, compared to humans, they don't seem to have a care in the world. Resolve to connect yourself to the wonder of the universe, to let go of things that you can't control.

You can't really do what I've just suggested with someone else. You have to do it alone. It's one of the most valued, healing therapies you can give yourself. It also helps to give you an "outerworld" focus that is the most rejuvenating of all to worried, introspective people, and to people who are always with others so that they are unable to stop and focus on the beauty of the world around them.

6. Go to the Library or Bookstore Alone

Going to a library is something that most people do alone, so if you're really afraid to do something in solitude, this might be the place to start. Think of a subject that interests you and ask the librarian where in the library those books are located. For example, if you're interested in flowers, you can go to the flower-book section and feast your eyes on the color-filled volumes. You may choose to browse through these books while standing by the shelves, or you can carry a bunch of them to a table and spend an hour or two vicariously surrounded by nature.

While you're in the library, take a look at the bulletin board. Most libraries have calendars of events—free lectures, plays, and so on. Note when the next community event will be and make up your mind to attend a gathering that is of interest to you—a play, a concert, a lecture—and to do it alone. After all, who is stopping you?

Nowadays there are many large bookstores that actually encourage browsing. In fact, they provide tables and chairs where you can sit and look at unpurchased books, and even order a snack.

After your visit to a library or bookstore, you will usually be in a better mood than you were before you went. Why? Unconsciously a message will have registered. You will remember that there is a whole world of books filled with ideas and experiences that you can enjoy alone.

7. Go to a Party, Dance, Game, or Club Alone

If you are single and you are invited to a party through a friend, make it your business to go alone instead of refusing to attend unless you can get a friend to go with you.

I was recently given a free ticket to a hockey game. Now, I don't like hockey, but I decided to go anyway. I thought, "Who knows? I might just enjoy the game and develop a new interest—and whom might I meet?"

After the first intermission, I had had enough of the game and went to the bar-restaurant. While looking around, I made eye contact with two good-looking men whom I soon engaged in a conversation. I ended up going out on a few dates with one of them. I know that if I had invited a friend, I would have been too engaged in conversation with her even to notice the man.

I go to dances, clubs, singles events, games—you name it—all by myself, and I always have an adventure. If it is a dance, I dance until I'm tired of it and then simply leave. I don't have to tell anyone I'm leaving. I don't have to ask my friend if she is ready to go; I just leave at will.

Rarely do I call a girlfriend when I want to go out. Why? Most of my friends need to make plans ahead of time, and I like to do things on the spur of the moment, as the mood hits me. I also like to be free to change my mind at the last minute, to cancel my plans and not to have to worry about disappointing a friend.

If you do go to a dance, party, or bar-restaurant alone, remember that the crowd does not remain static. No one really knows who came alone and who did not. But if you are embarrassed about being alone, until you feel more comfortable (and you will after a few times), if someone asks you who you're with, you can say you're meeting a girlfriend here—but she hasn't shown up yet. (You can even think of me as that friend—because I am truly there with you in spirit.)

In time, thankfully, you won't need these crutches because you'll eventually feel proud of yourself for being independent enough to go where you want to go when you want to go, and to do what you want to do when you want to do it.

8. GO TO A PLACE OF WORSHIP ALONE

No matter what the place of worship, any single person will be welcomed with open arms. I know this because a few years ago I conducted an experiment. Every weekend, for about six months, I selected a different place of worship. On each occasion, the people smiled at me, and made me feel welcome, and often I was invited to coffee or tea after the service. If I had wanted to do so, I could have made not just one friend, but a circle of friends.

But you can do more than meet people in a place of worship. You can talk to God and ask, "How am I doing?" Although you can talk to God anywhere anytime, a place of worship, an official place for talking to God, is very conducive to centering yourself and sensing if you are on the right path.

I remember a very tough time in my life, a time when I didn't even know if I believed in God. But I would wander into a church, light a candle, and look up to the ceiling and ask God to have his will in my life, and each and every time, I left that building feeling better, knowing full well that the candle itself had no power, but rather that what my lighting the candle symbolized—a cry to God to help me—was where the power lay.

I could not do that, at least not with the same clarity and intensity, if I had someone with me. I needed to be alone.

9. ATTEND A DINNER AT SOMEONE'S HOME OR A WEDDING ALONE

Most of us are reluctant to accept a dinner invitation alone, especially if everyone else will be in couples. This is a big mistake. If the people who invited you tell you that it is okay to come alone, then by all means do so.

Once at the dinner, you will find that you are a part of the conversation. The couples there may always be with each other and will probably be glad to talk to someone new, and certainly the host and or hostess will not neglect you.

Many people hesitate to go to a wedding alone. They say it depresses them to think that they don't have a partner when a couple is being joined together, so they will search out someone, anyone, to go to that wedding, just to be saved from having to go alone. But this is a big mistake. Why? Who knows? You may meet your future mate, who has also gone to the wedding single. More than one person has written to me telling me that this is exactly what happened to him or her.

In any case, if you are invited to a wedding, you are obviously attending to mark the celebration of a friend. You can do this alone very well. You don't need anyone there for moral support.

10. SEEK OUT AND JOIN A SOCIAL GROUP ALONE

Think of something you've always wanted to do—and then join a club or social group that does it. For example, I've always been interested in shooting, and finally I decided to do something about it. I called the NRA and got a listing of all the gun clubs in my area, then picked the closest one, found out when the next meeting was, and showed up.

When I arrived, I noticed that the club was filled with men—and every one of them appeared to be sixty or older. My first thought was, "What could I possibly have in common with these people?" I could feel their curious stares as I sat in the back of the room, hoping that no one would ask me to say anything.

Politely, the president acknowledged my presence and went on with the meeting. After it was over, the president volunteered to let me use his gun and to give me my first lesson in shooting. Other men talked to me and made me feel very much at home, very welcome.

The next week I decided to go back. I was again greeted warmly, and went through a lesson with the club president. In time, I joined the club and now I have a whole group of "shooting" friends. What I have in common with them is an interest in target shooting. At one point I even considered joining the "Combat League," but realized that I didn't have the extra time to commit. But in any case, I had expanded my circle of friends to include different people, and in so doing, I myself grew.

For you it may be a hiking club, a political association, or a sports-oriented group. Whatever it is, think of something that is of interest to you and look into it.

SOME PEOPLE NEED TO BE ALONE

My goal for you is that you become capable of doing for
yourself and being alone, whether you are a person who
needs a lot of solitude or not. However, some people actually thrive on being alone, and in fact would not be as effective or as creative or as devoted to their "call" in life if
they were with a partner. Small wonder that to this day the
Catholic Church requires priests and nuns to be single.

You don't have to be a religious person to need to be
alone. You may happen to be a gregarious person, one
who enjoys being around people, but who also needs a lot
of solitude. If you are this type, you will think not once, not
twice, but a hundred times before you agree to share your
living space with someone.

A WORD OF ADVICE TO
WOMEN ABOUT MONEY

I would be remiss if I wrote a whole chapter on autonomy
and neglected to mention the importance for women of not
making the mistake of becoming totally dependent upon a
man for income. No matter who you are, no matter what
your age, make it your business to begin moving toward the
education that will qualify you to earn an independent income so that, no matter what, you will never have to stay
with a man you don't love just for the money or the security.

And a special word of advice to you younger women,
who in the throes of romance may be tempted to give up
your education or your career for the one you love: Don't do
it. If that man really loves you, he'll encourage you to develop your potential and to pursue your interests, just as he
would want you to encourage him. If he insists that you
drop everything for him, I suggest that you drop him. If you
don't, in the long run you may have reason to regret it.

IS IT SELFISH TO WANT TIME ALONE?

Sometimes I worry about all of the wonderful women (and men too) who would love to have time alone, but due to family, business, and other responsibilities, simply cannot find the time to enjoy the solitude they crave. Is it selfish to want solitude, and if not, how can one find the precious time for it?

First, it's not at all selfish to want to be alone, no more selfish than wanting to take a shower or eat a hearty meal. Taking a shower cleanses the body; being alone for a time, even a short time, provides an opportunity to clear the mind and, in a sense, cleanse the soul. Eating a hearty meal provides nourishment for the body, just as spending some precious time alone can prove nourishing to the mind and the soul, especially if you use that time to sort out your thoughts and reflect upon your life.

But what can you do if you just can't find the time you would like to be alone? Well, chances are, if you thought about it and planned carefully, you could arrange for at least an hour or two alone a week. If you're a busy mother and housewife, you could arrange for a relative, friend, or reliable baby-sitter to come in, even if it is only for a couple of hours a week. Then you could get in the car and go for a drive, take a long walk, or hide somewhere and think, read, or just "be." If you are an overworked career person or businessperson, you can reexamine your calendar and arrange to have a few responsibilities delegated to reliable help. You may find that, although you are reluctant to give up control, it will be worth it in the long run.

We all need some time alone. In my view, you can't put a price on it, so even if you have to sacrifice to get it, by all means do it. And remember one thing: Nothing stays the same. Chances are the day will come when your schedule loosens up and you have the leisure of more time to yourself. You can look forward to that day, but in the meantime, start small and at least give yourself *some* time.

BEING ALONE HELPS TO
DEVELOP DISCIPLINE

People often ask me, "Where do you get all that discipline?" Well, one thing is for sure: I didn't get it by relying on the people around me. I developed discipline, over the years, by exercising my will and by doing things alone.

For example, years ago when I was trying to get in shape, I began a running regimen. I had to run at 4:30 in the morning in order to get to work on time, and I did it each morning, alone! What if I had waited for a friend to do it with me? Who in their right mind would run at 4:30 in the morning, anyway? If by some miracle I did find such a person, what if that person overslept—or changed schedules? So I did it alone, and doing it alone forced me to be disciplined. I had to push myself. I could not depend upon the knowledge that a friend was waiting for me, that I had no choice but to get up or disappoint a friend—unless of course that friend was myself, and it was.

Think of it for a moment. If you can work out alone, if you can study alone, if you can go on a vacation alone, if you can go to a bookstore or the library alone, you are developing discipline, training that will mold your character to be able to function without the help of others, to be self-reliant.

YOU ARE NEVER REALLY ALONE

I am delighted to end this chapter with a wonderful fact that seems like a contradiction: Even though you are alone, you are never really alone.

Sometimes I do get lonely. After all, I'm only human. For some reason, on some days, I'm overcome with a sadness that seems so deep it goes down to the core of my soul. When I catch myself feeling this way, I raise my mind to God and say with my thoughts, "Help me, God. I'm feeling so sad." I hold up my sadness to God and I give it to him. And you know what? It never fails. A few hours later (I never know when it happens, because I don't think of it until after the sadness has already passed) I realize that I'm not sad and lonely anymore. I wonder why I was so sad before. But the sadness is gone.

I am so comforted by that thought—that God is always there—that I could never feel extended, total despair. You will read much more about this in Chapter 9.

♀ **Key #6.**   The power of doing, being alone. Autonomize yourself.

NOTES

1. Carl G. Jung, *Memories, Dreams, Reflections*, ed. Anelia Jaffe (New York: Vintage Books, 1965), p. 357.

2. M. Scott Peck, M.D., *A World Waiting to Be Born* (New York: Bantam, 1993), p. 134.

8

THE POWER OF
SELF-MOTIVATION

HOW TO GET YOURSELF TO DO WHAT
YOU WANT TO DO

You've learned to trust yourself more, to listen to your inner voice. You've learned to love yourelf more; you've built your self-esteem. You've been able to free yourself; you've decided to bury the dead and move on. You've decided to become mature, to take responsibility for your own action. You've learned how to strengthen yourself; you've discovered the power of your will. You've increased your autonomy, the power to function independently without the presence or help of others. So now what? How do you apply all of this to your personal goals, to your daily life? How do you motivate yourself? How do you get yourself to do what you want to do, even when you least feel like doing it?

You need some special resources to call upon. In short, you need a "personal bag of tricks."

YOUR PERSONAL BAG OF TRICKS

In this chapter you will learn some self-motivation techniques or "tricks" that will help you to achieve your goals. You'll find out how to program your unconscious mind and to use visualization—and how to turn worry, fear, and unwanted change into positive forces. You will discover how to use psychology on yourself when you are tempted to break your diet, when you don't feel like working out, or when you are thinking of taking a day off from work. You will find out how to get the drive to finish a course in school when you are tempted to quit, and learn how to push yourself to continue taking the courses you need—until you complete your degree.

You'll find ways to motivate yourself to complete a tedious work assignment or conquer a dreaded chore when you are too tired to move. You'll gain the power to resist buying something you can't afford or to stop yourself from having one too many drinks. You'll learn how to turn off the TV when you have other, more important things to do—and find out how to spark the energy you need to do those things.

In order to get yourself to do what you want to do, first be sure you have read Chapter 6 regarding the power of your will. Next, read this chapter straight through and then go back and reread the sections that you feel will give you the most immediate help.

1. SET A CLEAR GOAL AND BECOME THE GENERAL CONTRACTOR OF THAT GOAL

A lost dog will often find his home after traveling for days across miles and miles. How can he do this? He has a goal. He has something very specific in mind, and come what may, he plods along, step after step, focused on his goal. Sometimes dogs are more single-minded than people.

What would happen if you got up in the morning and walked out of your house—with no idea in the world as to where you wanted to go? You would wander around aimlessly until the authorities caught up with you and carted you away. This seems like an extreme example, yet so many of us go through life in a similar manner. We have no clear idea of where we want to go—or of what we want to do.

Ask the next ten people you meet, "What is your goal in life?" Chances are, they will look at you "funny" and not be able to tell you. "What do you mean?" they will ask. Well, it's a very simple question. I can always answer it without hesitation—and so should you.

The human psyche can never be fully happy without goals, which enable us to use our skills and minds—our creative energy. Without a goal, we seek pleasure as a goal in and of itself, and we end up getting fat, drunk, addicted to drugs, and/or depressed. A goal helps us to organize our lives. It provides a purpose.

I divided goals into two categories: short-term goals, those that take a year or less to achieve, and long-term goals, those that usually take a year or more to achieve. Short-term goals include things like getting in shape or learning to dance. Long-term goals include things like finding a new career or graduating from a school.

Let's talk about long-term goals—and find out how to determine what are realistic and worthy goals.

The Magic Combination for Long-Term Goal-Setting

When I ask people "What is your goal—what do you want to do with your life?" I always cringe when I get the glib answer, "I want to become a millionaire." "Well, what's wrong with that?" you might ask. The answer is simple. The focus is all wrong. A worthy goal must first take into account your interests and talents. In other words, a person who tried to work at a job he hated in the hope of becoming a millionaire would probably never become a millionaire—because if you hate your job, you probably won't be good at it.

So you need to find a goal in life that utilizes your talent. But there's more to it than that. I have discovered that those people who get the most joy out of life, and at the same time eventually end up making a substantial income, choose jobs, professions, and goals that not only utilize their interests and talents, but at the same time provide a needed service for others. If you think about the people you know who seem happy, and who are at the same time doing well financially, you will find this to be true. Let me tell you about how I came to know this secret.

Some time ago, while struggling on a teacher's salary (doing a job I loved, but that didn't pay very much), I read a book that claimed that if you have a talent and use it to help people, that magic combination would end up making you wealthy—even if wealth was the last thing on your mind. Since I was struggling to pay the monthly bills and was in fact constantly juggling them around in order to make ends meet, I decided to take up the challenge. I asked myself what other talents I had besides teaching (which was using one of my talents to help people and at the same time was earning me a living). I asked myself what else I could do that could be used to help people and at the same time add to my income.

The longer I thought about it, the clearer it became. I had always had a strong interest in, if not talent for, writing. Wasn't it about time I did something about it? I was teaching in a high school at the time, so what better place than to start there, writing books for teenagers. So I wrote my first book and eventually got it published. After that followed seven more books. None of them made me a millionaire, but they did supplement my income so that I was able to pay all my bills and in the bargain take some wonderful vacations.

But how did those books help people? They were self-help books that advised teens on how to get along with parents, peers, and the opposite sex. To this day I get letters from teens thanking me for playing a major role in setting them on the right path. The money I made from those books is long gone, but I like to think that the impact on the teens who read them will last forever.

Continuing with the theme of using talent to help people, I later wrote fitness books designed to show my methods of getting in shape to women everywhere. My books eventually sold over a million copies, and I was able to devote myself full time to writing, lecturing, and doing seminars and television appearances. My income had grown to the point where I no longer had to worry about money—not because I focused on the money, but because I focused on helping others.

Now let's talk about you. What is it that you can do, that you are interested in, that you love to do, that would help others and at the same time earn you an income? Make a list here, and then we'll go through the process of elimination.

TALENTS, LOVE DOING	HELP PEOPLE	HOW TO MAKE $$
1.		
2.		
3.		
4.		
5.		

Suppose you wrote down singing in your "Talent" column. How can singing help people? You can bring joy to their hearts—in a church choir (but there you won't earn income), at weddings (you could get paid for this), at small supper clubs (definite money), or by making records (many singers dream of this, yes, but people break into the business every day).

Suppose you wrote down home decorating. This talent would prove a great help to many people who have only vague ideas of how they want to have their homes fixed, and no idea of how to go about doing it. You could make money doing this as a career. You could start by putting an ad in a local paper and, when people call, making a deal to redecorate charging either a flat rate or a percentage of what they buy (you could get them discounts so that your fee ends up not costing them money—and in fact, you could save them money in the long run).

Maybe you wrote down things like swimming, cooking, reading, or even telling jokes. At first glance, you may not be able to see how these things can help people and also earn you an income, but if you think hard enough, you will see how they can. Could you become a swim coach, a cook, a book reviewer, or a comedian?

Another thing to keep in mind is that we all have more than one talent. If one of your talents is not the ideal one for helping people and earning an income at the same time, another talent may be.

Short-Term Goals

Now let's talk about short-term goals. Think right now. What are some of the things you would like to accomplish in a year or less? List them here, and then pick one to three for immediate pursuit.

GOALS

1.

2.

3.

4.

5.

Your goal must be clear and well thought out, and you should decide on a time frame for that goal.

Think of Yourself as the General Contractor

Let's think about your goal, and how you can get there by planning it as you would an overall project if you were a general contractor. The general contractor looks over the plans for, say, renovating a kitchen, and sees that he or she will have to call in a carpenter, an electrician, a plumber, and so forth, and the contractor says, "Yes. I can do that," not "Oh my God, all those steps, all the different processes—the plumbing, the electrical work." Instead, the contractor pictures the process, step by step, being done, and he or she calmly proceeds to take each step that must be taken to accomplish the project.

You can achieve your goals by having the same attitude. Let's use the short-term goal of getting in shape as an example. You look at a picture of yourself (in your mind's eye) as the final product, how you want your body to look. You realize that lots of steps will go into achieving or building the final product (your new body), but you don't let that discourage you. Instead you draw up "the plans" by taking into account what is involved—by reading the workout book. Then you ascertain what tools or equipment will be needed. Next, you decide how much time you will have to allot each day for "the work." Finally, you determine the goal date for the finished product.

But most important, just as the general contractor of any project would do, you make sure that everything goes according to schedule. Day by day, you oversee the project, working out, keeping to your low-fat eating plan, and envisioning the day when you will see the finished product. And if there is a slip-up (you break your diet or miss a workout in this case) you don't abandon the project. You simply get back on track. After all, would a general contractor abandon the project just because one of his carpenters didn't show up for work one day—or even for a few days? You would proceed in the same manner for your long-term goals, the only difference being that it would take more time to achieve the result.

Even Mountains Can Be Moved

If your goal seems far away, if it seems like a mountain in front of you, don't look at the mountain and think, "This is impossible. It can't be done." Having lived in a big city all of my life, I've seen the equivalent of mountains moved every day. I've seen tall buildings demolished in a matter of days—and new buildings put in their place in a matter of months.

And in fact, literal mountains have been moved. With modern technology and equipment, water tunnels have been drilled through mountains, dams have been created, and mountains have been ground to powder. It didn't happen in a day, but over time; literal mountains were removed and projects or "goals" were put in their place. So whatever your goal, you can do it if you are patient, and you take the time to plan its execution carefully, and then carefully, day by day, take the steps necessary to see the project through.

2. JUMP INTO THE ENERGY OF YOUR DRIVE TOWARD SELF-ACTUALIZATION

As discussed in Chapter 6, one of the basic drives of the human being is self-actualization. It is right up there with the other three basic drives: food, safety, and love. When you are trying to motivate yourself to get yourself to do what you want to do, what you know you should do, you can remind yourself of your need for self-actualization.

If, when you are tempted to skip a class in school that will lead to a job promotion, you think about how miserable you will be if you stay at the job you are doing now until the day you die, and you remind yourself of how happy you will be when you are given the position that will better utilize your talents at work and at the same time raise your income and give you a more comfortable life, you will get just enough energy to push yourself to go to that class straight from work instead of driving home.

In other words, if at the moment when you are having a hard time getting yourself to do what you want to do, you could connect that goal to self-actualization, you would be able to use that reminder as an impetus to help you do what you should be doing. To help you along with this thinking, it's a good idea to collect the evidence ahead of time that will help to strengthen your will when you most need it—in your moments of weakness. Write down all the reasons you want to achieve your goal.

If it is your long-term goal you're tempted to neglect, think of how you would feel if you gave it up forever. For example, if you are trudging along in school, finishing the courses that will enable you to change careers and become a teacher, think about how you will feel if you remain forever a cafeteria worker. Think of how depressing it would be to know that forever you would remain in the position you hold now.

Every time you are trying to get yourself to do what you want to do, but are tempted to say, "Forget it. I'm too tired. It's too difficult. I'm feeling lazy, I have a hard life, no one understands," stop and ask yourself if you really want to improve your life. Remind yourself that in the long run, it is all *up to you and only you* whether or not anything in your life changes, and that nobody really cares as much about what happens to you as you do. And in any case, it can be fun to take up a challenge.

3. GET YOUR SUBCONSCIOUS MIND TO WORK FOR YOU TWENTY-FOUR HOURS A DAY

Your subconscious mind is a powerful force. It is a "worker," a willing servant that automatically does what your conscious mind tells it to do if given clear instructions. It can work for you twenty-four hours a day, even while you're sleeping. It functions as a homing torpedo. Once you "tell" your subconscious mind what to do, it gropes its way toward your goal, zigzagging its way around obstacles until it reaches its mark. The Tomahawk missile is such a device. It can be programmed to hit a certain target, not just on a certain date, but at a certain time—to the millisecond. But such missiles are only cheap imitations of the source that created them in the first place: the human mind.

You can use your subconscious mind to help you to get to a goal by a certain deadline. For example, suppose you are participating in amateur theater and have taken a part in a play. You know that you must have the lines memorized, but what's more, you must have the spirit of the character down pat by the date of the play. Here's what you can do to help yourself to achieve your goal by the target date.

Circle the target date on the calendar, and then "tell" yourself (your conscious mind tells your subconscious mind) to be up to your best performance by that date. Envision yourself on opening night, walking on stage, feeling fully at ease, and saying your lines with the greatest of enjoyment and calm. Then pencil practice sessions into your calendar, giving yourself every opportunity to achieve that goal by the target date. Then, one way or another, you will be at your best by opening night. How does this happen? Once you set the process in motion, your subconscious mind will automatically "remind" you to make whatever adjustments necessary in your practice schedule to get you to your goal on the target date. For example, if it should be necessary to call a friend and ask for help or for some advice in the practice sessions, instead of brushing it aside (as you might have done had you not engaged your subconscious mind), you will make that call.

Time and again I've seen people reach their goal on target dates by using this method, whether it be for a performance, a job interview, a test, a sporting event, or a slew of other things.

Your subconscious mind can also solve problems for you. I remember the time I was under pressure to find a title for my first fitness book. I had been racking my brain for a title for months, but could not come up with anything to satisfy me and my editor. The deadline was rapidly approaching. Eventually, I remembered to ask my subconscious mind to assist me with the task. "Give me the title to my book," I requested. But nothing seemed to happen.

Finally my editor called; it was 4:30 in the afternoon. She informed me that we must have a title by the following morning. Not exactly in a panic—looking back, it was a state of high excitement—I thought, "This is the real test. Now I'll see what my subconscious mind comes up with," and with that thought I got into my car to run an errand. The radio was on and my mind was just drifting. Suddenly the thought struck me, "Press any button on the radio dial and what you hear will give you the title to your book." Thinking it was a silly mind-game I was playing with myself, but curious enough to do it, I pressed the button. An old favorite was playing, a song I rarely hear on the radio these days, "It's Now or Never." I continued daydreaming, not really making the connection for a moment or two. Then it struck me: "Now or Never." That was it. That was the title for my new book, which was geared toward women over thirty-five. "Why didn't I think of this before?" I wondered. "It's so obvious," I thought.

I was so excited I could barely wait to get back to my house to call the editor, who luckily had not gone home for the day. She loved the title and it became the name of my first workout book.

Since then I have used my subconscious mind time and again to deliver to me answers to problems I could not figure out on a conscious level. Often I ask my subconscious mind the question weeks ahead of time. Other times I'll ask the night before, just before going to sleep. But no matter when I ask, my subconscious mind never lets me down— and neither will yours if you just give it a chance to work for you.

The "Gotcha" Card Trick

One way to key your subconscious mind to achieve your goals is the "gotcha" card trick. With this method, you plant "messages" in your subconscious mind that catch it unawares. It is a form of autosuggestion. Here's how it works: First, you think of what you want, a goal. It can seem so far away it feels like a dream, or be something less overwhelming, something you want to make yourself do. You write it down on three small cards—they could be index cards or business cards. The next step is to "plant" the cards in three different places where you will stumble upon them more than once during the day.

For example, when I wanted to get my first book, *I Dare You,* published, I wrote down, *Publisher for I Dare You* on the three cards and placed them strategically: one in the kitchen drawer where the silverware is kept; one pasted on my bedroom wall, where I would see it first thing in the morning and right before going to bed; and one in the top drawer of my desk at work, so every time I opened the drawer the subliminal message would seep into my mind. What were the results? As you already know from reading this book, I did get a publisher. Was it the cards alone? Of course not. It was a combination of techniques, all of them contained in this book. I used these techniques according to my own style. You will, of course, modify them to suit your purposes.

I used the cards to achieve many other goals. "Get Joe out of my life," I would state; "Meet new girlfriends," I would say; "Find right outfit for party," I would request; "Right place for vacation," I would demand, and so on and so on, and, seemingly miraculously, I achieved every single one of my requests. It got to the point where I was afraid to write something down unless I really meant it, because I began to realize that I would get it. In fact, one day I found myself writing, "Find right man to marry." As I was writing, I felt uncomfortable, but I forced myself to write the three cards anyway. But when it came time to plant the cards, I just couldn't do it. What did that mean? Apparently, at that time I wasn't ready to get married, and when I thought about it, it was true. The last thing I wanted at that point was to share my energy with someone else. I was too busy creating my own foundation. Later there would be time for marriage.

But how exactly do the cards work? Is there some special magic in the writing itself? Of course not. The message you write on the cards is reprocessed by your subconscious mind time and again during the day. You see the message when you are off guard and have openings in your conscious mind, and are unable to be defensive. This causes the subconscious process to go into operation. Having received the repeated message written on the cards, your subconscious mind goes on "red alert," attracting you to any and every idea or opportunity that will enable you to achieve the goal written on the card. It creates a seemingly magnetic field that works just like radar to put you in the right place at the right time. But there's really no mystery in it at all when you come to think about it. What you have done by using the cards was to give your mind the power to act upon "cues" and to be sensitized to your needs, so as not to miss any opportunity to achieve the goals you have in mind. By using the cards, you become highly sensitive and fully receptive to opportunities around you, whereas had you not put your mind on alert, those openings would have gone unnoticed.

When a Voice in Your Head Says "You'll Quit"

A woman who had just bought my book *Definition* wrote me, saying, "I really want to start this workout, but the scary part is that every time I think of starting, there's a voice in the back of my head saying, 'You'll quit just like all those other times.' It just doesn't let up."

How mean we are to ourselves sometimes. In fact, if you had a friend who was as mean to you as you can be to yourself, you would probably never want to talk to that friend again. Yet you say to yourself, time and again, "You can't, you won't, you'll fail." Instead say, "I believe, I believe, I believe." Don't just say it to yourself. Say it out loud. Why? Because by saying it out loud you will help yourself to overcome a lifetime of negative self-talk. At first you will feel silly saying it out loud, and think that nothing is happening, that it is an exercise in foolishness. But after saying it a few times, you'll find yourself feeling better. You will see that the very words have the power to begin melting the base of an iceberg that was blocking your energy flow, and soon you'll begin to think of the obstacle in front of you and say, "Maybe I can do that after all."

I wrote this woman back, telling her to use the method of shouting out "I believe, I believe, I believe" every time that silent, but yet so audible, negative self-talk started to act up, and she did it. She later admitted that she felt really silly at first, but then said, "I can't believe how it works—almost like magic. I start to laugh and my whole mood begins to change and I actually get the energy to work out." She is now well into the program, and planning to send me an "after" photo after three months.

4. USE VISUALIZATION IMAGERY

Visualization imagery can be a powerful tool in helping you to get yourself to do what you want to do. To understand how it works, let's think about how sound can be used to help a person visualize a peaceful environment, and, in turn, bring total relief from tension.

Today, on cassette tapes, you can buy a variety of sounds, such as the waves of the ocean beating against the shore, a breeze blowing through a forest, or the sound of a waterfall. It has been discovered that when someone listens to one of these relaxing sounds, even if they are in a barren, enclosed room, that person can have the psychological experience of being at the beach or out in the country—in the presence of the environment itself—and that person's entire body will relax, giving up the tension that held him or her captive all day. It is the lull of the sound of the ocean, the breeze, the waterfall, or some other peaceful environment, together with the images that are conjured up in the mind, that causes the physical and mental relaxation.

You can use visualization imagery not only to relax your body, but to achieve goals as well. In fact, specific visualization can help to improve one's performance in a given sport by as much as 50 percent. For example, if a basketball player practices visualization, imagining himself shooting the ball through the hoop, even though he has not practiced physically his performance will improve markedly.

You can use visualization to alter your behavior—and make yourself do what you want to do—even when you are too lazy to do it. For example, suppose you want to work out every day after you come home from work, but as soon as you walk through the door, you feel your resolve melting. You may be living the life I know so well: getting up at the crack of dawn, working all day, and trying to support a family. You may not have the moments to spare to get up even one minute earlier than you already get up to work out—and you may have no choice but to work out when you come home from work.

You can use visualization imagery to precondition your mind. During your lunch hour at work, when you are completely relaxed, think of yourself walking through your front door. Then think of yourself "thinking of yourself" working out—and imagine yourself getting on that "Oh no, I'm too tired; I'm not doing it" jag. Now "tell" your subconscious mind to shoot a sudden burst of energy into you at that very moment, and to give you the original excitement and determination you felt when you first decided to work out. Now picture yourself marching into the room where you keep your dumbbells, taking off your clothing, putting on your sweats and T-shirt, picking up the dumbbells, and beginning the workout.

When you get home and walk through the door, something strange will happen. Yes, just as usual, when you first think of working out, you will get that, "I have a hard life; I deserve a break today—I'm not doing it" feeling, but suddenly you will get a surprise change of mood. Something will energize you, and for some strange reason, (not so strange, actually) you'll do a turnaround and stubbornly walk into the room where you keep your dumbbells. You'll put on your old sweats and T-shirt, pick up the dumbbells, and begin the workout. Before you know it, the workout will be over, and later on in the evening, when you are prepared to relax on the couch and watch TV or read the paper, and you are ready to think, "Oh, I didn't work out," and you're prepared to feel guilty, how much better you will feel when you suddenly realize, "What am I thinking? I did work out today," and you can then relax on the couch without guilt.

You can use visualization imagery to help you not to skip a workout no matter what time you work out—morning, afternoon, or night. All you have to do is take the time to rehearse or "precondition" your mind, depending upon your specific situation.

Visualization can work to get your body to the ultimate size and shape you want it to be—within reason, of course. Obviously you cannot add one inch to your height, and obviously you cannot look like a Cindy Crawford type if you are a Joyce Vedral type. Now don't get me wrong. I think I look as good as Cindy Crawford, and in fact, I secretly (and I'm sure foolishly) believe I look better than she does. But I know why I feel this way. It is because I look the best I can look, and having achieved that point, I feel perfect for me.

You too can get your body into *your* ideal shape. The first step is to picture your ideal body. I would tell you to use an old photograph of yourself, one taken before you gained weight, but if you are following one of my workout books, after a while you will look much better than you did even at your thinnest, because the workout will reshape your body, improving areas that can't be improved just by diet. For a demonstration of this point, take a look at my twenty-four-year-old photo and a forty-nine-year-old photo on page 11 of my book *Bottoms Up*. That twenty-four-year-old photo was me at my best, before I got fat. Yet see how much better shaped and toned my body is at fifty.

So if you decide to use an old photograph of yourself, when you were at your thinnest, use a Magic Marker and draw in improvements. If you can't find a "thin" photograph, use a "fat" photograph and draw your thin body over it. If you're not much of an artist, or if you prefer it, find a picture of someone in a magazine, someone with a body type similar to yours but who is in the shape you imagine for yourself. The next step is to take the photo of yourself or the picture from the magazine and visualize your body evolving into that shape by a given date.

Take it a step farther. Stand in front of a mirror each morning, in the nude or in your underwear. Instead of allowing your mind to go through its usual ritual of attacking yourself and putting yourself down, and of saying things like, "You fat slob—look at those rolls of fat," look at the photograph or picture of your ideal body. Then look in the mirror and imagine the rolls of fat gradually shrinking down until finally they are gone. See your stomach turning into a strong, defined, sexy girdle of muscle. Envision your thighs slowly getting leaner and see them being reshaped into the thighs of your ideal body. See your buttocks becoming higher, harder, rounder, sexier. Do this for every part of your body until you imagine yourself standing in front of the mirror at a given date, delighted with what you see because you are in the form of your dreams.

She Pictured Herself Walking Into Victoria's Secret . . ."

You can use visualization to project yourself into a future time when you will be able to do something you only dared to think of in the past in your wildest fantasies. Some time ago, I got a letter from a reader who said, "I would love to be able to go to Victoria's Secret and be able to buy matching bras and panties instead of always having to go to the 'old ladies' section of my department store." I told her to use the visualization to picture herself walking into Victoria's Secret six months from now and picking out an array of lingerie, going into the fitting room, and trying it on. I told her to imagine herself in the lingerie, sexy, tight, toned, defined. I told her to picture herself buying the lingerie, and then going home and surprising her husband— and wearing the lingerie under a fuzzy robe, and having to beg him to stop.

She wrote me back and said she would try it—and she did. And now she tells me that she looks so good she wears Victoria's Secret lingerie all the time, and that her husband, who was rather blasé about her in the past, is now so attentive to her that when she goes on a business trip he calls her at least three times a day—in fear that she may have caught someone else's attention.

You can use visualization to help you to make quicker progress by practicing it during your actual workout. For example, as you are doing a buttocks exercise, picture your buttocks firming up and reshaping themselves. Picture your gluteus muscles responding to each repetition, and becoming high, tight, and toned. Do this with every body part you exercise. Focus on that body part and "see" in your mind's eye the shape you are "telling" that body part to become.

I Start a Diet Every Monday

A woman recently wrote me lamenting, "I start a diet every Monday!" I told her what I am going to tell you now. You can use visualization to help you to maintain your low-fat eating habits. Every night before you go to bed, picture yourself the next day, being tempted to eat one of your favorite "cheating" foods. Imagine yourself about to dig into the container of ice cream (that perhaps you keep around for your husband or the children). Envision yourself standing at the refrigerator with a spoon. No one is around to see you. You have the ice-cream container open. You are about to start shoveling it in.

But just as you are about to put the ice cream into your mouth, envision a wave of nausea coming over you. Imagine the thought going through your mind, "What am I doing? Why am I eating this repulsive fat?" Imagine yourself suddenly thinking, "I don't want to do this." And see yourself closing the ice-cream container, shutting the refrigerator door and putting the spoon down, and cutting up a few red peppers and cucumbers and enjoying the delicious treat, and then going about your business with a triumphant feeling.

Think of every food that may tempt you during the day and use the same method of visualization to second-guess yourself, to prevent yourself from automatically putting the wrong thing in your mouth.

You can use visualization to help you to overcome any temptation. For example, if you have to do some work at home in the evening and you know you will be tempted to turn on the television, picture yourself, after dinner, getting ready to do your work, but then saying, "I'm tired. I'm going to watch TV for a while." Imagine yourself turning on the TV and visualize that as soon as the picture and the sound of the TV come on, you get a powerful urge to turn it off, a sudden burst of excitement and diligence, a spirit of "attack" coming over you, an eagerness that you cannot control. Your only desire is to conquer the work you had planned to do. Envision yourself, with that burst of energy, turning off the television and heading straight for the work that is waiting to be done.

Use visualization for your long-term goals. Imagine yourself graduating from college. See yourself walking up and receiving the diploma in your hand. Picture yourself being congratulated on the promotion on your job, envision yourself being skilled in a sport you are trying to improve, envision yourself socializing and meeting friends or people of the opposite sex.

I'm not saying that visualization is a magic formula, that all you have to do is use the above techniques and you'll automatically be able to conquer any temptation, achieve any goal. Of course not. What I'm saying is that visualization helps. It helps a lot. When used in a comfortable combination with the other techniques in this book, it can work to make it that much easier for you to get yourself to do what you want to do. No one secret in this book got me where I am today, but rather a combination of them all.

5. TURN WORRY AND FEAR INTO PRODUCTIVE POWER

Worry and anxiety can drain your energy and hinder you from taking action. For example, say you are taking courses toward a degree that will net you a promotion on your job, and you are about to have a big test. You must put in an hour of study time each night for a week. But every time you get ready to study, you find yourself worrying, "What if I don't study the right things—and don't pass the test? I may fail the course, then I won't graduate, and I'll never get that promotion anyway. Maybe all of this is a waste of time." Such worry and anxiety saps your energy and defeats you before you even start the battle.

Worry and anxiety are never productive. They are always draining. So in order to get yourself to do what you want to do, whether it is to work out every day with the ultimate goal of getting your body into a certain shape, studying and reading on a regular basis in order to pass courses in school, practicing singing, playing a musical instrument, or even participating in a sport in order to perform in an event, what you need to do is "catch" the worry ball and turn it inside out. Then hold it up to God in the form of a prayer.

Let's see how this works using the above example. You are about to sit down and study for a test, but worry and fear assail you. Instead of giving in to those emotions, immediately say to yourself, "What am I thinking?" In other words, catch the thought. The thought was, "What if I don't study the right things, and fail the test? I may feel ashamed of myself. Maybe all of this is a waste of time." Now take that negative worry and fear and turn them inside out by making them into a positive statement. You can even hold them up to God as a prayer: "Help me to relax so that I can focus on and study the right things so that I get a good grade on the test. God, please help me to keep trying."

Once you do this, you are relieved of the paralyzing power of worry and fear, and in fact will feel renewed energy. By turning your worry inside out and holding it up as a prayer you stop the energy drain, thus creating a force that you can use to propel you toward your goal. You can do this each and every time you worry about something that is really not happening at all, even things unrelated to goals. For example, instead of worrying, "What if my daughter gets into a car accident tonight?" pray, "God, please protect my daughter and alert her to drive carefully." Instead of thinking, "Oh my God. What if I don't get that promotion?" pray, "God, please help me to do what is necessary to get that promotion." If you are single, and wish to get married, instead of worrying, "What if I never meet the right mate?" pray, "God, help me to be open and alert and to be ready to meet the right life partner."

Simple Exercises to Chase Worry and Fear Away

Positive thoughts will help you to dispel worry and fear. I could direct you to read a hundred different self-help books, among them *The Power of Positive Thinking,* the grandfather of them all. But I found a readily available source in the Gospels, the Psalms, and Proverbs of the Bible. You might want to try them too. To make your job simpler, I'll tell you exactly where I started: in the first book of The New Testament, Matthew.

Here's what I did, and I think you'll enjoy doing it too. With a pen or highlighter in your hand, begin reading. As you proceed, mark every verse that has to do with faith or positive thinking. Include all verses that are uplifting or are in any way inspiring. Next read the book of Mark, highlighting as you go. Do the same for the other two Gospels, Luke and John, and work your way to the Psalms and Proverbs (in the Old Testament). Also read Hebrews, Chapter Eleven. It's all about faith.

After you have done this, copy the passages onto index cards and carry them in your purse. Here are some quotations I find helpful: "According to your faith be it unto you" (Matthew 9:29); "Whosoever shall say unto this mountain, be thou removed, and be thou cast into the sea; and shall not doubt in his heart, but shall believe that those things which he saith shall come to pass; he shall have whatsoever he saith" (Mark 11:23); "Now faith is the substance of things hoped for, the evidence of things not seen" (He-brews 11:1). Every time you begin to worry, or to feel sad or depressed, take out the index cards and begin to read through them. They will cheer you up every time.

Another way to deal with worry and fear is to make a list of all the worries and fears you have regarding what you are trying to do, and then to knock down each worry and fear one by one with logical reasoning. For example, if you are trying to save up for a new car and you think "What if a year from now I still don't have the money?" Write down the rational answer to that: "I will at least have saved some money—and I'll be closer to getting a new car than I am now. But if I don't at least start saving, a year from now I'll be exactly where I am now in terms of getting a new car—at zero! I've got nothing to lose and everything to gain at least to begin saving."

If you are on your way to an interview for a job, and the worry comes, "What if I'm asked a question I can't answer?" write down the most reasonable answer to that: "Nobody is expected to know everything. I'll admit that I don't know, and continue to answer the other questions as intelligently and as confidently as I can. Perhaps the interviewer will be impressed with my forthrightness, integrity, and honesty." Also, think of it this way: It takes self-confidence to ac-knowledge not knowing something right up front.

As you practice writing down rational "comebacks" to worrying thoughts, you will soon realize that chances are that your worries are magnifications of irrational, childish fears and not pictures of predictions of reality. You will soon realize that no matter what happens to you, short of death, it's not the end of your world. In time, you will real-ize that in any given situation, if you want something, you might as well forge ahead and give it your best shot. It will become obvious that one thing is for sure: If you do noth-ing new, nothing new will happen, but if you keep trying different angles, sooner or later something's gotta give!

6. MAKE CHANGE WORK FOR YOU RATHER THAN AGAINST YOU

As if it isn't difficult enough sometimes to get ourselves to do what we need to do, along comes a change in our lives—and lo and behold, it's even more difficult to do what we must do.

Most people are afraid of change, or are at least uncomfortable with it. They experience fear when they think of change, a fear almost like a fear of death. Why is this so? In a way, change *is* a death, a little death, the death of a former way of doing things, or of a former way of life. So it is quite natural to feel insecure when we think of change. But we must learn to come to terms with change, because often we must deal with change in our lives, like the death of a loved one, or being forced to change jobs. If you think of each change as a forced opportunity to grow, you won't resent it as much.

You will recall the change that was forced upon former President Eisenhower (see Chapter 4 for the full story). He was on his way to becoming a professional football player, but he was suddenly cut down by an injury. Apparently the unwanted and unasked-for change that ended Eisenhower's football career was just what was needed to clear the path for Eisenhower's taking the steps he would eventually take to become president.

Other changes may not be forced upon us, but it may be in our best interests to choose them. For example, I used to write all my books on an old IBM typewriter. I knew I should switch to a computer, but I was afraid of change. When I thought about writing on a computer (word processor, actually), I experienced a sensation of fear—almost like a fear of death—that I would not write as well because my mind would be preoccupied with how to use the computer, and that my creativity would die. I knew the old way worked, and was given the promise by many people that the new way would work better, but how did I know it would really be better? I was tempted to stick to the tried and true.

But when I dared to take the plunge and make the transition, I was able to improve my writing to a great extent, and, in fact, I was able to get many more books published in a shorter time. I see now how that change was for the best, but like most people, I am a creature of habit and have to be highly motivated in order to choose change.

7. USE THE REWARD SYSTEM TO KEEP YOURSELF GOING

One of my favorite ways to get myself to do what I know I must do when I'm not in the mood to do it is to promise myself a reward after doing it. For example, when I was teaching all day and I had to come home from work, exercise, and then sit at my computer for an hour each evening to toil on a book I was writing, it was tough. In order to get myself to go to that computer, I would tell myself, "Okay, Joyce. Just sit at the computer for one hour. I don't care if you don't write a thing. Just sit there with your fingers on the keyboard. Then in exactly one hour you can get up and watch Larry King—and have a snack." (I love that show, but could barely spare the time to watch it.)

It worked. And guess what? I would always end up writing quite a bit during that hour, and sometimes I would get so carried away that I would write for two hours, even missing Larry King.

It's the carrot on the end of the stick, an old trick that people used to use in the days of the horse and buggy. The next time you're tempted to not keep an appointment, not to make a list of phone calls, not to read some important material, not to do a certain chore, think of a reward for yourself. Hold a carrot on a stick in front of yourself to motivate you to get the job done.

Carrots on the end of sticks can work to motivate you to work long and hard for bigger rewards, but you'll have to use bigger, juicier carrots. For example, if you are taking courses toward a degree, promise yourself a long weekend vacation on a tropical island when you get your degree—

even if it means you have to go into hock to do it. And chances are, now that you have a degree, you'll eventually get a higher-paying job to pay off the vacation.

I use carrots on the end of sticks all the time. I'm always having to get myself into "television" shape for book promotions. This means being five to ten pounds lighter than my normal happy weight, because television puts ten pounds on you. But because I love eating, I refuse to go as low as ten pounds below my happy weight of 120. Instead I go down to 115, but I resent even that. So in order to get myself to do what I must do—follow a very low-fat eating plan for months at a time—I promise myself a couple of months "off" in the winter, when no television appearances are coming up.

For example, I recently did a slew of shows for a fitness book, telling myself that when the shows were over, I could eat like a dog from February through March, and that "carrot" helped me to force my body down to its leanest form. Sure enough, when February came around, I gave myself the reward. Naturally, I eventually gained back the five pounds, but no problem. I always know how to lose it when I have to.

Once again, I am following a low-fat eating plan for an upcoming book and television tour, in order to melt away those five pounds. But had I not enjoyed the pleasure of that carrot at the end of the stick the last time, I would resent dieting now, and would in fact probably not be able to get myself to do it.

No matter what you are trying to do, there's no reason to turn it into a stark, joyless, military experience with no reward at the end. Think hard of something you can give yourself at the end of the job, something that will keep you going.

When you come to think of it, our economy and entire business system and even social structure are set up this way. After all, what else do we mean when we say, "Thank God it's Friday"?

Key #7.   The power of getting yourself to do what you want. Motivate yourself.

9

THE POWER OF SPIRITUALITY AND PRAYER

In beginning this chapter, I want to tell you, unabashedly, what you must already know: that I do believe in God. Call God by any name or gender—it doesn't matter to me. We're talking about the same creative, caring, all-knowing force that, thankfully, is more objective than we are, and is capable of intervening in our lives if we call upon him, and who sometimes intervenes in our lives even when we don't call on him. For the sake of simplicity, when I refer to God in this chapter I will use the male gender, not that I think God is a man (I believe God is a spirit, without gender), but because that is the traditional way of referring to God when using a pronoun.

I also want to separate myself from the New Age way of thinking about God, that we are really God ourselves. I believe that we have the potential to do good or evil (and yes, I believe that there *is* such a thing as evil), that we have Godlike qualities, and that we can develop those qualities to the utmost degree. But yet we can never *become* God. God, in my view, is both separate and superior to us. When we call upon God, I do *not* believe that we are really calling upon ourselves.

If you disagree with me, that is fine. I could be wrong. All I ask you to do is to read this chapter with an open point of view and then let what you read sit in your mind for a while, and see where it takes you. If what you read has no effect on your thinking or on your life, then so be it. If it is helpful and enlightening, I'm honored to have been of help to you.

WHAT IS PRAYER AND WHY SHOULD WE PRAY?

Prayer, in my view, is simply talking to God. Most people who pray don't just talk to God, they speak to God in order to ask for something. We ask for help for ourselves or loved ones, or even strangers—or we ask God to forgive us when we feel that we have done something wrong, or we ask God to give us wisdom to make the right choices. But some people never try to communicate with God. They think the whole idea of praying to a superior being is silly. In fact, some people believe that the very act of prayer takes away autonomy and causes one to feel like a puppet—without a will.

YOU CANNOT DIE BEFORE YOUR TIME!

Prayer, to me, does not mean you lose the power of your will. After all, prayer is a choice. It is an option that can be comforting but also capable of improving the quality of your life.

So many of us have heard theories about God. We've heard that if you don't believe in him or pray to him you will be condemned, and your life will be miserable. I don't look at it that way. The way I see it, if you don't avail yourself of the power of God in your life, you miss out on a comforting, guiding force that could insure that you spend your time on this earth in the most productive, peaceful, fulfilling way, all things considered.

For those of you who don't pray—and don't believe in God—I believe you may be subject to the tides of "luck." Both bad and good "luck" will come your way, mixed in, of course, with the recipe of your own doings—and your life will turn out to be either fulfilling or empty, joyful or sad, successful or failure-ridden, depending upon that combination. This, I believe, applies even to your fate. If you don't invite God into your life, the time and manner of your death may depend upon a combination of your health (which in turn will depend strictly on genetic components, the way you take care of your body) and environmental elements, in addition to good or bad fortune—being or not being in the wrong place at the right time.

If, on the other hand, you invite God into your life, if you ask God to have his will in your life and to cause you to fulfill the purposes for which you were born, and you communicate with him on a regular basis (pray), I believe you cannot die before your time. Cancer, heart disease, and a host of other ailments may invade your body, but they will be neutralized and you will never know you had the problem, or they will be lifted from you as you ask for healing—if it is not your time to go.

I'll take it a step farther. I believe that if you've committed your life to God, even if someone were planning to kill you they would not be able to complete their mission if it were not your time to die. They would be diverted to other problems in their life, or they would be stopped before the deed was done, perhaps by some seeming bit of "good luck" on your part. You may or may not ever know that the attempt was made on your life. The way I see it, the bottom line is that if you ask God to have his will in your life and not to let you leave this earth without fulfilling the purposes for which you were born, *you cannot die before your time*. You might in fact have many "close calls," and wonder why. But unless it is your time, you will not die.

What? Am I saying that those who do not believe in God and/or who do not choose to call upon him are completely unprotected? Certainly not. What about those who don't believe in God, who never prayed, and have close calls? What about those who escape death and other potential disasters and who have mysterious experiences that seem to lead them to a better path for their lives? I think these people are being urged by God to call upon him, because God wants them to invite him into their lives, or perhaps these people have been calling upon God to reveal himself to them, not consciously, but in the most remote and hidden thoughts of their minds, and God is hearing them.

I also admit to not knowing exactly what God is up to—or how he operates the universe. What I've said about God so far, and what I will say in the following paragraphs, I must remind you, is what my limited and very human insight has allowed up until this point of my life. And I want to share it with you, not impose it upon you.

THERE ARE NO ATHEISTS IN FOXHOLES

Does God hear you if you pray to him only in emergencies? You may have heard of the expression, "There are no atheists in foxholes." This phrase was coined during World War II, when soldiers were fighting battles in open fields, being shot at—and watching their buddies literally "drop like flies" while they hid in foxholes in the hope of avoiding the next round of fire. At such times everyone seemed to be able to conjure up at least a shred of faith—and even the most resistant unbelievers managed to pray.

But does God turn a deaf ear to such prayers? Is he disgusted because some people only pray when they are in emergency situations, or is he happy that at least then he is asked to be a part of the "caller's" life? I think the latter is true. I believe that if you never pray to God, but then blurt out a desperate call in the hope that God may just hear you and save you, God does hear and help.

And what's more, at such times I don't think it's necessary to make all kinds of promises to get help, because, let's face it, the very nature of God assumes that he knows everything—even the future. He knows whether or not you are going to keep those promises, so why make them? Why put pressure on yourself so that if you don't follow through, you will feel guilty later, driving a bigger psychological wedge between yourself and God? (The wedge, of course, would exist only in your mind, because God would have known ahead of time that you were not going to keep your promise, and he wouldn't be upset with you. The upset would be coming from your anger at yourself.) If you do insist upon making a promise, you can say something like, "God, if you get me out of this situation, I pray that you will help me to treat people with more kindness, spend more time with my family, stop drinking so much, be more honest, search for the purposes for which I was born and try to fulfill them," or some such thing. That's much more realistic. (By the way, you can tell a lot about what you know in your inner being needs improvement by the promises you make to God when you are in emergency situations.)

But why would God answer emergency or "foxhole"-type prayers? Why wouldn't he say, "Ah-ha, I know your game. You just call on me when you're desperate, otherwise you don't think about me at all. I'm not going to do a thing for you"? Apparently, God does not have the ego problems common to the human race. He does not behave like a rejected friend or lover who becomes offended if the only time you call him is when you need him—and he doesn't have a psyche that frets over such thoughts as "She's using me," or "He's only going to abandon me after I help him." That is not an issue with God.

I believe God sees emergency prayers as opportunities to introduce himself to you, and that he hopes you will be drawn to talk to him again. Perhaps you will call on him this time when the situation is not quite as dire; perhaps when you are feeling sad or lonely, or when you are questioning the meaning of life; or when you are trying to make a difficult decision and need wisdom as to which way to go. In other words, I think God sees emergency prayers as a way to start up a possible relationship with you.

But why would God like to have a friendship with you, to have you talk with him more often, even on a regular basis? I think he would like this not so much for himself, but for you. I imagine that God feels sorry to watch us struggle and suffer, often needlessly, when if we only called upon him, he could direct us to the best way to solve the problem at hand. He can save us so much strife, so much wasted time and energy.

IDEAS ON HOW TO PRAY

Not every prayer will be answered—but you already know that. For example, if you pray, "Dear God, please send me a million dollars. I want it delivered to my doorstep tomorrow morning, in hundred-dollar bills," or "God, I hate John. I want you to kill him tonight," of course God will not answer your prayer. But why?

The right, and in my view, the only, way to pray is *to pray according to God's will.* If you do that, you can pray for anything you want. You see, the condition that we must make in order for our prayers to be answered is to pray something like this: "God, you know how much I need a higher-paying job—to meet my bills and to have a better life. I pray that you will lead me to that job, unless you have a special purpose for me staying here for now—and if you do, your will be done—but please, give me peace about it and help me either to find a way to cover my bills or to live more simply." (And you might even add, "I, of course, would prefer the extra money," or "God, unless you have a special reason not to, I know you can heal me of this disease," or "God, lead me to the career that you know is best for me.")

Why does praying that way bother some people? Such prayer involves giving up a certain amount of control, and most people don't like to do that. It's just human nature. In addition, some people feel silly praying because they're not so sure God exists in the first place. But if you could think of God as follows, you could get over that "hump," so to speak: If there is a God, and if he does have a purpose for your life, and if he knows all things, what have you really got to lose in such prayer? Nothing. Even though you may be smart, God is smarter, and it will be worth giving up the control because your life will be guided into its best possible course. On the other hand, if there is no God and praying is just a mind game, what have you got to lose by such a prayer? Nothing again. You will merely be back to square one, in charge of your own destiny.

Still, some people will not want to try praying "according to God's will." Why? Some people can't let go of what they see as total control of their lives. In other words, there is no room in their minds for what is "meant to be." They have a plan and they intend to follow it. But in life, this kind of thinking can get one into trouble, while being open to God's will or to what is "meant to be" can *save* one from trouble.

I think of a recent example. A friend of mine had spotted and then made plans to purchase a wonderful dream home, a second home in the country. The closing date was set. But just before it arrived my friend read an article about old homes and the danger of radon contamination, how this could cause lung problems. She got a flashback: She had noticed a very strong lung medication sitting on the table in the house when she first visited. "I never snoop or look for such things. It was in plain sight and just caught my eye," she said.

She did some checking, had the home inspected, and sure enough, it was riddled with radon. She canceled her plans to purchase the home.

What is the significance of this story and what does it have to do with what is "meant to be" and praying according to God's will?

Even though my friend, during her negotiations and preparations for the final closing, may not have mouthed (and I'm sure she did not) the specific words to God, "Don't let this deal go through unless it is your will," knowing her, I'm sure she was throwing up "thoughts" to God. She may have been asking, "Don't let me make a mistake. Don't let this happen unless it is meant to be, unless it is right."

And sure enough, it didn't happen because it wasn't right. What I am saying is, if we can find within ourselves a small opening, a place for someone who knows more than we do to check our actions, whether we know it or not we are praying according to God's will.

I for one would never give up the privilege and joy of having God as a part of my life because with God you never feel completely alone and you always have peace of mind—or quick access to it. I know how I felt before I had a close connection with God, and I never want to feel that way again. If I had to give up everything I own, if I had to leave the country, wandering the earth in rags, I would do it rather than give up God. God is the secret of my joy and optimism, my happiness. I do not say this to try to convert you to anything. I only tell you how I feel because if I left that one cornerstone out of the book, I would not be telling you the full story, the truth about what motivates me, what keeps me going.

THE SAFETY OF PRAYING ACCORDING TO GOD'S WILL

Why is it important to pray according to God's will? It is an insurance policy, if you will, a guarantee that you will not "bite off more than you can chew." This idea is demonstrated in the proverb:

> Feed me with food that is convenient for me: Lest
> I be full and deny thee, and say, Who is the Lord?
> or lest I be poor, and steal, and take the name of
> my God in vain.
>
> (Proverbs 30:8–9)

We should not pray to be rich, but for just the right amount of wealth, the amount that we can cope with without "going off the deep end," so to speak, the amount of wealth that will still allow us to keep things in proper perspective—and to put our values first. In other words, the proverb indicates that we each have a different tolerance for wealth—or poverty—and only God knows what that tolerance is.

What happens if we don't preface our prayer with "according to your will"? We may find ourselves examples of what Oscar Wilde was talking about when he said, "There is only one thing worse than not getting what you want, and that is getting it."[1]

But what does this really mean? Suppose your wish is to become very rich and famous and to live in the lap of luxury. But perhaps if you were given such fortune, you would become an egotistical, self-centered, selfish miser, or worse. Perhaps you would succumb to a life of gambling, or drugs. Who knows? By praying according to God's will, you are acknowledging that only God knows—and that although you desire a given thing, you don't want it unless it is in your ultimate best interest, all things considered, because it is the all-knowing God who has insight into our particular nature. By asking God for "just the right amount" you are taking advantage of a safety valve.

Let's consider Oprah Winfrey. How many people could cope with the wealth that has been bestowed upon her and still remain true to principles of love and compassion—and even humility? Apparently, Oprah Winfrey can. She is one of the most generous affluent people alive today, and she is dedicated to helping those in need. She uses much of her abundance to better the human race. But some others who have gained incredible wealth—and we've all read the papers and watched the TV news reports—were destroyed by their wealth, while still other multimillionaries allow their wealth to bind them up in an endless "make-more-money" maze until their lives are over—and they wonder why they worked so hard and never got to enjoy their wealth.

Before we leave the proverb, let's take a look at the other side of the equation. Note that the biblical writer, in asking that God feed him with that which is "meet," or "right," for him, is covering the other end of the scale. He asks God, in a sense, please not to give him too little, either, "lest I be poor, and steal, and take the name of my God in vain." The biblical writer is implying that only God knows how far each of us can be tested before we may succumb to the temptation to do wrong—in order to survive.

Hidden within this part of the cry is the assurance that God would not allow us to be so poor as not to be able to cope. God and God alone knows how much we can take. If and when we are faced with the temptation to compromise our values because of financial need, we must cry out to God, "Feed me with that which is meet for me. . . . I am tempted to _____." And he will answer. He always does. But you have to ask. And yes, this prayer would certainly be according to his will.

But what might such praying mean for you? Will it mean that you will most likely be in poverty? Probably not, at least not in the long run. Jesus, in talking about material blessings, said, "Seek ye first the kingdom of God and his righteousness, and all these things shall be added unto you" (Matthew 6:33). In other words, put first things first— let go of materialism and put values and right living first, and ironically, you will also have more than your share of material wealth.

But praying according to God's will does not apply only to prayers for material well-being. It applies to every situation in which one might pray, situations that will be discussed in the following paragraphs. In each and every case, praying according to God's will is like taking out an insurance policy.

IDEAS ON WHEN AND WHERE TO PRAY

We already know that it's a good idea to preface, at least in our minds, every prayer with "according to your will," but what else is involved? When should we pray? What words should we use? What posture should we take?

I find that it is possible and convenient to pray anytime, anywhere, and in any position, in the most simple or complicated terms, in the most calm or desperate way, or anywhere in between. I believe that you can pray in spoken words or just by thought—or you can pray a specific prayer or a general "help" prayer that is not yet clear in your own mind. And God hears you, and will interpret your cry for help because he understands what is troubling you more clearly than you do.

You can pray sitting in a chair, kneeling, walking in the street, or lying in bed; God is not the least concerned about the position you take when you speak to him. He is more concerned that you *do* speak to him.

Most of the time, I pray not in words but with my thoughts, but those thoughts are clearly directed to God. For example, if I'm feeling down and I don't know why, I'll think—straight up to God—"God, I feel despondent, I'm sad, and I don't know why. Please, help me." If I'm worried about someone who is sick, I'll say, "God, I know you can heal so-and-so if it is your will. Please, unless you have another plan, right now I believe that your healing power is going through so-and-so." If I'm facing a difficult situation, say, an interview with an intimidating person, I'll ask, "God, give me wisdom and insight. Help this interview to go the way you want it to go. Don't let me get sidetracked. Keep me alert and on target." And so on.

When you pray, it helps a lot to imagine God looking at you compassionately and attentively and hearing every word you are saying—and then beginning to use his power to answer your prayer. Then, after you finish your prayer, leave it at that and enjoy the peace of mind that comes with knowing that "it's in the works." You'll soon find out that while all of your prayers may not be answered the way you had expected them to be answered, no prayer uttered sincerely is ignored by God.

LEGITIMATE REASONS TO PRAY

Anything that concerns you is proper prayer material. You can pray for wisdom about whether or not to stop seeing a boyfriend (or girlfriend), or for the power to let go of an unhealthy relationship that you already know is wrong for you. You can ask for the strength to get through the day. You can call upon God when you are about to do something that you know is wrong but you just don't seem to have the strength to stop yourself from doing. Instead of succumbing to the temptation without a struggle, you call out in your mind, "God, I can't resist. I'm about to do _____ but I know you can turn my mind in the right direction, so that I do not surrender."

I've suggested this to various people over the course of my life, and they often come back to tell me that, to their amazement, it works. For example, I once taught a student who was struggling to give up his cocaine habit. He felt guilty about doing cocaine because he was an *A* student and the drug was beginning to affect his ability to concentrate. He wanted me to pray with him; he told me that he was willing to promise God that he would never do the drug again.

To his surprise, I told him not to make any promises to God. Instead I advised him to ask God to take the habit away from him—confessing that he felt powerless to do it himself—and then just let it go until the next time he was faced with the temptation to do the coke. At such a time, I advised him to say, "God, I'm about to do this coke. I don't want to do it, but unless you help me, I don't think I can resist. I give it to you. Please help me." He tried it and it worked. He came back to me and told me that on three separate occasions, when he was faced with the temptation to do coke, situations in which in the past he surely would have done the coke, he was able to resist by praying that prayer. He gave me the details.

The first time, he was with a close friend and the friend threw some coke on the table and made some "lines," then rolled a dollar bill and started snorting. His first thought was, "Who am I kidding? Of course I have to do the coke. It's right here in front of me. How can I resist?" Then he remembered the prayer, so quickly in his mind he directed a thought up to God, telling him how he felt helpless and needed a miracle here. A minute later the phone rang and his friend became preoccupied with the call. While his friend was on the phone, he got the idea that he could brush his allotted six lines onto the floor and his friend would never know the difference. While he was thinking, "Are you kidding? That's crazy, wasting all that good coke," on impulse and as if on automatic pilot, he found himself raising his arm to the table, and before he knew it, he had brushed all of his allotment onto the floor. When his friend came back, he never thought to question whether or not he had done the coke.

The next temptation came at a party when everyone was doing cocaine. He was about to join the group, thinking, "It won't hurt to do just a couple of lines, just to be sociable and get a buzz." But as he was approaching the table, he got a heavy feeling in his chest and began to feel that if he did the coke it would lead to more coke and pull him back into his habit, so he quickly shot up the prayer of "Help!" Just at the moment when he was about to find a place at the table, an old girlfriend with whom he was still in love appeared in his view at the other side of the room—and he went over to speak to her. When he came back, all the greedy takers had consumed the cocaine!

His third temptation came when a friend of his, a guy for whom he had done a lot of favors, called and said, "Joe, I got a promotion on my job—and know where I can get some really great coke. Let's go out to dinner tomorrow night and celebrate—my treat. I'll bring the coke and we can do it in the men's room." "Great," Joe said. But the moment he hung up the phone he knew he had made a mistake. "Well, I'll just take my share and flush it down the toilet—he'll never know the difference," he said. But then another thought came to him, and he pictured himself in the bathroom stall, looking at the coke, being ready to throw it down the bowl, and then not being able to do so, but instead snorting it, and then later feeling guilty and being once again a captive of his habit.

With this thought, he jumped up from his chair and called his friend back, not really knowing exactly what he was going to say to get himself out of the situation because the last thing he wanted to do was not look cool in his friend's eyes. When his friend answered the phone, he found himself blurting out, "Jack, about tomorrow night, don't bring the coke. Instead I'll spring for a bottle of champagne." His friend immediately exclaimed, "What? I can't believe you said that. I used to have a big problem with drugs and I haven't done any in months, and I was about to break my clean run. I don't want to do the coke, either."

I haven't heard from this student in years, but I suspect that wherever he is, if he's facing a temptation, he knows who to call.

HOW TO TURN YOUR LUCK AND YOUR LIFE AROUND

If your life has not gone the way you have wished it would, if up until now you have been disappointed with events that have happened—and even if you have been disappointed *with yourself*—you can turn all of that around, but you must struggle for your "light," or for "the blessing."

I am reminded of a biblical tale of Jacob. He had battled all his days with his proclivity toward being deceptive, and his life was not going very well. He ended up on the run, with his father-in-law threatening to kill him because of his continual duplicity. Sick and tired of his life, Jacob determines to change things around. He calls out to God, asking him to transform his life and with it, his luck. Then Jacob has a dream, and in the dream, all night long, he wrestles with an angel. Finally, the dawn is breaking, and the angel tries to leave—but Jacob refuses to let the angel go, saying, "I will not let you go until you bless me" (Genesis 12–13, 22, 25, 27, and 32:26). Finally, the angel agrees to bless Jacob, and tells Jacob that his name will no longer be Jacob (which means deceiver) but will now be Israel, which means Prince with God (Genesis 32:24–28).

Whether or not Jacob wrestled with a literal angel is not at issue here. It is the symbolism of the story that is both graphic and compelling. The angel symbolizes the good that Jacob desired to bring out in himself and the change of lifestyle that he wished to accomplish. In refusing to let go of that angel, even until the break of dawn, Jacob showed his determination to choose light over darkness, to overcome his lower nature. Because of his determination, he was able to reverse a lifetime of misdeeds, and was given the promise that in the future he would no longer have to struggle in the same manner—because now he would be blessed of God.

The lesson is clear. Nothing is impossible with God. No matter how hopeless you think you are, no matter how many times you have failed to do or be right in the past, you can be transformed, but you must show that you mean business. You must, in a sense, "wrestle with an angel," refusing to let go until you are blessed—nagging, praying, and calling upon God until you are transformed.

WHEN YOU'RE BOUND AND DETERMINED TO DO THE WRONG THING

There's a story in the Bible where a man named Balaam is eagerly traveling along the wrong road, about to do the wrong thing, determined in his mind not to let anything stop him. Suddenly the jackass he's riding refuses to move another inch. After receiving many blows, the story goes, to Balaam's horror the mule begins to speak to him. But why? Let's take a closer look.

Balaam, a prophet of God for Israel, was on his way to meet the king of a foreign nation, after being told by God not to deal with that king, an evil man who wanted to seduce Balaam into betraying God and Israel. Although Balaam had been warned twice to have no dealings with this king, he continued to do so because the king was promising gifts and power for Balaam's betrayal of God and Israel.

Finally, I imagine, tired of Balaam's nagging, and ready to teach Balaam a lesson, God allows him to go to visit the king, but on his way, Balaam's jackass suddenly refuses to budge. Unbeknownst to Balaam, the poor beast saw an angel with crossed swords blocking his way. After three attempts to make the donkey move—via a reign of blows and kicks—the jackass began to speak to Balaam, asking him why he was beating a faithful servant for no reason. At this point, as the story goes, "the Lord opened the eyes of Balaam, and he saw the angel of the Lord, standing in the way, and his sword drawn in his hand: and he bowed down his head and fell flat on his face" (Numbers 22:31). The angel of the Lord then told Balaam to be thankful that the donkey was, in effect, smarter than he—because had he continued on his journey, he would have been killed.

What is the point of the story? It is human nature to want to do what we want to do, even if in our heart we know it is wrong, and sometimes we are fool enough to expect God to bless us in our wrongdoing. In other words, we half-heartedly pray that God will have his will, but in the meantime, we are not open to the answer to our prayer— what God's will may really be—because we already know what we want and are bound and determined to get it, not knowing that the very thing we were so hotly pursuing would have destroyed us. (Note that God said to Balaam, "Had you gone another step, you would have been killed.")

The moral of the story, as I see it, is that when we are bound and determined to do the wrong thing, even after asking God to have his will in a situation, God in his mercy can take into account the weakness of our human nature and stop us dead in our tracks, in a sense saving us from ourselves. I am reminded of the lyrics of a country-and-western song I once heard, that, as I recall, goes something like this: "Sometimes we have to thank God for unanswered prayers."

DO YOU REALLY HAVE TO BE AN IDIOT TO BELIEVE?

Is belief in God really a far-fetched idea that only the un-educated would even consider? Not by a long shot. In fact, scientists have been toying with the idea of God as origina-tor for years, and the more they learn about the origins of the universe, the closer many of them come to an outright declaration that there was indeed a creator. They are com-ing to realize that without this missing link they call the "God particle," none of their theories make sense. Yet many of these scientists are still hesitant to declare outright that they have boiled down their research to the point of saying, "Yes. There is a God."

A recent *USA Today* article discussed this very issue, pointing out how not one or two, but thousands of scien-tists are increasingly using terms such as "God particle" and "the mind of God" in their scientific explanations, and have joined organizations to discuss what they call the "en-chanted world" of science. Their goal, the article states, is to bridge the religion gap. Yet the article points out that many of these scientists admit that they feel reluctant to state their belief that there is a creator behind the universe because they think that other scientists might believe that they had "somehow gone soft in the brain."[2]

Why do so many of us, even when confronted with what we ourselves would admit are clear signs that there is a cre-ative force outside of ourselves, so often fight our instinct to reach out to that force, to establish a relationship with that higher power traditionally called "God"? Why must we continually feel obligated to apologize for our conviction that, based upon the evidence we see, there is a God? Aside from the fact that some of us may feel that it is too much of a sacrifice of pride or self-sufficiency to call upon or believe in God, could it be that we have out-intellectual-ized ourselves?

I am reminded of the story in the Bible of the blind man who was healed by Jesus and then challenged by the reigning intellectuals of the day, the Pharisees, who were a notoriously skeptical as well as highly respected religious group. Jesus had healed a man who had been blind from his birth, and the man was going around rejoicing about his good fortune. But the Pharisees were dubious, and refused to accept the marvelous event, and began asking questions regarding Jesus' authority to perform miracles, claiming that in any case, Jesus couldn't possibly have cured the man, because the so-called miracle took place on the sabbath, and according to religious law, to do "work" on the sabbath was a sin—and a sinner could not perform a miracle. Why, it was impossible, they asserted.

But in answer to the challenge about his healing, the man, in his simplicity, humbly declares, "Whether he be a sinner or no, I know not: one thing I know, that whereas I was blind, now I see" (John 9:25; John 9:1–38).

What is the lesson in this story? So many times we experience the wonder of God's intervention in our own lives, and just when we are ready to rejoice over it, along comes a skeptic and analyzes our experience to death, proving that it could not have possibly been God who intervened in our lives because of A, B, and C. What should we do in such cases? I say that, like the man who was blind from birth, we should answer, "Whether I can prove it was God or not, I know not. One thing I know, I asked for help, and I got it."

Do we really have to prove scientifically that God exists? Although we know that in fact, there can be, after all, no contradiction between "religious truth" and scientific or psychological truth, that there is only one truth, and that whatever it is, it is, we may never in our lifetime be able to understand this truth fully. For this reason, I feel that it is about time that religious leaders, psychologists, and scientists began making room for each others' findings and experiences—and treating each others' outlooks with an open mind.

NOT-SO-SILLY THINGS TO PRAY FOR

What are some legitimate things to pray for? We already know that it is quite natural to call upon God when it is a life-or-death issue, but what about asking for help in not-so-dreadful circumstances, such as finding your misplaced glasses or picking the right mechanic for your car? I don't think it's silly to pray for anything that concerns you, no matter how insignificant your problem may appear to others. In fact, I "bother" God all the time, and he doesn't seem to mind at all.

For example, whenever I can't find something—my keys (I'm in a mad rush and ready to leave the house), my reading glasses, an important document—after going crazy looking for the item, suddenly I remember, "Hey, wait a minute. If the item is in the house, the only problem I'm having is that I can't see where it is. But God sees everything, so if I ask him, I know he can direct me to where it is." Then I picture God looking down and seeing exactly where the missing item is. Next I think something like "God, you know where my (missing item) is. Help me to find it." I then calm down and relax for a minute, skimming through the newspaper or having a few sips of coffee. I then resume my search, and it almost never fails: In a few minutes, I find the missing item. (I know. You may be thinking that it was really only because I relaxed that I found the item, but who cares? I found it.)

But sometimes I don't find the missing item, and invariably when that happens, I later find out that the item was not in the house—like the time I had left my sunglasses at a friend's house (she later called saying she had them), or the time I had inadvertently thrown out some important tax documents (I later remembered that they were included in a box I had thrown away in the melee of having my office renovated).

I have learned through experience to ask God to help me find the right workers to do a job for me, but, interestingly, I don't always remember to take the few seconds to make that request of God—and I have to relearn the lesson.

For example, not long ago, I had a lot of odd painting jobs around the house, so I called a number advertised in the local paper. The man came over, and after an hour of analyzing, he gave me a price. Then he proceeded to call me ten times to ask questions about the job and to change the date the work would begin. I began to have serious misgivings about him—and I remembered that I hadn't bothered to ask God to help me find the right person for the job. I canceled and decided this time simply to ask God to direct me, and I did.

Later that day I was in the hardware store checking out an item, and for some reason, I blurted out to the cashier, "I'm having a terrible time finding a reliable painter. Can you recommend one?" He became highly animated and said, "Are you kidding? I've got the best people in town," and he gave me the name of a local company that he had used for the past ten years. I got the number and, to make a long story short, not only did they do an excellent job at a fair price, but they did many future jobs for me as well.

I guess I'm getting smarter these days, because more and more often I'm remembering that if I want to save precious time and energy, it makes sense to take a few seconds to shoot up a simple prayer of faith, asking God for his assistance. I recently bought a new home, and had so many odd jobs to be done that I would have had to call ten different "experts": plumbers, electricians, carpenters, and even someone to hang a heavy mirror—and whom do you call for that? When I looked around the house, all I wanted to do was turn on the television and eat! But instead I remembered to pray, and I did, saying, "God, help me with this problem—the quickest way to the best solution." The next thing you know (seconds later) I thought of calling the real-estate agent who had sold me the house.

After arguing with myself ("She won't want to be bothered with you now that the deal is done," and then, "She's probably not there anyway,") I picked up the phone and dialed. To my surprise, she answered the phone on the first ring, and I told her my problem. "I have the two greatest guys," she said. "They do everything—it's the strangest thing. I mean they unstop your toilet, hang a picture, or fix a sliding door. You name it, they'll do it." By the end of the day, all of the jobs were done, and plans were made for other nettlesome projects that would have to be done in the near future.

I have learned to ask God to help me when I'm writing a book, especially advice books like this one and *Get Rid of Him*. I was so excited about writing that book; I had so many stories to tell, so many ideas about how to advise women who were wasting their lives with men, sometimes a series of men, who were dragging them down. But once I started the book, I suddenly realized the awesomeness of the task in front of me. "How dare I propose to advise people whom I've never even met?" I thought. "Only God knows their situation," I realized. Then I understood that the only intelligent thing to do would be to ask God himself to give me the wisdom I needed to write the things that would help the most women.

Was my prayer answered? I think it was, because, interestingly, of the hundreds of letters I've gotten from women who read that book, most of them mention that although they had tried many ways to get out of the relationship—including reading a slew of other books and going to therapy—it was not until they read *Get Rid of Him* that they were able to take action. "Something about that book," they said, time and again, "made me see the light of day." And many of the women declared that the book has become a "Bible" to them, explaining how they copied certain passages of the book onto cards to carry around and read when they are tempted to go back.

I don't let this go to my head—not for one second—because I know deep in my heart that I got help with writing that book.

AMAZING GRACE:
FINDING GOD IN ANSWERS TO PRAYER

I talked about praying according to God's will in the above paragraphs. But what if you don't really know for sure that there is a God in the first place? How can you use prayer to help you find out for yourself if God is real, and how can you use prayer to begin to establish a relationship with God? I'll tell you how I did it—at the lowest point in my life—when I wasn't sure God existed at all, and, in fact, when I felt silly even talking to God, for fear that I was really only talking to myself.

I had just gotten through a divorce, and in the process had stupidly agreed to let my ex-husband have custody of my five-year-old daughter, thinking, "I'll see her all the time. Let him take the responsibility." After she had moved in with her father I suffered profusely. It felt as if my heart had been ripped out of me, and was in another place. At the same time, my father was dying of cancer. I was feeling miserable and very much alone, and the belief in God that was ingrained in me from the time of my childhood was shaky—very shaky—because up until that point, to me, God was not someone who was "on your side," but only a powerful force, a judge who lived in the sky, watching your every move. I had never really talked to him as a friend. I'd never dared to. It just didn't occur to me.

But now I felt so completely alone. I felt the loss of my daughter and I was afraid, and I was thinking of my father's death. I reached out to God—I guess instinctively—with a desperate prayer. It was close to the end for my father, and we all knew that it was only a matter of a few months before he would die. I tried to visit my father as often as I could—he was in and out of the hospital. Even so, I worried that no one would be there when he died, that he would die alone. Then the more I thought about it, the more I wished I could be the one with him when he died. I wanted to be alone with my father, holding his hand, so we could quietly say our last good-byes. I don't know exactly what gave me the courage, but I clearly remember (and this was twenty years ago) shooting up a prayer: "God, I know this is selfish, but unless you have another plan, please let me be alone with my father when he dies." And then I forgot I had even prayed the prayer.

On Thanksgiving weekend (I had just returned from a business trip), I got a call from my mother saying that my father had gone into a coma, but not to come to his bedside because the doctors were sure he would live at least another few weeks.

I felt horrible knowing that I had missed my last chance to talk to my father when he was in his full conscious mind, and I wanted to be alone to cry and think. I agreed that it would be foolish for me to come to the hospital at nine o'clock at night. I hung up the phone.

I was ready to get undressed, and to unpack from the trip and settle in so that I could deal with my guilt, and I was planning to get to bed early so that I could get up and go to the hospital first thing in the morning. But a strong foreboding kept making me feel uncomfortable about even getting undressed. Every time I went into the bedroom to remove my clothing, I just couldn't do it. There was a compelling force telling me that I must go to the hospital now. I called my mother again, hoping that she would say, "Yes, Joyce. Come now," but when I did, she reassured me that it was silly, and that she was only going there for a half hour to talk to the doctors. I should wait until the morning. I hung up the phone, but I still had no peace. Finally, I stopped resisting the feeling. I put on my lipstick, grabbed my purse, and, without another moment of hesitation, got in the car and drove to the hospital, arriving at 10:30 at night.

My mother and sister were at my father's bedside, and after a half hour were getting ready to leave, and were expecting me to do the same. But something came over me and I realized that I could not leave my father by himself, for fear that he would die with no family there. "I'm not leaving him alone," I said. After trying to talk me out of staying, my sister finally agreed that she and I would conduct a twenty-four-hour vigil at my father's bedside. I would stay until the morning, when she would return to relieve me, and so on, and then she and my mother left.

The doctors and nurses, seeing me remain behind, urged me to go home, assuring me that there was no indication that my father was very close to the end and reminding me that visiting hours were over, but I stubbornly refused, looking straight into their eyes and saying, "I'm staying." Somehow they must have known that I meant business, because one by one they left me alone to my vigil.

As I sat by my father's bedside, I held his hand, talking to him, assuring him that I would take care of my mother, and telling him how much I loved him, hoping all the time that what the doctors said was true—that even though he was in a coma, he could hear me. The time went by, and all the while I held his hand and kept my eyes riveted on the rhythmic rise and fall of his chest.

But as the morning came, I noticed that his breathing became erratic, and I could no longer see his chest rise and fall. I put my fingers on his wrist and found his pulse. It was faint, and becoming fainter by the minute. I kept my fingers on his pulse. I was telling him, "It's okay, Daddy. It's okay for you to go. I'll take care of Mother. We all love you. We'll be okay. You can go in peace." Then, at about 5:30 A.M., he gasped slightly and let out a breath of air—

and suddenly his face changed. Whereas before it had looked worried and furrowed, now a look of slight surprise and then incredible relief came over him. It was as if the sun came out in his face. And with that, his last heartbeat was gone. My father had passed on to another world.

I looked at my father's frail body, lying in the high hospital bed, guard rails around him, and could not resist a tremendous urge to give him one last hug, but in my nervous state, I couldn't figure out how to get the guard rails to come down, so I looked around wildly, and since no one was in sight, I climbed into the bed and hugged him and kissed him.

I then went to look for the nurse, and told her that he was gone, and she took over. I drove to my mother's house to tell her the news, half crying all the way. But then suddenly, in the midst of my state of upset, a calm came over me, and a voice in my mind said, "I did that for you." I looked up (all I could see was the roof of my car, of course) and said, "Did you do that?" Then it occurred to me as clear as day, that yes, God had answered my prayer, and I felt joy bubble up inside of me, a joy that for the moment made me start to laugh. I realized at that moment that only God could know how important it was for me to have those last moments alone with my father. This event was the beginning of my growing relationship with God.

WHEN GOD IS TRYING TO TELL YOU SOMETHING

As I've already mentioned, I agreed to let my ex-husband have custody of my daughter when I got divorced. The deal was that I would get to see her as much as I wanted to—for weekends, vacations, and so on—but she would live with him because he was at home most of the workday. I thought it would be a good arrangement, but I was never more wrong in my life.

As the months went by, I thought about asking for her back, but every time I did, I felt too guilty to do it, believing that since it was my idea to get the divorce, I would devastate my husband a second time by ripping his daughter away from his care. In addition, I believed that I would not be as good a parent as my ex-husband, who I thought to be rock-solid psychologically, while I was going through incredible emotional turmoil. Also, my ex-husband had met a woman who was helping him to care for my daughter, and they were talking about getting married.

As time went on, and as I continued to brood over the loss of the daily presence of my child, I became more and more depressed but I took no action. Eventually, my ex-husband remarried, and my daughter was given a family environment. Although I saw her every weekend, and in the summers, my life felt empty and "wrong." I tried to fill my life with work and projects, and to convince myself to leave well enough alone, but I couldn't do it. Not having her with me felt like an open wound that would never heal, and I imagined that it must be even worse for her, although my ex-husband kept reassuring me that she was fine.

Finally, after four years had gone by, I began to pray that if it was God's will that I get her back, he would by some miracle make it happen. After that, and I can only say this looking back, three things happened to me that, in combination, gave me the courage to stand up to my ex-husband and ask him to return my daughter to my custody.

The first event occurred on a plane when I was returning from a trip to Italy, where in every church I visited, I took the time to kneel at the altar and ask God to get my daughter back for me unless it was not his will.

On the plane going home, I got into a conversation with my seatmate, an old Italian woman. I told her my story, about my daughter, about my ex-husband and his happy family and his wife, and how guilty I felt about pulling her out of that home—and yet how miserable I felt without her. The woman listened patiently, and when I finished, I expected her to advise me to leave my daughter where she was—in a stable home, especially since I told her that my ex-husband was married to a good Italian woman. But instead, she leaned over her seat so she could face me eye to eye and, shaking her wrinkled hand and pointing her long, crooked finger at me, she commanded, "Take her back. She needs you." It felt like an order, not a suggestion, and the authority in her voice was more than that of a wizened old woman who just happened to be giving her opinion in idle conversation on a plane.

But when the plane landed, I did nothing. Instead, I continued to worry over my daughter, going about my business and trying to shake the depression.

The next message came a few days later. I was about to go out into my backyard to lie in the sun, but I decided instead not to completely waste that time and to read a book while sitting in the sun. I picked up *The Road Less Traveled*. I was up to a part in the book where Dr. Peck discusses the meaning of sin, and he talks about laziness as sin. "Laziness is sin?" I thought. "Well, surely that doesn't apply to me. If I am anything, I am not lazy." But then I read on, and he explained how fear is a disguised form of laziness when we allow it to stop us from acting, from doing what we know in our hearts we should do and, the way I read it, from taking responsibility. It was a form of willful immaturity.[3]

It was a revelation to me. I realized then and there that it was time for me to stop fooling myself into believing that my reason for not taking my daughter back was to protect her best interest, that she was better off with her father because he was a more stable person, or because he had remarried and could provide her with a family environment. It suddenly dawned on me that the truth was that my main reason for not taking my daughter back was laziness. I was too complaisant and self-centered to take responsibility for my own daughter. It was easier for me to be footloose and fancy-free and let others do the work of raising my daughter. I was allowing my fears that I would not be a good enough mother—and my belief that my ex and his wife were more capable—to stop me from doing what I knew I should do. I was very excited about what I had read—and almost embarrassed. Now that it was so clear, I was ashamed of myself "to myself," now that the truth was so obvious, if you can imagine what I mean. I stored my "revelation" away in my mind, thinking, "I can do it. It's time to dare to take responsibility." But the next morning I wasn't so sure.

My sister and I talk on the phone about twice a month, and I don't often go to her house, but the next day, for some reason, I had a strong urge to visit her. I called her and told her I was coming over.

Once in her house and after the small talk, I found myself spilling out the whole story, how I was thinking about getting my daughter back, but that I was scared to death. It was then that she said the words that broke the last link in the chain that was binding me from taking action. She said, "Joyce, I think you're afraid to take Marthe back because you think she is going to be a latch-key kid—like we were. But your situation is completely different from ours. You don't live in a tenement in a dangerous neighborhood. You don't work late into the day, or work nights, like our mother did. Marthe won't have to run up the stairs with a key—fearing for her life. She'll come home only an hour before you, to a sunny home in a quiet suburb, and she'll have friends to be with her for the hour she'll have to wait for you. After all, you're a teacher. You get home at almost the same time she does!"

That did it. I was free at last, free to do what I knew I must do from the day I let her go. I called my ex and told him about my resolve. He was very angry but said he would have to think about it. But by this time I had no doubt that he wouldn't fight me and, acting upon that conviction, while waiting for his "answer," I enrolled my daughter in the local elementary school and set up her new room. The next day he called me back and told me that he had spoken to her, and that she said she wanted to come live with me. He told me that since she was old enough to know what she wanted, he wasn't going to fight me. I picked her up the next day and lock, stock, and barrel, she moved in.

We were both so happy that words defy description. It felt for both of us as if a heavy burden had been lifted. My daughter began to flourish in a way that she never had before. And what's more, my life, which seemed to be on hold up until that point, began to move on. My career, over the years, slowly took off until I ended up where I am today.

But how did all of this come about, and why did it take so long? I believe that it came about because I prayed and asked God to have his will in the situation with my daughter. I also believe that it took so long—four and a half years—because I was not ready then to grow up and face my responsibility. I also believe that I needed to be so miserable that I could no longer stand the pain, and even my life, before I was able to say the prayer and mean it: "God, if it is your will, let me get my daughter back."

WHEN GOD SPEAKS IN STRANGE WAYS

Sometimes God speaks to us in very strange ways, ways that, although they are crystal clear to us and are undoubtedly healing, might cause others to look at us askance in the retelling.

One day I was very troubled, worried about a book I wrote for teenagers that was being considered by a publisher. Why was it taking so long for the editor to make a decision? I fretted. I was also concerned about my daughter, wondering whether to leave her in public school with her friends or try to scare up the money to put her into private school so that she would have a better chance to get into a good college eventually. In addition, I was concerned about my own career as a teacher. Was I on the right track remaining a high-school teacher, or should I try to switch to full-time college teaching?

With all of these things on my mind, I found myself walking alone on a near-deserted beach one Friday afternoon. I was thinking all of the above thoughts, and wistfully looking out to sea and up at the sky, and saying in my mind, "God, how am I doing? Am I on the right track?" when suddenly something very strange happened. Where the sky meets the ocean, it seemed as if the clouds and the sun came together and winked at me. It felt exactly as if God had winked at me and given me a kind of "A-okay" sign.

Instantly—and it really felt physical—all of the tension left my body and mind. I felt literally cleansed, the way we sometimes feel after a good, hard cry or after we make up with someone after having a big argument, and I started laughing out loud, even half crying in incredible relief. I saw or heard in that wink the clear message: "You're doing just fine. I'm proud of you. You're on the right track. Keep going. And don't worry. Many rewards are coming soon."

What makes me know that this was not some silly feeling I had, or that my mind was not playing tricks on me, is not so much the event itself and its immediate impact on me, but the impact it had on my attitude and my life for the next few years. Every time I was tempted to become weary, to start worrying too much, to allow anxiety to rule, the memory of that event would pass through my mind and I would have immediate reassurance that my hard work was not in vain. I was already blessed: I had my daughter back, I had my health, I had my talents, and I would soon be rewarded in ways that I had only dared to dream of. I was on my path—and not alone. God was with me.

That God speaks to us in epiphanies—divine appearances, in dreams, and even in an audible voice—is well illustrated in the Bible. God spoke to Moses from the midst of a burning bush. He spoke to the prophet Samuel in an audible voice, and he spoke to Joseph in some very graphic dreams.[4] And God can speak to you—but he may not bother you unless you want to hear from him.

THERE'S ALWAYS ROOM FOR A QUESTION MARK

How do we know when God is really speaking to us, and that it's not really our imaginations playing tricks on us or some such thing? In fact, we never do know for sure. But in my opinion, we never will have absolute proof when it comes to anything related to God, because from what I have learned about God, it is his style to leave a little room for doubt, so that your belief in him remains rooted in the choice of faith.

But why does God choose to leave this question mark? It seems as if the room for doubt is a test of our determination to stretch ourselves toward the light, a way of measuring our will to do right, a chance to resist the pull toward our lower natures—our laziness, our immaturity, and our self-centeredness.

WHEN PRAYERS SEEM TO BACKFIRE

What happens when you pray and things seem to turn out for the worse instead of for the better, and you wonder if the whole idea of prayer is a cruel joke invented to fool you into wishful thinking? At times like this we need to stop and ask ourselves, "What am I supposed to learn from this?" In other words, there is no guarantee when we pray that things will turn out exactly as we had fantasized, or even that things will go smoothly. When you pray, and in essence involve God in a situation, the result will eventually work into the entire fabric of your life for the best. Let me explain.

Not too long ago, I got the bright idea to go on a cattle drive. I had always dreamed of how it would feel to ride a horse for hours at a time, to be out in the real "Wild West," living like the cowhands of old. Like the true child that I am at times, I envisioned myself being with rough-and-tumble cowhands, with other adventure-seekers—and I fantasized having the escapade of my life as I drove the cattle along the Missouri River. With these fantasies in mind, and in the back of my mind asking God to help me to pick the best possible group from the brochure I had obtained, I signed up for a ten-day trip.

When I arrived in Montana to meet the other people who had signed up for the event, I was surprised to see, instead of rough-and-tumble adventurers like myself, what amounted to, in my view, a bunch of "yuppie intellectuals" out to have "an experience." I was disappointed, but I said to myself, "Oh, well, I'll just hang out with the workers—the cowhands." But I was in for a surprise there too. The so-called cowhands turned out to be what I quickly classified as a bunch of narrow-minded, judgmental rednecks (if cowboys could be called rednecks) who seemed to have been resurrected from the Middle Ages and who had very strict rules about "the place" of women and the way women should behave.

By the third night, after trying to find even a crumb of camaraderie with anyone in the group, I ended up hiding in my tent (pitched as usual on a hill of hard rocks—and a good walk from a nasty "outhouse") and crying to God, "Why, why, why?" I must admit, in my prayer there was a thread of, "Thanks a lot, God. I really appreciate this. Didn't I pray and ask you to help me to select the best cattle drive where I would meet the most adventurous people so that I could have the experience of my dreams?"

I began to cry, complaining to God that I didn't even want to talk to these people, that I was not having an adventure, and that I had spent my hard-earned money and valuable time only to be punished. Didn't God know that I had better things to do with my time and money? Then I began to worry that I had not really listened after I prayed about the trip. Maybe God had been trying to give me a sign not to go on the trip—and perhaps I was so dead-set on my plans that I didn't hear him.

I thought about going home. I had already checked into this—for a hefty price someone would come and fetch me from the middle of nowhere and drive me back to civilization, where I could catch a plane and go scurrying back to New York. "Should I do it?" I prayed, "or is there something I'm supposed to learn from this? If there is, don't let me run away from it. I don't want to have to learn it again."

Then I suddenly calmed down. I stopped sobbing and got a quiet, serene feeling. The answer was clear: "Stay. See what happens. Good will come of this." I then wanted to curl up in my tent and go to sleep, but instead I felt very strongly that I should get dressed and go out and join the party (every night, after dinner, they would have a country-and-western dance). So I did.

And that's when things turned around. Instead of being critical and standoffish toward everyone, I began to be more open. I danced with every cowboy who asked, old or young. I talked with various people—"hicks" or "yuppies," even the children in the group—and I listened to their stories, tales about their lives and troubles, and I found out about their joys, their hopes, their dreams. Suddenly these "narrow-minded, judgmental rednecks" and "yuppie intellectuals" became warm-blooded brothers and sisters trying to get along in a world filled with problems to be solved and challenges to be faced. "Why, they're just like me—only in different guises," I thought abashedly.

By the time the last day arrived, my view of the group had completely changed. Now, instead of judging and stereotyping them, I was feeling respect, love, and compassion for them. I found myself hugging various people and even telling some of them that I was going to pray for them.

What is the point of the story? It is this: Sometimes when you pray, and your prayer seems to backfire, when things don't turn out the way you had envisioned, it is because there is a lesson you must learn, a lesson that will help you to be better equipped to deal with life in the future and that will make you a better person.

In my case, that lesson was "Don't prejudge people, and don't be so opinionated," tendencies of mine that, before the cattle drive, I had never confronted in myself. Now when I meet people and I catch myself "reading them off," I check myself and open up to them, and get to know the "person," the soul behind the façade, and when I'm in the midst of pontificating about some "truth" I believe to be crucial to the lives of my listeners, I at least allow for another point of view.

But couldn't I have learned these things back in New York? I think not. I think that God knew that if I met such people in any situation where I could escape from them, I would have instantly removed myself from their presence. Apparently, for me, the best way to learn what I had to learn about people from different "worlds" was to live in their world for a few days (I had to be trapped in order to do it), where I was literally forced to eat, sleep, walk, talk, and ride with them, and finally to listen to them and get to know them.

LEARNING TO TALK TO GOD:
SOME SAMPLE PRAYERS

As mentioned in the above paragraphs, the best way to talk to God is in your own words and in your own way. But in case you're just starting out talking to God and you feel a little awkward, I'd like to offer a few sample prayers.

1. If you want to get to know God. "God, I'm not even sure that you exist. Please reveal yourself to me. You know me better than I know myself, so I trust you to find the way that will be best for me." (Then get ready—something will happen!)

2. In an emergency. "God, I'm scared. I know that if you want to, you can deliver me from this evil. Please help me to calm down. Give me peace. Solve this situation according to your will."

3. When you have a big or small problem, or a big or small decision to make. "God, I know that you know everything. You see the future, things I cannot see. Please give me wisdom in this situation. Solve this problem for me. Help me to make the right decision. No matter what, don't let me make a mistake."

4. When you are afraid that you have made a mistake in a decision you've made and there is still time to change your mind. "God, I'm feeling that I made a mistake in (choosing that school, getting engaged, saying yes to that new job, etc.). I know that you have the power to do whatever it takes to fix this if I've made a mistake. No matter what happens, don't let this event take place if it is not your will. If it is not a mistake, then please give me peace of mind about it."

5. When you can't find something. "God, you know exactly where I left my (missing item). I know that you see it. Unless you have a reason for me not to find it at this time, please help me to calm down and find it. If it is not retrievable, or if you don't want me to find it, please help me to have peace about it and to stop searching."

6. When you want a better life. "God, I'm tired of my life. Please change my life around and guide me to the paths that you have for me. Don't let me go out of this world without fulfilling the purposes for which I was born. Have your will in my life."

7. When you are feeling sad, lonely, or depressed. "God, you see how sad I am. Help me. I can't go on this way. I hold myself up to you. Restore my soul."

8. When you are tempted to do something wrong. "God, I am about to do this thing, and I feel as if I have no willpower to stop myself. Please, I give this situation to you. Have your will in the situation. Help me. Deliver me from evil."

9. When praying for something you want. "God, you know all things. I would really love to have this (item, job, relationship) and I know that if it is your will, you can help me to get it. If it's not your will, I know that in the long run it will not be best for me, but help me to see that and to let it go and to have peace about it."

10. When praying for healing for yourself or others. "God, I know that you have the power over sickness and health, life and death. If you want, you can even raise the dead. If it is your will, I know that you can heal me (Joe, Jane, etc.) from this sickness (or even fatal disease). Please, right now, let your healing power surge through me (him, her). God, I trust that you know the big picture, and what must be. If it is not your will that I (Joe, Jane, etc.) be healed, help me (us) to deal with the situation in the best possible way, and to have peace of mind."

Once you get used to inviting God into your life, you may find yourself automatically "shooting up a prayer" in your mind—quite often during the day. Some people do it so automatically that in sense, they live in constant state of mental prayer. Perhaps this is what the biblical writer meant when he said, "Pray without ceasing" (1 Thessalonians 5:17).

Before closing this section on prayer, let's take a fresh
look at what is perhaps the best sample prayer, one that is
recited week after week in churches around the world: the
Lord's Prayer. Although it is traditionally a Christian invoca-
tion, clearly it can be used by anyone. Jesus offered this
prayer as an example of how, when talking to God, we
don't need lengthy diatribes or fancy words. He said:

After this manner therefore pray ye: Our Father which art
   in heaven, Hallowed be thy name.
Thy kingdom come. Thy will be done on earth as it is in
   heaven.
Give us this day our daily bread.
And forgive us our debts as we forgive our debtors.
And lead us not into temptation, but deliver us from evil:
For thine is the Kingdom, and the power, and the glory,
   forever. Amen.

(Matthew 6:9–13)

And what is Jesus really advising? He's reminding us to
give due respect to the power of God. He's reminding us to
pray according to God's will. He's telling us that it is perfectly legitimate to pray for our daily needs. He's telling us
that we can ask for forgiveness—but that we must also remember to forgive those who have wronged us. He's ad-
monishing us to ask God to help us to avoid evil and
temptation. And he's ending his advice with a second reminder of the power of God.

I often "think" the Lord's prayer to God in the morning—
as I walk or run—looking up at the sky and meaning every
word. That's when the prayer becomes real to me.

IS IT NECESSARY TO GO TO
A PLACE OF WORSHIP?

Going to a place of worship once a week can be thought of
as having a date or an appointment, a special weekly conference with God. It's a time when you can, in the privacy

of your own thoughts, in your mind, look up and say, "How am I doing, God?" You can reaffirm your determination to be kind to others and to accomplish the purposes for which you were born. You can ask God to restore your energy and your faith. Chances are that you will leave the place of worship feeling spiritually refreshed and with renewed peace of mind.

Of course you can have a similar weekly appointment with God in your own home. (And in fact, if you practice the ideas in this chapter, you probably have regular conversations with God.) But going to a place of worship to congregate with other people who have the common purpose of communicating with God is often comforting and refreshing. We are able to feel our connection not only to God, but to other human beings. We see that indeed we are not alone. In addition, if we tune in, we can almost "feel" the presence of God because we are in his official place of worship, his "house," and the people who are there are there for one purpose, and one purpose alone—to communicate with God. That concentrated energy focused on God can help us to concentrate too—and to get in touch.

Why, then, don't more people go to a place of worship? Perhaps for them a place of worship has become a social or political club where the last thing on people's minds is communicating with God. Perhaps being sensitive and intuitive, such people perceive this and feel closer to God in the privacy of their own homes. If this is you, perhaps you can try what I did some years ago: walking into "strange" places of worship where you don't know a soul and just sitting in the pew, or kneeling down and talking to God. After trying a number of places of worship, you may eventually find one where you feel comfortable enough to return on a weekly basis. If not, you can continue to move around, or you may decide that for you, an occasional visit to a place of worship is enough.

A SPIRITUAL AWAKENING

In concluding this chapter, I feel it is important to think about why we would want to consider exploring the spiritual side of ourselves. The answer, I believe, is found in what too often seems to happen if we rely only upon the tangible, material world. The following biblical passage demonstrates the experience of a person who tried to find fulfillment in the material—the physical—without consideration for the spiritual:

> Vanity of vanities . . . all is vanity. I said in mine heart Go to now, I will prove thee with mirth, therefore enjoy pleasure, and behold, this is also vanity. . . . Therefore I hated life; because the work that is wrought under the sun is grievous unto me: for all is vanity and vexation of spirit.
>
> (Ecclesiastes 1–2:17)

We've all met people who have become so cynical that they've lost their passion for living. The "juice" has gone out of life for them, and they seem to go around with an "Is that all there is?" attitude. This attitude, I believe, is the result of cutting off the energy flow that keeps us excited about life until the day we die, the energy we get from opening up to the spiritual side of ourselves and in turn reaching beyond ourselves to a relationship with God.

In addition, a spiritual life seems to help to put everything else into perspective: fun, pleasure, work, and material things—in short, the human experience. Without a spiritual life, most people seem to become too preoccupied with possessions, and what's worse, if they lose those possessions, they become totally devastated. Small wonder that Jesus advised:

> Lay not up for yourself treasures upon earth, where moth and rust doth corrupt, and where

thieves break through and steal: But lay up for
yourselves treasures in heaven, where neither
moth nor rust doth corrupt, and where thieves do
not break through and steal: For where your treasure is, there will your heart be also.

(Matthew 6:19–21)

What is Jesus really talking about? Clearly, he is saying
that if your "treasure" (that which you value the most in
life) is tangible and hence ephemeral, and can be taken
away from you (possessions, pleasures, recognition, and
fame) you are most vulnerable—because it is the nature of
our world to threaten these things—and they may very well
be taken away from you. On the other hand, if your "treasure" (that which you value most in life) is intangible, is indeed spiritual—a simple faith in God, a relationship with
him, and an interest in doing what he has for you to do in
this life—you are not defenseless, but instead are invulner-
able. I don't mean to say that we should go to the other extreme and deny ourselves material blessings; I'm talking
here about spiritual versus material emphasis.

As the year 2000 approaches, people seem to be reaching out toward the spiritual. This was predicted by the biblical prophets:

And it shall come to pass afterward, that I will
pour out my spirit upon all flesh; and your sons
and your daughters shall prophesy, your old men
shall dream dreams, your young men shall see vi-
sions.

(Joel 2:28)

It seems to me that the forecast is coming true. Today we
are beginning to accept the possibility of a whole other
world, a spiritual world, that years ago only those labeled
as "kooks" dared to discuss. More and more people are
talking about having had spiritual experiences, whether

they be seeing angels, near-death encounters where they pass on to the other side and come back to tell about it, or just talking to God on a daily basis. Books on prayer and angels abound and are often found on best-seller lists all over the country, whereas years ago, the only place you could find such books was in religious bookstores.

There is a spiritual awakening in this country, and to me, that's good news.

Key #8. The power of spirituality and prayer. Inspire yourself.

NOTES

1. Edward Edinger, *Ego and Archetype* (New York: G. P. Putnam's Sons, 1972), p. 33. (Edinger quotes Oscar Wilde.)

2. Leslie Miller, "Scientists Reluctant to Discuss Religion Publicly," (*USA Today*, cover story, April 3, 1994), pp. 1–2.

3. M. Scott Peck, *The Road Less Traveled* (New York: Simon & Schuster, 1978), pp. 273–274.)

4. Exodus 3:1–10; 1 Samuel 3:1–11; Genesis 37:5–11.

10

LIVING A LIFE OF POWER: THE EIGHT GOLDEN KEYS

How can you be sure to live the rest of your life to its fullest potential, to be the person you were meant to be? You can take the dare and look within—and learn to trust and love yourself—and take the greater dare and look up, and ask God for his wisdom, and his will in your life.

Growing and changing is not always easy. It means facing uncharted territory. It means looking into yourself and facing old fears, and indeed "lies," that you've come to believe about yourself—and thinking when thinking is painful. In other words, it means deciding to live "consciously" as opposed to "unconsciously," or, to put it another way, actively or "smart," instead of passively or "stupid."

Introspection, looking in and facing one's "skeletons," *is* scary. It isn't safe. But safe is boring. So even though it isn't safe, think of it this way: It might be fun. And yes, it is fun. Once you start to realize that you can trust and love yourself—and that you can once and for all be free of the invisible chains that held you captive—you'll begin to take chances you've never dared to take before, and to succeed in ways you never dreamed. Your life will become more adventurous and exciting. Finally, you'll realize that you are becoming the person you were meant to be, and you'll know that anything can happen.

IT'S NOT THE SHORT RUN BUT THE LONG RUN THAT COUNTS

We've all heard the expression, "Life is short." But a wise older friend told me, "Life is long," and I when I thought about it for a while I realized what he meant. It's not the immediate event that makes the life, not the one stitch in the cloth, but the whole pattern woven into the fabric over one's entire life that tells the story. There's room for many mistakes along the way. It's the "big picture" that tells the tale.

THE EIGHT GOLDEN POWER KEYS FOR BECOMING THE PERSON YOU WERE MEANT TO BE

By way of review, here are the eight golden power keys, keys that you can develop and place on your *inner-strength key ring*, keys that you can use to help you to become the person you were meant to be, and in turn, to get, do, and be what you want in life—in spite of the odds.

Separately, but especially in combination, these keys will open up the doors and empower you to achieve the life of your dreams. They are:

Key #1 The power of your inner voice. Know and trust yourself.
Key #2 The power of self-esteem. Respect, value and love yourself.

Key #3 The power of letting go of the **p**ast and moving on. Liberate and free yourself.

Key #4 The power of admitting it—**o**wning up and taking responsibility. Mature yourself.

Key #5 The power of your **w**ill. Strengthen yourself.

Key #6 The power of doing, being **a**lone. Autonomize yourself.

Key #7 The power of getting yourself to do what you want. **M**otivate yourself.

Key #8 The power of spirituality and **p**rayer. Inspire yourself.

Notice the boldface letters. I've done this to provide an easy way for you to remember the main idea of the eight golden power keys. Think of the three words: *is pow amp*. What do they mean? They convey the message that the cumulative effect of the eight golden power keys *is a powerful amp* of positive energy in your life that will give you the power to "be the person you were meant to be."

Key #1 *I* = Inner voice (Listen to it.)
Key #2 *S* = Self-esteem (Build it.)

Key #3 *P* = Past (Let go of it.)
Key #4 *O* = Own up (Take responsibility.)
Key #5 *W* = Will (Use it.)

Key #6 *A* = Alone (Do it.)
Key #7 *M* = Motivation (Use your personal bag of tricks.)
Key #8 *P* = Prayer (The insurance policy that you're on the right track.)

Each time you choose to listen to your *inner voice*, you build self-trust. Every time you make an effort to increase your *self-esteem*, you learn to love and value yourself more. Whenever you choose not to wallow in *past* injustices, and instead forgive and, to the best of your ability, forget, you free yourself to move on. Each time you dare to *own up* and take responsibility for your own actions, even if there were others involved who bear some of the culpability, you empower yourself with maturity. Every time, by an act of *will,* you do what you want to do, in spite of the forces that would pull you in the opposite direction, you solidify your inner strength.

Whenever you do something *alone,* without the help or comfort of someone else, overcoming your tendency to lean on others, you build autonomy, and every time you struggle to achieve your goals, using whatever method necessary to activate yourself, you develop the power to *motivate* yourself. Every time you take a moment to look up and direct a simple *prayer* of faith to God, inviting him into the situation for his wise advice, you provide yourself with insurance that you will not make a mistake.

Make it a habit to use the eight golden power keys, and with God's help, make your dreams happen and become the person you were meant to be, because yes, you can indeed get it, do it, be it, in spite of the odds. And let me know how you're doing. I'd love to hear from you—and if you include a stamped, self-addressed envelope, I'll personally answer your letter. Your letter will be forwarded to me if you address it to:

Joyce Vedral
P.O. Box 7433
Wantagh, NY 11793

Bibliography

I could list hundreds of books here, but I've decided instead to list only the ones I have read over and over, the ones that have most influenced my life. If you like any given book on the list, check for other books by the same author. In most cases there are many more written by that author. Also, don't be fooled for one moment by the early copyright date of some of the books. Their message is timeless. I can't imagine how anyone could read any of the books on this list and not be permanently influenced for the better.

BIBLES

Please note that I use the King James Version of the Bible throughout the text. I chose this translation because it is the most poetic and indeed the most "traditional." In fact, it is the most quoted version in English literature. I love to quote it myself because it sounds so—well, authoritative. However, if you wish to read the Bible at length for understanding, you may be more comfortable with one of the more modern translations. I list my favorite here.

The Holy Bible. King James Version: New York: The American Bible Society.

Good News Bible. New York: The American Bible Society.

INSPIRATIONAL, EMPOWERING, AND INFORMATIVE BOOKS

Branden, Nathaniel. *How to Raise Your Self-Esteem*. New York: Bantam, 1987.

Bristol, Claude M. *The Magic of Believing*. New York: Pocket Books, 1948.

Horney, Karen. *Self Analysis*. New York: W. W. Norton & Company, 1942.

Horney, Karen. *Our Inner Conflicts*. New York: W. W. Norton & Company, 1945.

Jung, Carl G. ed., Anelia Jaffe. *Memories, Dreams, Reflections*. New York: Vintage, 1965.

Maltz, Maxwell, M.D., F.I.C.S. *Psychocybernetics*. New Jersey: Prentice Hall, 1960.

Maslow, Abraham. *Toward a Psychology of Being*. 2nd ed. New York: Van Nostrand, 1968.

Rogers, Carl R. *On Becoming a Person*. Boston: Houghton Mifflin, 1962.

Peck, Scott M., M.D. *The Road Less Traveled*. New York: Simon & Schuster, 1978.

Peale, Norman Vincent. *The True Joy of Positive Thinking*. New York: Ballantine, 1984.

Peale, Norman Vincent. *The Power of Positive Thinking*. New York: Fawcett Crest, 1956.

Siegel, Bernie S. *Love, Medicine & Miracles*. New York: Harper & Row, 1988.

Schwartz, David J. *The Magic of Thinking Big*. New York: Simon & Schuster, 1965.

BOOKS BY JOYCE VEDRAL

Definition: Shape without Bulk in Fifteen Minutes a Day. New York: Warner Books, 1995.

Top Shape. New York: Warner Books, 1995.

With Marthe S. Vedral. *The College Dorm Workout.* New York: Warner Books, 1994.

Bottoms Up! New York: Warner Books, 1993.

Gut Busters. New York: Warner Books, 1992.

The Fat-Burning Workout. New York: Warner Books, 1991.

The Twelve-Minute Total-Body Workout. New York: Warner Books, 1989.

Now or Never. New York: Warner Books, 1986.

Get Rid of Him. New York: Warner Books, 1993, paperback 1994.

VIDEOS BY JOYCE VEDRAL

The Bottoms Up Workout: Upper Body. New York: Good Times Video, 1994.

The Bottoms Up Workout: Middle Body. New York: Good Times Video, 1994.

The Bottoms Up Workout: Lower Body. New York: Good Times Video, 1994.

Note: *Bottoms Up* videos are $9.98 each, and can be ordered by calling 1-800-433-6769 on mainland USA and 612-571-5840 elsewhere, or check your local video store.

The Fat-Burning Workout: Volume I. The Regular Workout. Time-Life Video.

The Fat-Burning Workout: Volume II. The Intensity and Insanity Workout. Time-Life Video.

The Fat-Burning Workout videos can be ordered directly only through Joyce Vedral. For each video, send a check for $24.98 to Joyce Vedral, P.O. Box 7433, Wantagh, NY 11793-7433. This includes two-day express mailing.